Taste of Home

# CLASSIC
# FAMILY
# FAVORITES

**TASTE OF HOME BOOKS • RDA ENTHUSIAST BRANDS, LLC • MILWAUKEE, WI**

© 2024 RDA Enthusiast Brands, LLC.
1610 N. 2nd St., Suite 102, Milwaukee WI 53212-3906
All rights reserved. Taste of Home is a registered
trademark of RDA Enthusiast Brands, LLC.

Visit us at **tasteofhome.com** for other Taste of Home
books and products.

**International Standard Book Number:**
979-8-88977-025-1

**Content Director:** Mark Hagen
**Creative Director:** Raeann Thompson
**Senior Art Director:** Courtney Lovetere
**Assistant Art Director:** Carrie Peterson
**Deputy Editor, Copy Desk:** Ann M. Walter
**Copy Editor:** Suchismita Ukil
**Contributing Art Director:** Monya Mollohan

**Cover Photography:**
**Photographer:** Mark Derse
**Set Stylist:** Stacey Genaw
**Food Stylist:** Shannon Norris

**Pictured on front cover:**
Potluck Fried Chicken, p. 172; No-Bake Mango
Strawberry Cheesecake, p. 316; Super Italian Chopped
Salad, p. 140

**Pictured on back cover:**
Quick Bean & Rice Burritos, p. 221; Over-the-Top
Baked Ziti, p. 225; Strawberry Pretzel Dessert Minis,
p. 304; Pork Chops with Parmesan Sauce, p. 191;
Lemon Popovers with Pecan Honey Butter, p. 80;
Jalapeno Sloppy Joes, p. 113; Ganache-Topped
Pumpkin Tart, p. 308; Zucchini-Cornbread Fritters,
p. 125

INSTANT POT is a trademark of Double Insight Inc.
This publication has not been authorized, sponsored
or otherwise approved by Double Insight Inc.

Printed in China
1 3 5 7 9 10 8 6 4 2

CHOCOLATE
OAT SQUARES,
PAGE 258

> "
> **I've made
> these over and
> over again.
> My family and
> friends love
> them.**
> —MAAN, TASTEOFHOME.COM

# Grab a Seat Because These Family Cooks Are Sharing Their Best!

For generations, families have passed down their all-time favorite recipes, tantalizing taste buds decade after decade. Now, home cooks are letting you in on their secrets—the sensational recipes they've enjoyed for years.

With *Taste of Home Classic Family Favorites*, you'll discover 277 must-try heirloom dishes. Legendary bites such as Mom's oven-fresh Italian bread, Grandma's classic potato salad and sweet cookie-jar treats ... these are just a few of the hallmark dishes that promise to become staples at your own table.

**Take a peek inside for ...**

• Tried-and-true recipes ideal for busy weeknight dinners, holiday menus and everything in between.

• At-a-glance icons that highlight dishes made in the slow cooker 🍲, air fryer 🍱 and Instant Pot® 🍲.

• Contest winners 🏆, in addition to dozens of appetizers, snacks, soups and popular sandwiches piled high with flavor.

• A complete set of nutrition facts with every recipe, as well as diabetic exchanges where applicable.

Serve (and savor) every delicious dish in this keepsake cookbook, knowing that everything was tested and approved by the experts in the *Taste of Home* Test Kitchen. After preparing and enjoying any of these wonderful dishes, you'll quickly see why they landed in this delightful collection. With the new *Classic Family Favorites*, you'll relish the best of the best at every meal.

# TABLE OF CONTENTS

VEGGIE
FRITTATA,
PAGE 17

"
I love this
recipe. I will
definitely
make it again!
—ANNR
TASTEOFHOME.COM

# CHAPTER 1

# FAVORITE BREAKFASTS

Rise and shine! When it's time to kick off the day with a hearty bite, why not turn to a time-tested family favorite? Whether you need a quick weekday breakfast, a hearty weekend brunch or a special menu for a holiday-morning celebration, turn to these eye-openers.

# MINI ITALIAN FRITTATAS

I created this recipe when my friends and I had a picnic breakfast. I wanted an egg meal
that was portable and easy to make. These crowd-pleasing frittatas were the result!
—*Jess Apfe, Berkeley, CA*

PREP: 20 MIN. • BAKE: 20 MIN. • MAKES: 1 DOZEN

½ cup boiling water
¼ cup sun-dried tomatoes
(not packed in oil)
¾ cup shredded part-skim
mozzarella cheese, divided
½ cup chopped fresh spinach
⅓ cup water-packed artichoke hearts,
rinsed, drained and chopped
⅓ cup chopped roasted
sweet red peppers
¼ cup grated Parmesan cheese
¼ cup ricotta cheese
2 Tbsp. minced fresh basil
1 Tbsp. prepared pesto
2 tsp. Italian seasoning
¼ tsp. garlic powder
8 large eggs
½ tsp. pepper
¼ tsp. salt

1. Preheat oven to 350°. Pour boiling water over tomatoes in a small bowl;
let stand 5 minutes. Drain and chop tomatoes.

2. In a small bowl, combine ½ cup mozzarella cheese, fresh spinach, artichoke
hearts, roasted red peppers, Parmesan cheese, ricotta cheese, minced basil,
pesto, Italian seasoning, garlic powder and tomatoes. In a large bowl, whisk
eggs, pepper and salt until blended; stir in the cheese mixture.

3. Fill 12 greased or foil-lined muffin cups three-fourths full. Sprinkle with
remaining mozzarella cheese. Bake until set, 18-22 minutes. Cool 5 minutes
before removing from pan. Serve warm, with additional pesto if desired.

**1 mini frittata:** 95 cal., 6g fat (3g sat. fat), 149mg chol., 233mg sod., 2g carb.
(1g sugars, 0 fiber), 8g pro. **Diabetic exchanges:** 1 lean meat, 1 fat.

# BANANA FRENCH TOAST BAKE

Hamburger buns and bananas come together beautifully in this whimsical
make-ahead dish that the whole family will love. It's the ultimate breakfast for dinner.
—*Nancy Zimmerman, Cape May Court House, NJ*

PREP: 20 MIN. + CHILLING • BAKE: 55 MIN. + STANDING • MAKES: 8 SERVINGS

6 whole wheat hamburger buns
1 pkg. (8 oz.) reduced-fat
cream cheese, cut into
¾-in. cubes
3 medium bananas, sliced
6 large eggs
4 cups fat-free milk
¼ cup sugar
¼ cup maple syrup
½ tsp. ground cinnamon

1. Preheat the oven to 350°. Cut buns into 1-in. cubes; place half in a 13x9-in.
baking dish coated with cooking spray. Layer with cream cheese, bananas
and the remaining cubed buns.

2. In a large bowl, whisk eggs, milk, sugar, syrup and cinnamon; pour over top.
Refrigerate, covered, 8 hours or overnight.

3. Remove from refrigerator; let stand 30 minutes. Bake, covered, 30 minutes.
Uncover; bake 25-30 minutes longer or until a knife inserted in the center comes
out clean. Let stand 10 minutes before serving.

**1 piece:** 341 cal., 12g fat (6g sat. fat), 181mg chol., 379mg sod., 47g carb.
(28g sugars, 4g fiber), 15g pro.

MINI ITALIAN
FRITTATAS

BUTTERMILK-BEER
PANCAKES

# BUTTERMILK-BEER PANCAKES

A friend of mine shared these pancakes with me when I was in college. His dad had made them for as long as he could remember. I love them because they are so light and fluffy!
—*Carrie Auldridge, Hudson Oaks, TX*

**PREP: 10 MIN. • COOK: 5 MIN./BATCH • MAKES: 36 PANCAKES**

5   cups all-purpose flour
2   Tbsp. sugar
2   tsp. salt
2   tsp. baking soda
4   large eggs, room temperature
4   cups buttermilk
¼   cup canola oil
1   bottle (12 oz.) beer

**1.** In a large bowl, whisk flour, sugar, salt and baking soda. In a second bowl, whisk eggs, buttermilk and oil until blended. Add to dry ingredients, stirring just until moistened. Stir in beer.

**2.** Lightly grease a griddle; heat over medium heat. Pour batter by ¼ cupfuls onto the griddle. Cook until bubbles on the top begin to pop and bottoms are golden brown. Turn; cook until second side is golden brown.

**3 pancakes:** 308 cal., 7g fat (1g sat. fat), 65mg chol., 784mg sod., 47g carb. (7g sugars, 1g fiber), 10g pro.

# ARTICHOKE & ONION FRITTATA

Fresh flavors make this pretty egg bake a perfect entree for a special-occasion brunch or a light luncheon.
—*Joyce Moynihan, Lakeville, MN*

**PREP: 15 MIN. • BAKE: 40 MIN. • MAKES: 8 SERVINGS**

1   pkg. (8 oz.) frozen artichoke hearts
1   Tbsp. butter
1   Tbsp. olive oil
1   medium onion, chopped
1   garlic clove, minced
¼   tsp. dried oregano
¾   cup shredded Parmesan cheese, divided
6   large eggs
½   cup 2% milk
¼   tsp. salt
⅛   tsp. white pepper
⅛   tsp. ground nutmeg
1   cup shredded Monterey Jack cheese
    Minced chives, optional

**1.** Cook artichokes according to the package directions; drain. Cool slightly; coarsely chop. Preheat oven to 350°.

**2.** In a large skillet, heat butter and oil over medium-high heat. Add onion; cook and stir until tender. Add garlic; cook 1 minute longer. Stir in oregano and artichokes; remove from heat.

**3.** Sprinkle ¼ cup Parmesan cheese into a greased 11x7-in. baking dish. Top with artichoke mixture.

**4.** In a large bowl, whisk eggs, milk, salt, pepper and nutmeg. Stir in Monterey Jack cheese and ¼ cup Parmesan cheese. Pour over artichoke mixture.

**5.** Bake, uncovered, 30 minutes. Sprinkle with remaining Parmesan cheese. Bake until a knife inserted in the center comes out clean, 6-8 minutes longer. If desired, sprinkle with minced chives.

**1 piece:** 192 cal., 13g fat (7g sat. fat), 163mg chol., 373mg sod., 5g carb. (2g sugars, 2g fiber), 13g pro.

# MUSHROOM-HERB STUFFED FRENCH TOAST

This recipe transforms French toast into a savory delight with mushrooms and cheese. Its ooey-gooey texture is irresistible!
—*Lisa Huff, Wilton, CT*

**PREP:** 25 MIN. • **COOK:** 5 MIN./BATCH • **MAKES:** 8 SERVINGS

1 lb. thinly sliced baby portobello mushrooms
4 Tbsp. butter plus 2 Tbsp. melted butter, divided
1 pkg. (8 oz.) reduced-fat cream cheese
2 cups shredded Gruyere or Swiss cheese, divided
4 Tbsp. minced chives, divided
1 Tbsp. minced fresh tarragon or 1 tsp. dried tarragon
1 garlic clove, minced
⅛ tsp. salt
⅛ tsp. pepper
16 slices Texas toast
4 large eggs
2 cups 2% milk

**1.** In a large skillet, saute mushrooms in 1 Tbsp. butter until tender; set aside.

**2.** In a small bowl, beat cream cheese, 1 cup Gruyere cheese, 2 Tbsp. chives, tarragon, garlic, salt and pepper until blended. Spread over bread slices. Spoon mushrooms over half of the slices; place remaining bread slices over the top, spread side down.

**3.** In a shallow bowl, whisk eggs, milk and 2 Tbsp. melted butter. Dip both sides of sandwiches into egg mixture.

**4.** In a large skillet, toast sandwiches in remaining 3 Tbsp. butter in batches until golden brown, 2-3 minutes on each side. Sprinkle with remaining cheese and chives.

**1 sandwich:** 531 cal., 30g fat (17g sat. fat), 185mg chol., 757mg sod., 41g carb. (8g sugars, 2g fiber), 24g pro.

## TEST KITCHEN TIP

*Baby portobello mushrooms are also known as cremini mushrooms. They can be used instead of white mushrooms for a flavor boost in many family-favorite recipes.*

# BRIE & SAUSAGE BRUNCH BAKE

I've made this brunch bake for holidays as well as for a weekend at a friend's cabin, and I am always asked to share the recipe. It is make-ahead convenient, reheats well and even tastes great the next day.

—*Becky Hicks, Forest Lake, MN*

**PREP:** 30 MIN. + CHILLING • **BAKE:** 50 MIN. + STANDING • **MAKES:** 12 SERVINGS

- 1 lb. bulk Italian sausage
- 1 small onion, chopped
- 8 cups cubed day-old sourdough bread
- ½ cup chopped roasted sweet red peppers
- ½ lb. Brie cheese, rind removed, cubed
- ⅔ cup grated Parmesan cheese
- 2 Tbsp. minced fresh basil or 2 tsp. dried basil
- 8 large eggs
- 2 cups heavy whipping cream
- 1 Tbsp. Dijon mustard
- 1 tsp. pepper
- ½ tsp. salt
- ¾ cup shredded part-skim mozzarella cheese
- 3 green onions, sliced

**1.** In a large skillet, cook sausage and onion over medium heat until meat is no longer pink, 5-7 minutes; drain.

**2.** Place bread cubes in a greased 13x9-in. baking dish. Layer with the sausage mixture, red peppers, Brie and Parmesan cheeses, and basil. In a large bowl, whisk eggs, cream, mustard, pepper and salt; pour over top. Cover and refrigerate overnight.

**3.** Remove from the refrigerator 30 minutes before baking. Preheat the oven to 350°. Bake, uncovered, until a knife inserted in the center comes out clean, 45-50 minutes.

**4.** Sprinkle with mozzarella cheese. Bake until cheese is melted, 4-6 minutes. Let stand 10 minutes before cutting. Sprinkle with green onions.

**1 piece:** 451 cal., 34g fat (18g sat. fat), 217mg chol., 843mg sod., 16g carb. (3g sugars, 1g fiber), 19g pro.

# PEANUT BUTTER & BANANA WAFFLES

These are a refreshing change from your everyday waffles. I like to make big batches
so I can freeze the leftovers and reheat them later for a quick breakfast.
—Christy Addison, Clarksville, OH

PREP: 10 MIN. • COOK: 5 MIN./BATCH • MAKES: 16 WAFFLES

1¾ cups all-purpose flour
2 Tbsp. sugar
3 tsp. baking powder
¼ tsp. salt
¾ cup creamy peanut butter
½ cup canola oil
2 large eggs, room temperature
1¾ cups 2% milk
1 cup mashed ripe bananas (about 2 medium)
Maple syrup, optional

1. In a large bowl, whisk flour, sugar, baking powder and salt. Place peanut butter in another bowl; gradually whisk in oil. Whisk in eggs and milk. Add to the dry ingredients; stir just until moistened. Stir in bananas.

2. Bake in a preheated waffle maker according to manufacturer's directions until golden brown. Serve with syrup if desired.

**Freeze option:** Cool waffles on wire racks. Freeze between layers of waxed paper in freezer containers. Reheat waffles in a toaster on medium setting. Or microwave each waffle on high for 30-60 seconds or until heated through. If desired, serve with maple syrup.

**2 waffles:** 299 cal., 19g fat (3g sat. fat), 34mg chol., 266mg sod., 26g carb. (8g sugars, 2g fiber), 8g pro.

## TEST KITCHEN TIP

*Maple syrup makes a great addition to these savory waffles, but consider serving them with jelly to really mix up your breakfast routine. A few banana slices make for a quick, flavorful garnish.*

# ORANGE-GLAZED BACON

Just when you thought bacon couldn't get any tastier, we whipped up this sensational recipe starring the favorite breakfast side drizzled with a sweet orange glaze.
—Taste of Home *Test Kitchen*

**PREP:** 20 MIN. • **BAKE:** 25 MIN. • **MAKES:** 8 SERVINGS

¾ cup orange juice
¼ cup honey
1 Tbsp. Dijon mustard
¼ tsp. ground ginger
⅛ tsp. pepper
24 bacon strips (1 lb.)

**1.** Preheat oven to 350°. In a small saucepan, combine the first 5 ingredients. Bring to a boil; cook until liquid is reduced to ⅓ cup.

**2.** Place bacon on a rack in an ungreased 15x10x1-in. baking pan. Bake for 10 minutes; drain.

**3.** Drizzle half of glaze over bacon. Bake for 10 minutes. Turn bacon and drizzle with remaining glaze. Bake until golden brown, 5-10 minutes longer. Place bacon on waxed paper until set. Serve warm.

**3 glazed bacon strips:** 146 cal., 8g fat (3g sat. fat), 21mg chol., 407mg sod., 12g carb. (11g sugars, 0 fiber), 7g pro.

# MIGAS, MY WAY

My family loves any foods with a southwestern kick, so this recipe gets a big thumbs-up from them. I have substituted fresh corn tortillas for the chips by cutting the tortillas into strips and sauteing them with pepper and onion. It makes for a nice change.
—Joan Hallford, North Richland Hills, TX

TAKES: 25 MIN. • MAKES: 2 SERVINGS

¼ cup chopped onion
¼ cup chopped green pepper
1 Tbsp. bacon drippings or canola oil
4 large eggs
1 Tbsp. water
1 Tbsp. salsa
½ cup crushed tortilla chips
½ cup shredded cheddar cheese, divided
Optional: Chopped green onions, additional salsa and warm flour tortillas

1. In a large skillet, saute onion and green pepper in drippings until tender. In a small bowl, whisk eggs, water and salsa. Add to skillet; cook and stir until set. Stir in tortilla chips and ¼ cup cheese.

2. Sprinkle with remaining cheese. If desired, top with green onions and additional salsa and serve with tortillas.

**1 serving:** 385 cal., 27g fat (12g sat. fat), 459mg chol., 411mg sod., 15g carb. (2g sugars, 1g fiber), 20g pro.

## TEST KITCHEN TIP

*Crushed tortilla chips are a good way to dress up scrambled eggs as well as soups and chowders.*

# WAFFLE MONTE CRISTOS

We love the sweet, smoky flavor of these morning sandwiches. I use store-bought frozen waffles to save time, but have at it if you want to put your waffle maker to good use.
—Kelly Reynolds, Urbana, IL

TAKES: 20 MIN. • MAKES: 4 SERVINGS

½ cup apricot preserves
8 frozen waffles
4 slices deli turkey
4 slices deli ham
4 slices Havarti cheese (about 3 oz.)
4 bacon strips, cooked
2 Tbsp. butter, softened
Maple syrup

1. Preheat griddle over medium heat. Spread preserves over 4 waffles. Layer with turkey, ham, cheese and bacon; top with remaining waffles. Lightly spread outsides of waffles with butter.

2. Place on griddle; cook 4-5 minutes on each side or until golden brown. Serve with syrup for dipping.

**1 sandwich:** 511 cal., 23g fat (10g sat. fat), 70mg chol., 1163mg sod., 57g carb. (22g sugars, 2g fiber), 21g pro.

# VEGGIE FRITTATA

I was impressed with myself that I could omit dairy and still create something so good! Use any vegetables in this recipe, then add a fruit cup or almond yogurt on the side.
—*Kizmet Byrd, Fort Wayne, IN*

**TAKES: 30 MIN. • MAKES: 6 SERVINGS**

- 9 large eggs
- ½ tsp. salt, divided
- ¼ tsp. pepper, divided
- 1 Tbsp. olive oil
- ½ cup chopped carrot
- ½ cup chopped sweet red pepper
- ⅓ cup chopped red onion
- ½ cup sliced zucchini
- 2 Tbsp. chopped fresh basil, divided
- 2 garlic cloves, minced
- ½ cup grape tomatoes, halved

1. Preheat broiler. In a large bowl, whisk eggs, ¼ tsp. salt and ⅛ tsp. pepper until blended.

2. In a 10-in. broiler-safe skillet, heat oil over medium-high heat. Add carrot; cook and stir until crisp-tender, 4-5 minutes. Add red pepper and red onion; cook and stir until crisp-tender, 1-2 minutes. Add zucchini, 1 Tbsp. basil, garlic, and the remaining ¼ tsp. salt and ⅛ tsp. pepper; cook and stir until vegetables are tender.

3. Reduce heat to medium low; pour in egg mixture. Cook, covered, until nearly set, 4-6 minutes. Add tomatoes; cook, uncovered, until edge begins to pull away from the pan, about 3 minutes.

4. Broil 3-4 in. from heat until eggs are completely set, 1-2 minutes. Let stand 5 minutes. Sprinkle with remaining 1 Tbsp. basil; cut into wedges.

**1 piece:** 145 cal., 10g fat (3g sat. fat), 279mg chol., 313mg sod., 4g carb. (2g sugars, 1g fiber), 10g pro. **Diabetic exchanges:** 1 medium-fat meat, 1 vegetable, 1 fat.

**SAUSAGE & APPLE CORNBREAD BAKE**

66

Love this. It's so easy. The combination of spicy/salty sausage, tangy apple and sweet cornbread is very tasty.

—LENINE277
TASTEOFHOME.COM

# SAUSAGE & APPLE CORNBREAD BAKE

I make a cornbread-style bake with sausage, maple syrup and apples when we want a hearty breakfast casserole. It's sweet, savory and easy to make.
—*Stevie Wilson, Fremont, IA*

PREP: 15 MIN. + CHILLING • BAKE: 30 MIN. + STANDING • MAKES: 4 SERVINGS

1 lb. bulk pork sausage
4 medium tart apples, peeled and sliced (about 4 cups)
1 pkg. (8½ oz.) cornbread/muffin mix
⅓ cup 2% milk
1 large egg, room temperature
Maple syrup

1. Preheat oven to 400°. In a large skillet, cook sausage over medium heat until no longer pink, 6-8 minutes, breaking into crumbles; drain. Transfer to a greased 8-in. square baking dish. Top with apples.

2. In a small bowl, combine muffin mix, milk and egg just until moistened. Pour over apples. Bake, uncovered, until edges are golden brown and a toothpick inserted in center comes out clean, 30-40 minutes. Let stand 10 minutes before serving. Serve with maple syrup.

**1 serving:** 618 cal., 34g fat (10g sat. fat), 111mg chol., 1209mg sod., 61g carb. (27g sugars, 6g fiber), 19g pro.

**Make ahead:** Refrigerate unbaked casserole, covered, several hours or overnight. To use, preheat oven to 400°. Remove casserole from refrigerator while oven heats. Bake as directed, increasing time as necessary until edges are golden brown and a toothpick inserted in center comes out clean. Serve with syrup.

# PUFF PANCAKE WITH BOURBON PEACHES

I could make this breakfast every weekend when we are smack-dab in the middle of peach season.
—*James Schend, Pleasant Prairie, WI*

PREP: 20 MIN. • COOK: 20 MIN. • MAKES: 6 SERVINGS

1 Tbsp. butter
3 large eggs, room temperature, lightly beaten
½ cup 2% milk
1 tsp. vanilla extract
⅛ tsp. salt
½ cup all-purpose flour
1 cup water
4 Tbsp. bourbon or peach nectar, divided
2 Tbsp. honey
2 Tbsp. peach preserves
3 cups sliced peeled peaches (about 5 medium) or frozen unsweetened sliced peaches

1. Preheat oven to 400°. Place butter in a 9-in. deep-dish pie plate; heat in oven until butter is melted, 2-3 minutes. Meanwhile, in a small bowl, whisk eggs, milk, vanilla and salt until blended; gradually whisk in flour. Remove pie plate from oven; tilt carefully to coat bottom and sides with butter. Immediately pour in egg mixture. Bake until puffed and browned, 18-22 minutes.

2. Meanwhile, in a large saucepan, combine water, 3 Tbsp. bourbon, honey and preserves. Bring to a boil; reduce heat. Add peaches; cook and stir until tender, 3-4 minutes. Remove peaches to a bowl; set aside. Bring sauce mixture to a boil; cook and stir until reduced to ½ cup. Remove from heat; stir in peaches and remaining 1 Tbsp. bourbon.

3. Remove pancake from oven. Serve immediately with warm peach sauce.

**1 serving:** 192 cal., 5g fat (2g sat. fat), 100mg chol., 110mg sod., 27g carb. (17g sugars, 1g fiber), 6g pro.

# MINI-CHIP COCOA PANCAKES

Whip up a batch of cocoa pancakes dotted with mini chocolate chips
to satisfy your chocolate cravings first thing in the morning. Yum!
—*Joyce Moynihan, Lakeville, MN*

**TAKES:** 30 MIN. • **MAKES:** 4 SERVINGS

1¼ cups all-purpose flour
¼ cup baking cocoa
¼ cup sugar
3 tsp. baking powder
½ tsp. salt
2 large eggs, room temperature
1 cup 2% milk
3 Tbsp. butter, melted
1½ tsp. vanilla extract
⅔ cup miniature semisweet
chocolate chips
Optional: Confectioners' sugar and
whipped cream

**1.** In a large bowl, whisk the first
5 ingredients. In another bowl, whisk eggs, milk, butter and vanilla until blended. Add to flour mixture; stir until moistened. Fold in chocolate chips.

**2.** Coat a griddle with cooking spray; heat over medium heat. Pour batter by ¼ cupfuls. Cook until bubbles on top begin to pop. Turn; cook until lightly browned. If desired, dust with confectioners' sugar and serve with whipped cream.

**3 pancakes:** 489 cal., 22g fat (12g sat. fat), 133mg chol., 725mg sod., 67g carb. (32g sugars, 4g fiber), 12g pro.

TURKEY & MUSHROOM SPICY SCOTCH EGGS

# TURKEY & MUSHROOM SPICY SCOTCH EGGS

I grew up in Scotland, where greasy Scotch eggs were often sold alongside pies in bakeries. I decided to make my own version with less grease and more taste, and the air fryer helped me achieve my goal.
—*Fiona Green, Keller, TX*

PREP: 30 MIN. • COOK: 10 MIN./BATCH • MAKES: 6 SERVINGS

1 lb. ground turkey
½ cup shredded part-skim
  mozzarella cheese
½ cup finely chopped
  fresh mushrooms
¼ cup oil-packed sun-dried tomatoes,
  chopped
1 jalapeno pepper, seeded and minced
2 tsp. taco seasoning
½ tsp. garlic powder
6 hard-boiled large eggs
⅓ cup all-purpose flour
1 large egg, beaten
1 cup seasoned bread crumbs
¼ cup olive oil
  Spicy dipping sauce

1. Preheat air fryer to 400°. In a large bowl, mix the first 7 ingredients lightly but thoroughly. Divide mixture into 6 portions; flatten. Shape each portion around a peeled hard-boiled egg.

2. Place flour, beaten egg and bread crumbs in separate shallow bowls. Dip eggs into flour to coat all sides; shake off excess. Dip in beaten egg, then in crumbs, patting to help coating adhere. Brush with oil.

3. In batches, place eggs on greased tray in air-fryer basket; brush with oil. Cook until golden brown and turkey is no longer pink, 10-12 minutes. Serve with sauce.

**Note:** In our testing, we find cook times vary dramatically among brands of air fryers. As a result, we give wider than normal ranges on suggested cook times.

**1 egg:** 364 cal., 23g fat (6g sat. fat), 271mg chol., 402mg sod., 11g carb. (2g sugars, 1g fiber), 26g pro.

# BAKED FRENCH TOAST WITH BLUEBERRY SAUCE

French toast has a special-occasion feel, but why save it for company? Top it with a homemade blueberry sauce to make any day festive.
—*Debbie Johnson, Centertown, MO*

PREP: 20 MIN. • BAKE: 20 MIN. • MAKES: 4 SERVINGS (1 CUP SAUCE)

¼ cup butter, melted
4 large eggs
1 cup 2% milk
1 tsp. vanilla extract
½ tsp. ground nutmeg
8 slices Texas toast

**BLUEBERRY SAUCE**
¼ cup sugar
1½ tsp. cornstarch
¼ tsp. ground cinnamon
⅛ tsp. ground cloves
1½ cups fresh or frozen blueberries
2 Tbsp. orange juice concentrate

1. Pour melted butter into a 15x10x1-in. baking pan; lift and tilt pan to coat bottom evenly. In a large shallow bowl, whisk eggs, milk, vanilla and nutmeg. Dip both sides of Texas toast into egg mixture; place on prepared pan. Bake at 375° until lightly browned, 20-25 minutes.

2. For sauce, in a large saucepan, combine sugar, cornstarch, cinnamon and cloves. Stir in blueberries and thawed orange juice concentrate. Bring to a boil; cook and stir until thickened, about 2 minutes. Serve with French toast.

**2 pieces French toast with ¼ cup sauce:** 481 cal., 20g fat (10g sat. fat), 225mg chol., 549mg sod., 63g carb. (27g sugars, 3g fiber), 14g pro.

# SWEET POTATO WAFFLES WITH NUT TOPPING

These tender waffles are ready in just minutes and have a
wonderfully sweet and crunchy topping. What a mouthwatering
way to get your family out of bed in the morning!
—*Christine Keating, Norwalk, CA*

**PREP:** 20 MIN. • **COOK:** 5 MIN./BATCH • **MAKES:** 6 SERVINGS

2 cups biscuit/baking mix
2 Tbsp. brown sugar
½ tsp. ground cinnamon
¼ tsp. ground ginger
¼ tsp. ground nutmeg
1 large egg, room temperature
1⅓ cups 2% milk
1 cup canned sweet potatoes, mashed
2 Tbsp. canola oil
1 tsp. vanilla extract

**TOPPING**
1 Tbsp. butter
½ cup chopped pecans
½ cup chopped walnuts
2 Tbsp. brown sugar
1 Tbsp. water
⅛ tsp. ground cinnamon
  Dash salt
  Dash ground nutmeg
  Maple syrup

**1.** In a large bowl, combine biscuit mix, brown sugar, cinnamon, ginger and nutmeg. In another bowl, whisk egg, milk, sweet potatoes, oil and vanilla. Stir into the dry ingredients just until combined.

**2.** Bake waffles in a preheated waffle maker according to manufacturer's directions until golden brown.

**3.** Meanwhile, in a small skillet, melt butter over medium-high heat. Add pecans and walnuts. Cook and stir for 2 minutes. Add brown sugar, water, cinnamon, salt and nutmeg. Cook and stir until sugar is dissolved. Serve waffles with topping and syrup.

**2 waffles with about 2 Tbsp. nut topping:** 457 cal., 28g fat (5g sat. fat), 44mg chol., 598mg sod., 46g carb. (17g sugars, 3g fiber), 9g pro.

## TEST KITCHEN TIP

*If you and your family are pumpkin lovers, try this recipe but consider swapping in an equal amount of canned pumpkin for the canned sweet potatoes.*

# WILD MUSHROOM & BACON PIE

Rustic flavors of roasted garlic and mushrooms make this savory pie a perfect option for brunch or weeknight dinner. A mixture of mushrooms gives the pie depth of flavor—feel free to use your favorites!
—*Barbara Estabrook, Appleton, WI*

**PREP:** 25 MIN. • **BAKE:** 30 MIN. + STANDING • **MAKES:** 8 SERVINGS

3  garlic cloves, peeled
1  tsp. canola oil
1  sheet refrigerated pie crust
4  bacon strips, cut into ½-in. pieces
1  lb. sliced assorted fresh mushrooms
¼  cup finely chopped sweet onion
3  large eggs, room temperature
1  pkg. (8 oz.) cream cheese, softened
½  tsp. salt
¼  tsp. pepper
1  cup shredded sharp cheddar cheese
2  Tbsp. grated Parmesan cheese
⅛  tsp. paprika

**1.** Preheat oven to 425°. Place garlic on a double thickness of heavy-duty foil; drizzle with oil. Wrap foil around garlic. Bake 15-20 minutes or until softened. Cool. Reduce oven setting to 375°. Unroll crust into a 9-in. pie plate; flute edge.

**2.** In a large skillet, cook bacon over medium heat for 3-5 minutes or until crisp. Remove to paper towels with a slotted spoon; drain, reserving 2 tsp. drippings. Saute mushrooms and onion in drippings until tender, about 3 minutes; set aside.

**3.** In a large bowl, whisk eggs and cream cheese until blended. Stir in salt, pepper and the mushroom mixture. Squeeze softened garlic into mixture and mix well.

**4.** Sprinkle cheddar cheese over crust; top with bacon. Pour egg mixture over top. Sprinkle with Parmesan cheese and paprika.

**5.** Bake until a knife inserted in the center comes out clean, 30-35 minutes. Let stand 15 minutes before cutting.

**1 piece:** 468 cal., 35g fat (19g sat. fat), 181mg chol., 719mg sod., 24g carb. (3g sugars, 1g fiber), 16g pro.

# CROISSANT BREAKFAST CASSEROLE

Turning croissants and marmalade into a classic overnight casserole
makes a wonderful treat for family and guests in the morning.
—Joan Hallford, North Richland Hills, TX

PREP: 15 MIN. + CHILLING • BAKE: 25 MIN. • MAKES: 10 SERVINGS

1 jar (18 oz.) orange marmalade
½ cup apricot preserves
⅓ cup orange juice
3 tsp. grated orange zest
10 croissants, split
5 large eggs
1 cup half-and-half cream
1 tsp. almond or vanilla extract
  Optional: Quartered fresh
  strawberries and whipped cream

1. In a small bowl, mix marmalade, preserves, orange juice and zest. Spread croissant bottoms with marmalade mixture; replace tops. Cut croissants in half; arrange in a greased 13x9-in. baking dish.

2. In another bowl, whisk eggs, cream and extract; pour over croissants. Refrigerate, covered, overnight.

3. Preheat oven to 350°. Remove from refrigerator while the oven heats. Bake, uncovered, 25-30 minutes or until a knife inserted in the center comes out clean. Let stand 5 minutes before serving. Serve with strawberries and whipped cream.

**1 serving:** 376 cal., 12g fat (6g sat. fat), 128mg chol., 242mg sod., 62g carb. (43g sugars, 1g fiber), 7g pro.

# CINNAMON ROLLS WITH COOKIE BUTTER FILLING

I created this recipe when I had a jar of cookie butter on hand and I was craving cinnamon rolls. Using frozen bread dough cuts down on time and effort, and the cookie butter makes a nice, even filling with a touch of something special.
—Kallee Krong-McCreery, Escondido, CA

PREP: 20 MIN. + RISING • BAKE: 15 MIN. • MAKES: 1 DOZEN

½ cup Biscoff creamy cookie spread
3 Tbsp. butter, softened
½ tsp. vanilla extract
⅓ cup sugar
1 Tbsp. ground cinnamon
1 loaf (1 lb.) frozen bread dough,
  thawed

ICING
1⅓ cups confectioners' sugar
1 to 2 Tbsp. 2% milk
2 tsp. light corn syrup
1 tsp. vanilla extract

1. In a small bowl, mix the first 5 ingredients. On a lightly floured surface, roll dough into a 12x7-in. rectangle. Spread butter mixture over dough to within ½ in. of edges. Roll up jelly-roll style, starting with a long side; pinch seam to seal. Cut into 12 slices. Place in a greased 13x9-in. baking pan, cut side down. Cover and let rise in a warm place until doubled, about 45 minutes.

2. Preheat oven to 350°. Bake until edges are lightly browned, 15-20 minutes. Place pan on a wire rack. Combine icing ingredients; drizzle over warm rolls. Let stand until set.

**1 roll:** 272 cal., 8g fat (3g sat. fat), 8mg chol., 236mg sod., 44g carb. (25g sugars, 2g fiber), 4g pro.

CROISSANT
BREAKFAST
CASSEROLE

" 
I make this frequently. It's so easy to prep the night before then just pop it into the oven.

—BECKYJCARVER
TASTEOFHOME.COM

> "This sauce sounded so good, I had to try it. We weren't disappointed. It was delicious.
> —SUELLENPATTON
> TASTEOFHOME.COM

GRILLED
CHERRY-GLAZED
CHICKEN WINGS,
PAGE 37

CHAPTER 2

# SNACKS & APPETIZERS

Turn the page and you'll find more than 30 sensational bites and beverages guaranteed to impress! These most-requested classics make any occasion a bit more special. See why when you set them out for your gang.

# BENEDICTINE SPREAD

This version of a traditional Kentucky cucumber spread is
always a hit. Serve it as an appetizer dip or sandwich filling.
—Taste of Home *Test Kitchen*

TAKES: 15 MIN. • MAKES: 1¾ CUPS

1  pkg. (8 oz.) cream cheese, softened
1  Tbsp. mayonnaise
¼  tsp. salt
⅛  tsp. white pepper
⅛  tsp. dill weed
1  drop green food coloring, optional
¾  cup finely chopped peeled
    cucumber, patted dry
¼  cup finely chopped onion
    Optional: Snack rye bread,
    pita bread wedges and assorted
    fresh vegetables

In a small bowl, combine cream cheese, mayonnaise, salt, white pepper, dill and, if desired, food coloring; beat until smooth. Stir in cucumber and onion. Cover and refrigerate until serving. Serve with snack rye bread, pita bread wedges and vegetables as desired.

**2 Tbsp.:** 65 cal., 6g fat (3g sat. fat), 16mg chol., 98mg sod., 1g carb. (1g sugars, 0 fiber), 1g pro.

## TEST KITCHEN TIP

*Benedictine spread is delicious as a veggie dip or as a spread for crackers and mini rye breads. But it can also be the foundation of cucumber tea sandwiches. Just spread a little on a piece of bread. Place thinly sliced cucumbers on top of the spread, and top with another piece of bread.*

---

# GRILLED SHRIMP-STUFFED MUSHROOMS

I love this recipe because it's fast and easy. The mushrooms
can also be cooked on an indoor grill or grill pan.
—Patti Duncan, Colorado Springs, CO

TAKES: 30 MIN. • MAKES: 1 DOZEN

6   uncooked shrimp (16-20 per lb.),
     peeled and deveined, tails removed
6   bacon strips
12  baby portobello mushrooms,
     stems removed
2   Tbsp. barbecue sauce

Cut shrimp and bacon strips in half. Place 1 piece of shrimp on each mushroom cap. Wrap each mushroom with a piece of bacon; secure with a toothpick. Grill, covered, over indirect medium heat or broil 4 in. from heat until bacon is crisp and mushrooms are tender, 10-15 minutes, turning occasionally. Brush with barbecue sauce; grill 5 minutes longer. Discard toothpicks before serving.

**1 stuffed mushroom:** 77 cal., 6g fat (2g sat. fat), 25mg chol., 137mg sod., 2g carb. (1g sugars, 0 fiber), 4g pro.

66
We really liked
this spread!
It has a very
fresh flavor and
was excellent
with baby carrot
dippers as well
as crackers.
—DEBGLASS11
TASTEOFHOME.COM

# BIG-BATCH BLOODY MARYS

Tailgates, game-day parties and big brunches call for a Bloody Mary recipe that caters to a bunch. This one has a little bit of a kick—just enough to get the crowd cheering.
—Taste of Home *Test Kitchen*

TAKES: 20 MIN. • MAKES: 8 SERVINGS

8 cups tomato juice
½ cup lemon juice
¼ cup lime juice
2 Tbsp. Worcestershire sauce
1 tsp. celery salt
1 tsp. pepper
1 tsp. hot pepper sauce
4 tsp. prepared horseradish, optional
2 cups vodka

**OPTIONAL GARNISHES**
Celery ribs, pickle spears, green and ripe olives, cucumber slices, pickled mushrooms, cubed cheese, beef sticks, cherry tomatoes, cocktail shrimp

In a pitcher, stir together the first 7 ingredients. Stir in horseradish if desired. For each serving, pour about 1 cup over ice with ¼ cup vodka; add garnishes as desired.

**1¼ cups:** 180 cal., 1g fat (0 sat. fat), 0 chol., 817mg sod., 12g carb. (7g sugars, 1g fiber), 2g pro.

## TEST KITCHEN TIP

*The sky is the limit when it comes to garnishing a Bloody Mary. Consider offering guests sticks of string cheese, cocktail onions, beef jerky, pickled asparagus spears or even bacon-wrapped water chestnuts.*

# CHEESE & PIMIENTO SPREAD

My mother made delicious pimiento cheese, but this is a spicy, modern version of her recipe. Serve it stuffed in celery or spread on crackers or a sandwich.
—Elizabeth Hester, Elizabethtown, NC

TAKES: 15 MIN. • MAKES: 2¾ CUPS (22 SERVINGS)

12 oz. sharp white cheddar cheese
8 oz. reduced-fat cream cheese, softened
2 tsp. Worcestershire sauce
2 tsp. white vinegar
¼ tsp. white pepper
¼ tsp. garlic powder
¼ tsp. cayenne pepper
1 jar (4 oz.) diced pimientos, undrained
Assorted crackers and vegetables

Shred the cheddar cheese; transfer to a large bowl. Add cream cheese, Worcestershire sauce, vinegar, pepper, garlic powder and cayenne; beat on low speed until blended. Drain pimientos, reserving 2 Tbsp. juice. Stir in pimientos and reserved juice. Serve with crackers and vegetables.

**2 Tbsp.:** 90 cal., 7g fat (4g sat. fat), 23mg chol., 150mg sod., 1g carb. (1g sugars, 0 fiber), 5g pro.

# SLAW-TOPPED BEEF SLIDERS

When I was working full time, I would rely on these delicious, fast-to-fix beef sliders for simple meals.
To ease on prep time and avoid extra cleanup, I use bagged coleslaw mix and bottled slaw dressing.
—*Jane Whittaker, Pensacola, FL*

**PREP: 20 MIN. • COOK: 6 HOURS • MAKES: 1 DOZEN**

3 cups coleslaw mix
½ medium red onion, chopped
   (about ⅔ cup)
⅛ tsp. celery seed
¼ tsp. pepper
⅓ cup coleslaw salad dressing

**SANDWICHES**
1 boneless beef chuck roast (2 lbs.)
1 tsp. salt
½ tsp. pepper
1 can (6 oz.) tomato paste
¼ cup water
1 tsp. Worcestershire sauce
1 small onion, diced
1 cup barbecue sauce
12 slider buns or dinner rolls, split

1. Combine coleslaw, red onion, celery seed and pepper. Add coleslaw salad dressing; toss to coat. Refrigerate until serving.

2. Sprinkle chuck roast with salt and pepper; transfer roast to a 5-qt. slow cooker. Mix tomato paste, water and Worcestershire sauce; pour over roast. Top with onion. Cook, covered, on low 6-8 hours or until meat is tender.

3. Shred meat with 2 forks; return to slow cooker. Stir in barbecue sauce; heat through. Place beef on buns; top with coleslaw. Replace bun tops.

**1 slider:** 322 cal., 12g fat (4g sat. fat), 67mg chol., 726mg sod., 34g carb. (13g sugars, 3g fiber), 20g pro.

---

# WATERMELON & CUCUMBER SALSA

The combo of watermelon and cucumber may sound unusual—
it tastes anything but! Eat the salsa with chips, or serve it as a topper
with hot dogs or chicken tacos for a refreshing change of pace.
—*Suzanne Curletto, Walnut Creek, CA*

**TAKES: 15 MIN. • MAKES: 3 CUPS**

1½ cups seeded chopped watermelon
¾ cup finely chopped cucumber
½ cup finely chopped sweet onion
¼ cup minced fresh cilantro
1 jalapeno pepper, seeded and minced
2 Tbsp. lime juice
¼ tsp. salt

In a small bowl, combine all of the ingredients; refrigerate until serving.

**Note:** Wear disposable gloves when cutting hot peppers; the oils can burn skin. Avoid touching your face.

**¼ cup:** 10 cal., 0 fat (0 sat. fat), 0 chol., 50mg sod., 3g carb. (2g sugars, 0 fiber), 0 pro. **Diabetic exchanges:** 1 free food.

# BAKED EGG ROLLS

These egg rolls are low in fat but the crispiness from
baking will fool you into thinking they were fried!
—*Barbara Lierman, Lyons, NE*

**PREP:** 30 MIN. • **BAKE:** 10 MIN. • **MAKES:** 16 SERVINGS

2  cups grated carrots
1  can (14 oz.) bean sprouts, drained
½  cup chopped water chestnuts
¼  cup chopped green pepper
¼  cup chopped green onions
1  garlic clove, minced
2  cups finely diced cooked chicken
4  tsp. cornstarch
1  Tbsp. water
1  Tbsp. light soy sauce
1  tsp. canola oil
1  tsp. brown sugar
   Pinch cayenne pepper
16  egg roll wrappers
   Cooking spray

1. Coat a large skillet with cooking spray; heat pan over medium heat. Add the first 6 ingredients; cook and stir until vegetables are crisp-tender, about 3 minutes. Add chicken; heat through.

2. In a small bowl, combine the cornstarch, water, soy sauce, oil, brown sugar and cayenne until smooth; stir into chicken mixture. Bring to a boil. Cook and stir for 2 minutes or until thickened; remove from the heat.

3. Spoon ¼ cup chicken mixture on the bottom third of 1 egg roll wrapper; fold sides toward center and roll tightly. (Keep remaining wrappers covered with a damp paper towel until ready to use.) Place seam side down on a baking sheet coated with cooking spray. Repeat.

4. Spritz tops of egg rolls with cooking spray. Bake at 425° for 10-15 minutes or until lightly browned.

**Freeze option:** Freeze cooled egg rolls in a freezer container, separating layers with waxed paper. To use, reheat rolls on a baking sheet in a preheated 350° oven until crisp and heated through.

**1 egg roll:** 146 cal., 2g fat (0 sat. fat), 18mg chol., 250mg sod., 22g carb. (1g sugars, 1g fiber), 9g pro. **Diabetic exchanges:** 1½ starch, 1 lean meat, ½ fat.

# TEQUILA SUNRISE

Everyone loves the pretty sunset layers in this refreshing
cocktail classic. It's like a mini vacation in a glass!
—Taste of Home *Test Kitchen*

**TAKES:** 5 MIN. • **MAKES:** 1 SERVING

1  to 1¼ cups ice cubes
1½  oz. tequila
4½  oz. orange juice
1½  tsp. grenadine syrup
   Optional garnish:
   Orange slice and
   maraschino cherry

Place ice in a Collins or highball glass. Pour the tequila and orange juice into the glass. Slowly pour grenadine over a bar spoon into the center of the drink. Garnish as desired.

**¾ cup:** 184 cal., 0 fat (0 sat. fat), 0 chol., 0 sod., 17g carb. (15g sugars, 0 fiber), 1g pro.

# EASY STRAWBERRY SALSA

My salsa is sweet and colorful, with just a little bite from jalapeno peppers. I use fresh strawberries and my own home-grown vegetables, but you can also use produce available year round. It's a wonderfully unique treat.

—*Dianna Wara, Washington, IL*

PREP: 20 MIN. + CHILLING • MAKES: 16 SERVINGS

- 3 cups chopped seeded tomatoes (about 4 large)
- 1⅓ cups chopped fresh strawberries
- ½ cup finely chopped onion (about 1 small)
- ½ cup minced fresh cilantro
- 1 to 2 jalapeno peppers, seeded and finely chopped
- ⅓ cup chopped sweet yellow or orange pepper
- ¼ cup lime juice
- ¼ cup honey
- 4 garlic cloves, minced
- 1 tsp. chili powder
  Baked tortilla chip scoops

In a large bowl, combine the first 10 ingredients. Refrigerate, covered, at least 2 hours. Serve with chips.

**Note:** Wear disposable gloves when cutting hot peppers; the oils can burn skin. Avoid touching your face.

¼ **cup:** 33 cal., 0 fat (0 sat. fat), 0 chol., 4mg sod., 8g carb. (6g sugars, 1g fiber), 1g pro. **Diabetic exchanges:** ½ starch.

## TEST KITCHEN TIP

*This salsa is great with tortilla chips, but try it with grilled chicken or pork or even cooked white fish.*

# GRILLED CHERRY-GLAZED CHICKEN WINGS

SHOWN ON PAGE 28

When I take these grilled wings to events, there are never any leftovers! Friends and family love them. The sweet and spicy glaze is delicious.

—*Ashley Gable, Atlanta, GA*

PREP: 20 MIN. • GRILL: 15 MIN. • MAKES: 2 DOZEN

- 12 chicken wings (about 3 lbs.)
- 3 Tbsp. canola oil, divided
- 1 garlic clove, minced
- 1 cup ketchup
- ½ cup cider vinegar
- ½ cup cherry preserves
- 2 Tbsp. Louisiana-style hot sauce
- 1 Tbsp. Worcestershire sauce
- 3 tsp. coarse salt, divided
- 1 tsp. coarsely ground pepper, divided

**1.** Using a sharp knife, cut through the 2 wing joints; discard wing tips. In a small saucepan, heat 1 Tbsp. oil over medium heat. Add garlic; cook and stir 1 minute. Stir in ketchup, vinegar, preserves, hot sauce, Worcestershire sauce, 1 tsp. salt and ½ tsp. pepper. Cook and stir until heated through. Brush wings with remaining 2 Tbsp. oil; sprinkle with remaining 2 tsp. salt and ½ tsp. pepper.

**2.** Grill, covered, over medium heat 15-18 minutes or until juices run clear, turning occasionally and brushing with glaze during the last 5 minutes of grilling. Serve with remaining glaze.

**1 piece:** 107 cal., 6g fat (1g sat. fat), 18mg chol., 439mg sod., 7g carb. (7g sugars, 0g fiber), 6g pro.

> **"**
> Really good!
> They had the
> perfect blend
> of sweet and
> savory. They
> are perfect
> for a party!
> Make these,
> you'll be happy!
> —GITRUMMN
> TASTEOFHOME.COM

# CRAB WONTON CUPS

These tasty little tarts make excellent appetizers served warm
and crispy from the oven. They're true crowd-pleasers.

—Connie McDowell, Greenwood, DE

**TAKES: 30 MIN. • MAKES: 32 APPETIZERS**

32 wonton wrappers
   Cooking spray
1 pkg. (8 oz.) cream cheese, softened
½ cup heavy whipping cream
1 large egg, room temperature
1 Tbsp. Dijon mustard
1 tsp. Worcestershire sauce
5 drops hot pepper sauce
1 cup lump crabmeat, drained
¼ cup thinly sliced green onions
¼ cup finely chopped sweet red pepper
1 cup grated Parmesan cheese
   Minced chives, optional

**1.** Preheat oven to 350°. Press wonton wrappers into miniature muffin cups coated with cooking spray. Spritz wrappers with cooking spray. Bake until lightly browned, 8-9 minutes.

**2.** Meanwhile, in a small bowl, beat the cream cheese, cream, egg, mustard, Worcestershire sauce and pepper sauce until smooth. Stir in crab, green onions and red pepper; spoon into wonton cups. Sprinkle with Parmesan cheese.

**3.** Bake until filling is heated through, 10-12 minutes. Serve warm. If desired, garnish with minced chives. Refrigerate leftovers.

**1 wonton cup:** 77 cal., 5g fat (3g sat. fat), 26mg chol., 153mg sod., 5g carb. (0 sugars, 0 fiber), 3g pro.

# CLASSIC SWISS CHEESE FONDUE

This rich and fancy fondue is a great appetizer for the holidays. Or let it warm
you up on a wintry day. Don't be surprised when the pot is scraped clean!

—Taste of Home *Test Kitchen*

**TAKES: 30 MIN. • MAKES: ABOUT 4 CUPS**

1 garlic clove, halved
2 cups white wine, chicken broth or unsweetened apple juice, divided
¼ tsp. ground nutmeg
7 cups shredded Swiss cheese
2 Tbsp. cornstarch
   Cubed bread and assorted fresh vegetables

**1.** Rub garlic clove over the bottom and side of a fondue pot; discard garlic and set fondue pot aside. In a large saucepan over medium-low heat, bring 1¾ cups wine and nutmeg to a simmer. Gradually add cheese, stirring after each addition until cheese is melted (cheese will separate from wine).

**2.** Combine cornstarch and remaining wine until smooth; gradually stir into cheese mixture. Cook and stir until thickened and mixture is blended and smooth. Transfer to prepared fondue pot and keep warm. Serve with bread cubes and vegetables.

**¼ cup:** 214 cal., 15g fat (9g sat. fat), 44mg chol., 90mg sod., 2g carb. (0 sugars, 0 fiber), 13g pro.

# MAI TAI

This party favorite has been around for quite some time. It's not overly fruity and features a good blend of sweet and sour. For a splash of color, garnish with strawberries and lime.
—Taste of Home *Test Kitchen*

TAKES: 5 MIN. • MAKES: 1 SERVING

1½ to 2 cups ice cubes
2 oz. light rum
¾ oz. Triple Sec
½ oz. lemon juice
1½ tsp. lime juice
1½ tsp. amaretto
Optional garnish: Lime slice, lime twist, edible flowers and fresh pineapple

**1.** Fill a shaker three-fourths full with ice. Place remaining ice in a rocks glass; set aside.

**2.** Add the rum, Triple Sec, juices and amaretto to shaker; cover and shake for 10-15 seconds or until condensation forms on outside of shaker. Strain into prepared glass. Garnish as desired.

**⅔ cup:** 241 cal., 0 fat (0 sat. fat), 0 chol., 7mg sod., 15g carb. (13g sugars, 0 fiber), 0 pro.

# POTATO LATKE FUNNEL CAKES

This savory funnel cake incorporates mashed potatoes and ranch seasoning into the dough. It's delicious. Just try it and you'll see!
—Chanie Apfelbaum, Brooklyn, NY

PREP: 30 MIN. • COOK: 5 MIN./BATCH • MAKES: 15 SERVINGS

1½ cups sour cream or plain Greek yogurt
1 envelope ranch salad dressing mix (1 oz.), divided
2 lbs. russet potatoes (about 3 large), peeled and cubed
3 Tbsp. all-purpose flour
1 large egg
½ to 1 tsp. kosher salt
½ to 1 tsp. pepper
½ cup 2% milk, optional
Oil for deep-fat frying
Grated Parmesan cheese, optional

**1.** Stir together sour cream and 1 Tbsp. ranch dressing mix; refrigerate, covered, until serving.

**2.** Place potatoes in a large saucepan; add water to cover. Bring to a boil. Reduce heat; cook, uncovered, until just tender, 15-20 minutes. Drain potatoes; return to pan and stir over low heat 1 minute to dry. Mash potatoes; stir in the flour, egg, salt, pepper, remaining ranch dressing mix and, if desired, milk until smooth.

**3.** In a deep cast-iron or electric skillet, heat oil to 350°. Transfer potato mixture to a pastry bag fitted with a small round pastry tip. Pipe batter in a spiral motion. Fry until golden brown, 1-2 minutes on each side. Drain on paper towels. Sprinkle with Parmesan cheese if desired; serve warm with dip.

**1 cake:** 165 cal., 11g fat (3g sat. fat), 18mg chol., 231mg sod., 14g carb. (1g sugars, 1g fiber), 3g pro.

> This was a major hit with friends and family. Easy to throw together and tastes stunning.
> —MOLLY491
> TASTEOFHOME.COM

# PISTACHIO & DATE RICOTTA CROSTINI

My husband and I regularly have date night at home where we make a four-course meal.
For appetizers, I like to keep things simple but dressed up. I've found that making a special appetizer
helps transform the atmosphere into a fancy meal. Fresh figs can be used in lieu of dates.
—*Kristin Bowers, Gilbert, AZ*

**PREP:** 20 MIN. • **BAKE:** 15 MIN. • **MAKES:** 3 DOZEN

36 slices French bread baguette
   (¼ in. thick)
2 Tbsp. olive oil
⅛ tsp. plus ¼ tsp. salt, divided
1 cup whole-milk ricotta cheese
4 oz. cream cheese, softened
3 Tbsp. honey, divided
4 tsp. grated lemon zest, divided
10 pitted medjool dates, chopped
   (about 1½ cups)
½ cup shelled pistachios,
   finely chopped

1. Preheat oven to 400°. Place bread slices on a large ungreased baking sheet. Brush tops with olive oil and sprinkle with ⅛ tsp. salt. Bake until golden brown, 12-15 minutes. Cool on baking sheet.

2. Meanwhile, place ricotta, cream cheese, 2 Tbsp. honey, 2 tsp. zest and remaining ¼ tsp. salt in a food processor; process until almost smooth. Spread mixture over bread slices. Top with dates and pistachios. Drizzle with remaining 1 Tbsp. honey and 2 tsp. zest. Serve immediately.

**1 piece:** 57 cal., 3g fat (1g sat. fat), 6mg chol., 74mg sod., 6g carb. (3g sugars, 0 fiber), 1g pro.

# SOUTH-OF-THE-BORDER BRUSCHETTA

I like to get creative in the kitchen, and this is one of
the first dishes I threw together without using a recipe.
It boasts a zesty Mexican flavor everyone is sure to love.
—*Rebecca Spoolstra, Pilot Point, TX*

**PREP:** 20 MIN. + CHILLING • **BROIL:** 5 MIN. • **MAKES:** 12 SERVINGS

2 medium ripe avocados,
   peeled and finely chopped
3 Tbsp. minced fresh cilantro
1 to 2 red chili peppers, finely chopped
¼ tsp. salt
2 small limes
12 slices French bread baguette
   (½ in. thick)
   Crumbled Cotija cheese, optional

1. In a small bowl, mix avocados, cilantro, chili peppers and salt. Grate zest from limes. Cut limes crosswise in half; squeeze juice from limes. Stir lime zest and juice into avocado mixture. Refrigerate 30 minutes.

2. Preheat broiler. Place bread slices on an ungreased baking sheet. Broil 3-4 in. from heat 1-2 minutes on each side or until golden brown. Top with avocado mixture. If desired, sprinkle with cheese.

**1 appetizer:** 62 cal., 4g fat (0 sat. fat), 0 chol., 100mg sod., 7g carb. (0 sugars, 2g fiber), 2g pro.

# MAC & CHEESE CUPS

I started making these for a close friend's daughter when she started eating solid food.
She loves mac and cheese and could hold these in her tiny hands to feed herself.
Now the adults like them more than the kids! They're always requested at potlucks.
—Karen Lambert, Weaverville, NC

**PREP: 20 MIN. • BAKE: 25 MIN. • MAKES: 24 SERVINGS**

1    lb. uncooked elbow macaroni
3    cups sharp cheddar cheese, finely
     shredded
5    Tbsp. butter, softened
3    large eggs
1    cup half-and-half cream
½    cup sour cream
1    tsp. salt
½    tsp. pepper

**1.** Preheat oven to 350°. Cook macaroni according to package directions, drain. Transfer to a large bowl. Stir in cheese and butter until melted.

**2.** In another bowl, whisk the eggs, cream, sour cream, salt and pepper until blended. Add to macaroni mixture; stir until well blended. Spoon macaroni into 24 well-greased muffin cups. Bake until golden brown, 25-30 minutes.

**1 piece:** 178 cal., 10g fat (6g sat. fat), 50mg chol., 226mg sod., 15g carb. (1g sugars, 1g fiber), 7g pro.

# DOMINICAN GREEN & YELLOW FRIED PLANTAINS

Fried plantains are a tradition in most Caribbean countries. In the Dominican Republic they are served with almost everything. In our home they're almost always served as a snack or an appetizer before dinner. The mojo dipping sauce adds extra flavor to the plantains so it is an absolute must!
—Belqui Ortiz-Millili, Mesa, AZ

**TAKES: 15 MIN. • MAKES: ABOUT 2 DOZEN (¼ CUP SAUCE)**

1    green plantain
1    yellow plantain
     Oil for deep-fat frying

**MOJO SAUCE**
¼    cup corn oil
½    tsp. minced fresh cilantro
¼    tsp. minced garlic

**1.** In a deep cast-iron or electric skillet, heat oil to 375°. Peel plantains. Cut green plantain into 1-in. slices. Cut yellow plantain into ½-in. slices.

**2.** Add both plantains to oil, a few at a time, and cook until lightly browned, 30-60 seconds. Remove with a slotted spoon; drain on paper towels.

**3.** Place fried green plantain pieces between 2 sheets of aluminum foil. With the bottom of a glass, flatten to ½-in. thickness. Fry until golden brown, 2-3 minutes longer.

**4.** In a small bowl, combine mojo sauce ingredients. Serve with plantains.

**1 piece with ½ tsp. sauce:** 50 cal., 4g fat (0 sat. fat), 0 chol., 1mg sod., 5g carb. (2g sugars, 0 fiber), 0 pro.

# HEALTHY SPINACH ARTICHOKE DIP

I love this recipe because you get all of the deliciousness of spinach artichoke dip without the heaviness of too much cheese and cream! It's great with cut-up whole wheat pitas for dipping.
—*Kristyne Mcdougle Walter, Lorain, OH*

TAKES: 20 MIN. • MAKES: 3 CUPS

1 jar (7½ oz.) marinated quartered artichoke hearts
1 can (15 oz.) white kidney or cannellini beans, rinsed and drained
1 pkg. (10 oz.) frozen chopped spinach, thawed and squeezed dry
1 Tbsp. Italian seasoning
3 Tbsp. grated Parmesan and Romano cheese blend
1 tsp. extra virgin olive oil
Carrot and celery sticks

Drain artichokes, reserving marinade. In a small saucepan, cook and stir beans, spinach, artichokes and Italian seasoning over medium heat until aromatic and heated through, 4-5 minutes. Remove from heat; cool slightly. Transfer to a food processor, add reserved artichoke marinade; pulse until mixture reaches a texture of thick hummus. Pour into a serving bowl; stir in cheese and drizzle with oil. Serve warm with carrots and celery.

**¼ cup:** 70 cal., 3g fat (1g sat. fat), 2mg chol., 182mg sod., 7g carb. (0 sugars, 3g fiber), 3g pro. **Diabetic exchanges:** ½ starch, ½ fat.

## TEST KITCHEN TIP

*Add a dollop of this dip to your next grilled cheese sandwich or use it in a deli-meat wrap, panini or even quesadilla.*

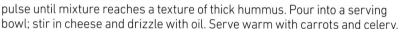

# CHEESE-STUFFED CHERRY TOMATOES

We grow plenty of tomatoes, so my husband and I often handpick enough cherry tomatoes for these easy-to-fix appetizers. This is one of our favorite recipes, and it's impossible to eat just one.
—*Mary Lou Robison, Greensboro, NC*

PREP: 15 MIN. + CHILLING • MAKES: 1 DOZEN

1 pint cherry tomatoes
1 pkg. (4 oz.) crumbled feta cheese
½ cup finely chopped red onion
½ cup olive oil
¼ cup red wine vinegar
1 Tbsp. dried oregano
Salt and pepper to taste

**1.** Cut a thin slice off the top of each tomato. Scoop out and discard pulp. Invert tomatoes onto paper towels to drain. Combine cheese and onion; spoon into tomatoes.

**2.** In a small bowl, whisk the oil, vinegar, oregano, salt and pepper. Spoon over tomatoes. Cover and refrigerate for 30 minutes or until ready to serve.

**1 tomato:** 111 cal., 11g fat (2g sat. fat), 5mg chol., 93mg sod., 2g carb. (1g sugars, 1g fiber), 2g pro.

# PEPPERONI FOCACCIA BREAD

This focaccia bread recipe is perfect to serve with a pasta dinner, either as an appetizer or sliced for sandwiches. You will love the smell of it baking—it's hard to wait for it to be done!
—*Trisha Kruse, Eagle, ID*

PREP: 25 MIN. • BAKE: 20 MIN. + COOLING • MAKES: 8 SERVINGS

1 pkg. (3½ oz.) sliced pepperoni, chopped
½ medium onion, thinly sliced
1 large egg, room temperature
1 cup 2% milk
½ cup plain Greek yogurt
¼ cup olive oil
2½ cups all-purpose flour
2½ tsp. baking powder
½ tsp. garlic powder
¼ tsp. salt
¾ cup shredded Parmesan cheese, divided
Optional: Marinara sauce and fresh basil leaves

1. Preheat oven to 425°. Heat a 10-in. cast-iron or ovenproof skillet over medium-high heat. Add pepperoni and onion; cook and stir until pepperoni is crisp and onion is tender, 6-8 minutes. Remove and keep warm. In a large bowl, beat egg, milk, yogurt and oil until well blended. In another bowl, whisk flour, baking powder, garlic powder and salt; gradually beat into egg mixture. Stir in ½ cup cheese and pepperoni mixture (batter will be thick).

2. Transfer to same skillet; sprinkle with remaining ¼ cup cheese. Bake until bread is golden brown and a toothpick inserted in center comes out clean, 20-25 minutes. Cool 10 minutes in skillet on a wire rack. Serve warm. If desired, serve with marinara sauce and top with fresh basil leaves.

**1 piece:** 339 cal., 18g fat (6g sat. fat), 47mg chol., 580mg sod., 33g carb. (3g sugars, 1g fiber), 12g pro.

# VANILLA CHAI TEA

An aromatic chai is comfort in a cup. It's extra special with a dollop of fresh whipped cream and a sprinkling of ground allspice on top.
—*Taste of Home Test Kitchen*

TAKES: 25 MIN. • MAKES: 6 SERVINGS

8 whole peppercorns
½ tsp. whole allspice
2 cardamom pods
1 cinnamon stick (3 in.)
4 whole cloves
8 tea bags
1 Tbsp. honey
4 cups boiling water
2 cups 2% milk
1 Tbsp. vanilla extract
½ cup heavy whipping cream
1½ tsp. confectioners' sugar
Ground allspice

1. Place the first 5 ingredients in a large bowl. With end of a wooden spoon handle, crush mixture until aromas are released. Add tea bags, honey and boiling water; steep, covered, 6 minutes.

2. In a small saucepan, heat milk. Strain tea into a heatproof pitcher; stir in milk and vanilla.

3. In a small bowl, beat cream until it begins to thicken. Add confectioners' sugar; beat until soft peaks form. Top servings with whipped cream; sprinkle with allspice.

**1 cup (with 2½ Tbsp. topping):** 131 cal., 9g fat (6g sat. fat), 33mg chol., 48mg sod., 9g carb. (7g sugars, 0 fiber), 3g pro.

PEPPERONI
FOCACCIA BREAD

# BRANDY OLD-FASHIONED SWEET

Here in Wisconsin, we make this old-fashioned favorite using brandy in place of whiskey and soda instead of water for a milder sweet cocktail.
—Taste of Home *Test Kitchen*

TAKES: 10 MIN. • MAKES: 1 SERVING

1 orange slice
1 maraschino cherry
1½ oz. maraschino cherry juice
1 tsp. bitters
¼ to ⅓ cup ice cubes
1½ oz. brandy
2 tsp. water
1 tsp. orange juice
3 oz. lemon-lime soda

In a rocks glass, muddle orange slice, cherry, cherry juice and bitters. Add ice. Pour in the brandy, water, orange juice and soda.

**1 serving:** 277 cal., 0 fat (0 sat. fat), 0 chol., 18mg sod., 36g carb. (17g sugars, 0 fiber), 0 pro.

## TEST KITCHEN TIP

*The typical old-fashioned garnish is a speared cherry with an orange slice. A cinnamon stick is another classic complement.*
—CATHERINE WARD, *TASTE OF HOME* PREP KITCHEN MANAGER

# TERRIFIC TOMATO TART

Fresh, colorful tomatoes, feta cheese and prepared pesto perfectly complement this appetizer's crispy phyllo dough crust.
—*Diane Halferty, Corpus Christi, TX*

PREP: 15 MIN. • BAKE: 20 MIN. • MAKES: 8 SERVINGS

12 sheets phyllo dough (14x9 in.)
2 Tbsp. olive oil
2 Tbsp. dry bread crumbs
2 Tbsp. prepared pesto
¾ cup crumbled feta cheese
1 medium tomato, cut into ¼-in. slices
1 large yellow tomato, cut into ¼-in. slices
¼ tsp. pepper
5 to 6 fresh basil leaves, thinly sliced

**1.** Preheat oven to 400°. Place 1 sheet of phyllo dough on a baking sheet lined with parchment. (Keep remaining phyllo covered with a damp towel to prevent it from drying out.) Brush with ½ tsp. oil and sprinkle with ½ tsp. bread crumbs. Repeat layers, being careful to brush oil all the way to edges.

**2.** Fold each side ¾ in. toward center to form a rim. Spread with pesto and sprinkle with half the feta cheese. Alternately arrange the red and yellow tomato slices over cheese. Sprinkle with pepper and remaining feta.

**3.** Bake until crust is golden brown and crispy, 20-25 minutes. Cool on a wire rack for 5 minutes. Remove parchment before cutting. Garnish with basil.

**1 piece:** 135 cal., 7g fat (2g sat. fat), 7mg chol., 221mg sod., 13g carb. (1g sugars, 1g fiber), 5g pro.

# MUSTARD PRETZEL DIP

This flavorful dip is addictive, so be careful! It's also delicious served with pita chips, crackers and fresh veggies.
—*Iola Egle, Bella Vista, AR*

**PREP:** 10 MIN. + CHILLING • **MAKES:** 3½ CUPS

1 cup sour cream
1 cup mayonnaise
1 cup prepared mustard
½ cup sugar
¼ cup dried minced onion
1 envelope (1 oz.) ranch salad dressing mix
1 Tbsp. prepared horseradish
Sourdough pretzel nuggets

In a large bowl, combine the first 7 ingredients. Cover and refrigerate for at least 30 minutes. Serve with pretzels. Refrigerate leftovers.

**2 Tbsp.:** 95 cal., 8g fat (2g sat. fat), 2mg chol., 342mg sod., 6g carb. (4g sugars, 0 fiber), 1g pro.

## TEST KITCHEN TIP

*Since you need an entire cup of prepared mustard for this dip, any texture will transfer to the finished recipe. Look for a smooth mustard, avoiding anything that says course ground or whole grain on the label.*

# GRILLED ZUCCHINI WITH PEANUT CHICKEN

Zucchini slices make perfect finger food. It's fun to make a topping for zucchini and a good solution for a never-ending crop.
—*Elisabeth Larsen, Pleasant Grove, UT*

**TAKES:** 30 MIN. • **MAKES:** ABOUT 16 APPETIZERS

2 medium zucchini, cut diagonally into ½-in. slices
⅛ tsp. salt
⅛ tsp. pepper

**TOPPING**
¼ cup water
3 Tbsp. brown sugar
2 Tbsp. reduced-sodium soy sauce
1 Tbsp. creamy peanut butter
1 tsp. lime juice
¼ tsp. ground ginger
¼ tsp. cayenne pepper
1 cup shredded cooked chicken
2 Tbsp. finely chopped red onion
Julienned carrot and chopped fresh cilantro

**1.** Place zucchini on an oiled grill rack over medium heat; grill, covered, until tender, 3-4 minutes per side. Sprinkle with salt and pepper.

**2.** In a small saucepan, whisk together first 7 topping ingredients; bring to a boil. Reduce heat; simmer, uncovered, until slightly thickened, 2-3 minutes, stirring occasionally. Stir in chicken and onion; heat through.

**3.** To serve, top zucchini slices with chicken mixture. Sprinkle with carrot and cilantro.

**1 appetizer:** 38 cal., 1g fat (0 sat. fat), 8mg chol., 110mg sod., 4g carb. (3g sugars, 0 fiber), 3g pro.

> "
> I make this
> dip frequently.
> It's always
> a hit, and
> someone
> usually asks
> for the recipe.
> —BDC63
> TASTEOFHOME.COM

# ALMOND BONBON COOKIES

Almond paste is wrapped in cookie dough for these bite-sized treats. Dip cooled cookies into one frosting or dip each side into different flavors of frosting. Get creative with sprinkle toppings!
—Teri Rasey, Cadillac, MI

PREP: 20 MIN. • BAKE: 10 MIN./BATCH + COOLING • MAKES: 4 DOZEN

1 cup butter, softened
⅔ cup confectioners' sugar
¼ cup 2% milk
1 tsp. vanilla extract
3 cups all-purpose flour
1 pkg. (7 oz.) almond paste

**VANILLA ICING**
1 cup confectioners' sugar
4½ tsp. 2% milk
1 tsp. vanilla extract

**CHOCOLATE ICING**
1 cup confectioners' sugar
1 oz. unsweetened chocolate, melted and cooled
3 Tbsp. 2% milk
1 tsp. vanilla extract
Assorted sprinkles

**1.** Preheat oven to 375°. In a large bowl, cream butter and confectioners' sugar until light and fluffy, 3-4 minutes. Beat in milk and vanilla. Gradually beat in flour.

**2.** Cut almond paste into 12 slices (about ¼ in. thick); cut each into quarters. Shape into balls. Wrap tablespoons of cookie dough around almond paste to cover completely. Place 2 in. apart on ungreased baking sheets.

**3.** Bake 10-12 minutes or until golden brown. Remove cookies to wire racks to cool completely.

**4.** In a small bowl, mix vanilla icing ingredients until smooth. For chocolate icing, mix confectioners' sugar, cooled chocolate, milk and vanilla until smooth. Dip cookies in icings as desired; allow excess to drip off. Decorate cookies with assorted sprinkles. Place on waxed paper; let stand until set. Store in airtight containers.

**1 cookie:** 112 cal., 5g fat (3g sat. fat), 10mg chol., 29mg sod., 15g carb. (8g sugars, 1g fiber), 1g pro.

# TOM COLLINS

This cocktail has been popular for a long time, but the origin of the name is still up for debate. Some think it was named after a sweet gin called Old Tom, and others believe the drink was named for the bartender who invented it.
—Taste of Home Test Kitchen

TAKES: 5 MIN. • MAKES: 1 SERVING

1½ to 2 cups ice cubes, divided
2 oz. gin
1½ oz. sour mix
½ cup club soda, chilled
Optional garnish:
Orange slice and maraschino cherry

**1.** Fill a shaker three-fourths full with ice. Place remaining ice in a Collins or highball glass; set aside.

**2.** Add the gin and sour mix to shaker; cover and shake until condensation forms on outside of shaker, 10-15 seconds. Strain into prepared glass. Pour club soda into glass. If desired, garnish with orange slice and cherry.

**1 serving:** 213 cal., 0 fat (0 sat. fat), 0 chol., 29mg sod., 22g carb. (21g sugars, 0 fiber), 0 pro.

# BUFFALO WING DIP

All the signature flavors of Buffalo chicken wings are waiting to be scooped up in this warm dip. We love it with tortilla chips.
—*Lisa Delmont, Lititz, PA*

PREP: 15 MIN. • BAKE: 25 MIN. • MAKES: 24 SERVINGS

2 pkg. (8 oz. each) cream cheese, softened
1 bottle (5 oz.) Louisiana-style hot sauce
2 cups chopped cooked chicken breast
2 cups shredded cheddar cheese, divided
1 cup crumbled blue cheese
¾ cup chopped celery
  Tortilla chips and celery sticks

Preheat oven to 350°. In a large mixing bowl, beat cream cheese and hot sauce until smooth. Stir in chicken, 1 cup cheddar cheese, blue cheese and celery. Transfer to a greased 2-qt. baking dish. Sprinkle with remaining cheddar cheese. Bake, uncovered, until heated through, 25-30 minutes. If desired, top with additional blue cheese and chopped celery. Serve with tortilla chips and celery sticks.

**¼ cup:** 143 cal., 12g fat (7g sat. fat), 42mg chol., 232mg sod., 2g carb. (1g sugars, 0 fiber), 8g pro.

---

# COCONUT SHRIMP

Jumbo shrimp is the perfect vehicle for crunchy, tropical coconut flakes. The fruity salsa is delightful as a dip for this island-influenced appetizer.
—*Marie Hattrup, Sonoma, CA*

PREP: 20 MIN. • COOK: 5 MIN./BATCH • MAKES: 1½ DOZEN

18 uncooked jumbo shrimp (about 1 lb.)
⅓ cup cornstarch
¾ tsp. salt
½ tsp. cayenne pepper
3 large egg whites
2 cups sweetened shredded coconut
  Oil for deep-fat frying

**APRICOT-PINEAPPLE SALSA**
1 cup diced pineapple
½ cup finely chopped red onion
½ cup apricot preserves
½ cup minced fresh cilantro
2 Tbsp. lime juice
1 jalapeno pepper, seeded and chopped
  Salt and pepper to taste
  Lime wedges, optional

**1.** Peel and devein shrimp, leaving tails intact. Make a slit down inner curve of each shrimp, starting with the tail; press lightly to flatten. In a shallow dish, combine the cornstarch, salt and cayenne; set aside. In a bowl, beat egg whites until stiff peaks form. Place the coconut in another shallow dish. Coat shrimp with cornstarch mixture; dip into egg whites, then coat with coconut.

**2.** In an electric skillet or deep-fat fryer, heat oil to 375°. Fry shrimp, a few at a time, 1 to 1½ minutes on each side or until golden brown. Drain on paper towels.

**3.** In a bowl, combine the 7 salsa ingredients. Serve with shrimp and, if desired, lime wedges.

**Note:** Wear disposable gloves when cutting hot peppers; the oils can burn skin. Avoid touching your face.

**1 shrimp with 1 Tbsp. salsa:** 141 cal., 7g fat (4g sat. fat), 31mg chol., 170mg sod., 16g carb. (11g sugars, 1g fiber), 5g pro.

RHUBARB
BRUSCHETTA

# RHUBARB BRUSCHETTA

Fresh rhubarb jam is spooned over cheese-topped bruschetta for a delightful spring appetizer.
Spread the goat cheese on bread slices as soon as they are removed from the broiler.
—*Margee Berry, White Salmon, WA*

TAKES: 30 MIN. • MAKES: 1½ DOZEN

5  tsp. olive oil, divided
1½ cups chopped fresh
    or frozen rhubarb
½  cup chopped red onion
¼  cup sugar
3  Tbsp. lemon juice
1  tsp. grated lemon zest
½  tsp. dried lavender flowers
18 slices French bread baguette
    (¼ in. thick)
½  cup crumbled goat cheese
¼  cup chopped pistachios

1. In a large skillet, heat 1 tsp. oil over medium-high heat. Add rhubarb, onion, sugar and lemon juice; cook and stir until tender, 5-7 minutes. Stir in zest and lavender. Remove from the heat. Mash to a chunky consistency; set aside.

2. Brush bread slices on both sides with remaining 4 tsp. oil. Place bread on ungreased baking sheets. Broil 3-4 in. from heat until golden brown, 1-2 minutes on each side. Spread with goat cheese. Top with rhubarb mixture and pistachios.

**Note:** Look for dried lavender flowers in spice shops. If using lavender from the garden, make sure it hasn't been treated with chemicals.

**1 appetizer:** 62 cal., 4g fat (1g sat. fat), 8mg chol., 60mg sod., 6g carb. (3g sugars, 1g fiber), 2g pro.

# PINEAPPLE CHEESE BALL

Pineapple lends a fruity tang to this fun and tasty appetizer. Instead of forming one large
cheese ball, you could make two smaller balls, one to serve before a meal and one to take to a party.
—*Anne Halfhill, Sunbury, OH*

PREP: 20 MIN. + CHILLING • MAKES: 1 CHEESE BALL (3 CUPS)

2  pkg. (8 oz. each) cream
    cheese, softened
1  can (8 oz.) unsweetened
    crushed pineapple, drained
¼  cup finely chopped green pepper
2  Tbsp. finely chopped onion
2  tsp. seasoned salt
1½ cups chopped walnuts
    Assorted crackers and
    fresh vegetables

In a small bowl, beat cream cheese, pineapple, green pepper, onion and seasoned salt until blended. Cover and refrigerate for 30 minutes. Shape into a ball (mixture will be soft); coat in walnuts. Cover and refrigerate overnight. Serve with crackers and vegetables.

**2 Tbsp.:** 87 cal., 8g fat (2g sat. fat), 10mg chol., 155mg sod., 3g carb. (1g sugars, 1g fiber), 3g pro.

## TEST KITCHEN TIP

*Be sure to drain the pineapple as well as possible to help keep this cheese ball together. If you find that you didn't drain it quite enough, simply scoop the mixture into a bowl and serve as a dip.*

# BEER & PRETZEL CARAMELS

Beer and pretzels are a natural combination—mix them with smooth caramel and you have an awesome candy. The guys will go wild over these crunchy, chunky chews.

*—Jenni Sharp, Milwaukee, WI*

**PREP:** 1 HOUR + COOLING • **COOK:** 50 MIN. + STANDING • **MAKES:** ABOUT 3 LBS. (81 SERVINGS)

## PRETZELS

- ⅓ cup sugar
- ½ tsp. salt
- 2 cups miniature pretzels
- 1 Tbsp. canola oil
- 1 Tbsp. vanilla extract

## CARAMELS

- 4 cups dark beer
- 1 tsp. plus 1 cup butter, divided
- 3 cups sugar
- ⅔ cup corn syrup
- 2 cups heavy whipping cream, divided
- ⅓ cup water
- 1 tsp. salt
- ½ tsp. kosher salt

**1.** Preheat oven to 350°. For pretzels, in a small bowl, combine sugar and salt; set aside. In a large bowl, combine the pretzels, oil and vanilla. Add sugar mixture; toss to coat. Transfer to a 15x10x1-in. foil-lined pan coated with cooking spray.

**2.** Bake until sugars have melted and caramelized, 10--13 minutes, stirring occasionally. Do not over-cook or sugar may burn. Cool completely. Coarsely chop pretzels; set aside.

**3.** In a large saucepan, bring beer to a boil; cook until reduced to ⅔ cup. Set aside to cool.

**4.** Meanwhile, line a 9-in. square pan with foil; grease the foil with 1 tsp. butter and set aside.

**5.** In a Dutch oven, combine the sugar, corn syrup, ⅔ cup cream, water, salt and remaining 1 cup butter. Cook and stir over medium heat until a candy thermometer reads 238°, about 20 minutes. In a small bowl, combine the reduced beer and remaining 1⅓ cup cream; slowly stir into sugar mixture.

**6.** Using a pastry brush dipped in cold water, wash down the side of the pan to eliminate sugar crystals. Cook, stirring constantly, until a candy thermometer reads 245° (firm-ball stage), about 30 minutes.

**7.** Remove from the heat. Pour into prepared pan (do not scrape saucepan); sprinkle with candied pretzels and kosher salt. Let stand until firm, about 5 hours or overnight. Using foil, lift candy out of pan. Discard foil; cut candy into 1-in. squares using a buttered knife. Wrap individually in waxed paper; twist ends.

**Note:** We recommend that you test your candy thermometer before each use by bringing water to a boil; the thermometer should read 212°. Adjust your recipe temperature up or down based on your test.

**1 piece:** 90 cal., 5g fat (3g sat. fat), 14mg chol., 91mg sod., 12g carb. (9g sugars, 0 fiber), 0 pro.

## TEST KITCHEN TIP

*if you like your caramel candies a bit more on the traditional side, simply leave out the pretzels and enjoy the creamy goodness these treats offer.*

66
This recipe
turned out
great! I made
these for a
potluck at
work and
everyone was
impressed!
—DERBIE
TASTEOFHOME.COM

# FRESH HERB VEGETABLE DIP

I entertain a lot and am always looking for an easy crowd-pleaser. If it's one where
I use fresh ingredients from my herb and vegetable garden, it's even better!
—Isabel Minunni, Poughkeepsie, NY

**TAKES: 15 MIN. • MAKES: 3 CUPS**

¼ cup olive oil
3 Tbsp. lemon juice
1½ cups sour cream
2 medium ripe avocados,
   peeled and cubed
2 Tbsp. chopped chives
2 Tbsp. chopped fresh parsley
2 Tbsp. chopped fresh basil
1 Tbsp. chopped fresh tarragon
1 Tbsp. chopped fresh thyme
1 garlic clove, halved
½ tsp. salt
¼ tsp. pepper
  Assorted fresh vegetables

Place the first 12 ingredients in a food processor; process until smooth.
Refrigerate until serving. Serve with vegetables.

**¼ cup:** 140 cal., 14g fat (5g sat. fat), 21mg chol., 111mg sod., 3g carb. (1g sugars,
2g fiber), 2g pro.

## TEST KITCHEN TIP

*Not only does this dip refrigerate well, but allowing it to sit in the
fridge overnight may actually help blend the flavors even more.*

# CRANBERRY-PECAN BRIE CUPS

These appetizer cups are great for entertaining since you can make them
ahead of time and refrigerate until you're ready to pop them in the oven.
—Trisha Kruse, Eagle, ID

**PREP: 25 MIN. • BAKE: 10 MIN. • MAKES: 2 DOZEN**

24 wonton wrappers
   Cooking spray
1 cup whole-berry cranberry sauce
¼ cup orange marmalade
¼ cup honey
2 Tbsp. brandy
½ tsp. ground ginger
½ tsp. apple pie spice
½ lb. Brie cheese (rind removed),
   cut into 24 pieces
½ cup chopped pecans

**1.** Preheat oven to 350°. Press wonton
wrappers into miniature muffin cups
coated with cooking spray. Spritz
wrappers with cooking spray. Bake
6-8 minutes or until edges brown.

**2.** Meanwhile, in a small saucepan,
combine cranberry sauce, marmalade,
honey, brandy and spices; heat through
over medium heat, stirring frequently.
Remove from heat.

**3.** Divide cheese among wonton cups; top with cranberry mixture. Sprinkle with
pecans. Bake 8-10 minutes or until heated through and wonton wrappers are
golden brown.

**1 appetizer:** 110 cal., 4g fat (2g sat. fat), 10mg chol., 113mg sod., 15g carb. (8g sugars,
1g fiber), 3g pro.

GRANDMA'S
BISCUITS
PAGE 79

# CHAPTER 3

# BEST-SHARED BREADS

Talk about lovin' from the oven! Few things offer heartwarming appeal like a golden, aromatic loaf of freshly baked bread. Turn here for breads that are sure to satisfy as well as homemade rolls, bagels, cornbreads, breadsticks, muffins and more.

# LEMON BLUEBERRY COFFEE CAKE

Baking mix eases preparation of this quick coffee cake.
Fresh blueberries, lemon peel and a fast glaze really perk up the flavor.
It's among the treats I always make for guests and family.
—*Nancy Brown, Dahinda, IL*

PREP: 15 MIN. • BAKE: 25 MIN. + COOLING • MAKES: 8 SERVINGS

1 large egg, room temperature, lightly beaten
⅓ cup sugar
1 tsp. grated lemon zest
⅔ cup 2% milk
2¼ cups biscuit/baking mix
1 cup fresh or frozen blueberries
¾ cup confectioners' sugar
4 tsp. lemon juice

1. Preheat oven to 350°. In a large bowl, combine egg, sugar, lemon zest and milk; mix well. Stir in biscuit mix just until moistened. Fold in blueberries. Pour into a greased 9-in. round baking pan.

2. Bake until a toothpick inserted in the center comes out clean, 25-30 minutes. Cool for 10 minutes before removing from pan to a wire rack.

3. Combine confectioners' sugar and lemon juice until smooth; drizzle over warm cake. Garnish with additional blueberries. Cut into wedges.

**1 piece:** 234 cal., 4g fat (1g sat. fat), 25mg chol., 343mg sod., 47g carb. (24g sugars, 0 fiber), 4g pro.

## TEST KITCHEN TIP

*The trick to baking with frozen berries is to keep them from tinting the entire batter blue. The best way to do so is to rinse the berries with cold water 2-3 times, until the water runs clear. Pat dry before gently folding them into your batter, just until combined—if you see blue streaks starting to form, stop.*

—HAZEL WHEATON, *TASTE OF HOME* BOOK EDITOR

HAZELNUT
CHOCOLATE CHIP
SCONES

66
Love this
recipe.
I've made
these scones
a few times.
Everybody
loves them!
—KAREN8987
TASTEOFHOME.COM

# HAZELNUT CHOCOLATE CHIP SCONES

With chocolate, hazelnuts and the tangy taste of buttermilk, these delicious scones
are easy to make, come together fast and taste so good with your morning coffee.
—*Trisha Kruse, Eagle, ID*

**PREP: 20 MIN. • BAKE: 15 MIN. • MAKES: 8 SCONES**

2 cups all-purpose flour
¼ cup packed brown sugar
1½ tsp. baking powder
½ tsp. baking soda
½ tsp. salt
½ cup cold butter, cubed
1 large egg, room temperature
½ cup buttermilk
1½ tsp. vanilla extract
1 cup semisweet chocolate chips
1 cup hazelnuts, coarsely chopped

1. Preheat oven to 400°. Whisk together first 5 ingredients; cut in butter until mixture resembles coarse crumbs. In another bowl, whisk together egg, buttermilk and vanilla; stir into crumb mixture just until moistened. Stir in chocolate chips and hazelnuts.

2. Turn onto a lightly floured surface; knead gently 8 times. Pat dough into a 6-in. circle. Cut into 8 wedges; place on a greased baking sheet. Bake until golden brown, 15-20 minutes. Serve warm.

**Note:** To substitute for each cup of buttermilk, use 1 Tbsp. white vinegar or lemon juice plus enough milk to measure 1 cup. Stir, then let stand 5 min. Or, use 1 cup plain yogurt or 1¾ tsp. cream of tartar plus 1 cup milk.

**1 scone:** 409 cal., 23g fat (10g sat. fat), 76mg chol., 327mg sod., 47g carb. (20g sugars, 3g fiber), 8g pro.

# SLOW-COOKER BANANA BREAD

I love to use my slow cooker. I started to experiment with making bread in it so I wouldn't have to
heat up my kitchen by turning on my oven. It's so easy and simple. I now make it this way all the time.
—*Nicole Gackowski, Antioch, CA*

**PREP: 10 MIN. • COOK: 2½ HOURS • MAKES: 16 SERVINGS**

5 medium ripe bananas
2½ cups self-rising flour
1 can (14 oz.) sweetened condensed milk
1 tsp. ground cinnamon
Cinnamon sugar, optional

1. Place a piece of parchment in a 5-qt. slow cooker, letting ends extend up sides. Grease paper with cooking spray. Combine the first 4 ingredients in a large bowl. Pour batter into prepared slow cooker. If desired, sprinkle cinnamon sugar over the top of batter. Cover slow cooker with a double layer of white paper towels; place lid securely over towels.

2. Cook, covered, on high until bread is lightly browned, 2½-3 hours. To avoid scorching, rotate slow cooker insert a half turn midway through cooking. Remove bread from slow cooker using parchment to lift; cool slightly before slicing.

**Note:** As a substitute for each cup of self-rising flour, place 1½ tsp. baking powder and ½ tsp. salt in a measuring cup. Add all-purpose flour to measure 1 cup.

**1 piece:** 210 cal., 3g fat (2g sat. fat), 11mg chol., 276mg sod., 41g carb. (23g sugars, 2g fiber), 5g pro.

# PARMESAN-SAGE BEER BREAD

I'm asked to bring this savory loaf to nearly every function I attend. It's great as a side dish, but if you're in the mood for an extraordinary sandwich, start with two slices of beer bread.
—*Elizabeth King, Duluth, MN*

PREP: 10 MIN. • BAKE: 45 MIN. • MAKES: 1 LOAF (12 PIECES)

2½ cups all-purpose flour
1 cup grated Parmesan cheese
2 Tbsp. sugar
3 tsp. baking powder
1 Tbsp. chopped fresh sage
1 tsp. salt
1½ cups beer
¼ cup melted butter, divided

**1.** Preheat oven to 375°. In a small bowl, whisk the first 6 ingredients. Add beer and 3 Tbsp. melted butter; stir just until moistened.

**2.** Transfer to a greased 8x4-in. loaf pan. Drizzle with remaining butter. Bake 45-50 minutes or until a toothpick inserted in center comes out clean. Cool in pan 5 minutes before removing to a wire rack to cool.

**1 piece:** 177 cal., 6g fat (4g sat. fat), 16mg chol., 469mg sod., 24g carb. (3g sugars, 1g fiber), 5g pro.

# LOUISIANA PECAN BACON BREAD

One Christmas, the babysitter brought gifts for my daughter and a basket of goodies, including pecan bread. When I make this bread, I remember that kind soul.
—*Marina Castle-Kelley, Canyon Country, CA*

PREP: 20 MIN. • BAKE: 50 MIN. + COOLING • MAKES: 1 LOAF (16 PIECES)

6 bacon strips, chopped
6 oz. cream cheese, softened
⅓ cup sugar
1 large egg
2 cups all-purpose flour
2½ tsp. baking powder
½ tsp. salt
¾ cup 2% milk
1 cup chopped pecans
¼ cup finely chopped onion
¼ cup chopped green pepper

**1.** Preheat oven to 350°. In a large skillet, cook bacon over medium-low heat until crisp, stirring occasionally. Remove with a slotted spoon; drain on paper towels. Reserve 2 Tbsp. drippings; cool slightly.

**2.** In a large bowl, beat cream cheese, sugar and reserved drippings until smooth. Beat in egg. In another bowl, whisk flour, baking powder and salt; add to cream cheese mixture alternately with milk, beating well after each addition. Fold in pecans, onion, pepper and bacon. Transfer to a greased 9x5-in. loaf pan.

**3.** Bake until a toothpick inserted in center comes out clean, 50-60 minutes. Cool in pan 10 minutes before removing to a wire rack to cool.

**1 piece:** 198 cal., 12g fat (4g sat. fat), 29mg chol., 242mg sod., 18g carb. (6g sugars, 1g fiber), 5g pro.

> 66
> **This quick bread is very good and has an almost biscuit-like consistency.**
> —RWIPPEL
> TASTEOFHOME.COM

> "I made these for our church's progressive supper and they were a big hit."
> —TKUEHL
> TASTEOFHOME.COM

# ASIAGO BAGELS

Discover a cheesy alternative to the usual sweet bread brunch offerings.
There's no need to stop by a bakery when you can make these bagels at home.

*—Tami Kuehl, Loup City, NE*

**PREP:** 30 MIN. + RESTING • **BAKE:** 15 MIN. • **MAKES:** 1 DOZEN

1   cup water (70° to 80°)
2   large eggs, room temperature
¼   cup plus 1 Tbsp. olive oil
2   Tbsp. honey
¾   cup shredded Asiago cheese, divided
⅓   cup nonfat dry milk powder
1½  tsp. salt
1   tsp. dried basil
2   cups whole wheat flour
1½  cups plus 2 Tbsp. all-purpose flour
4   tsp. active dry yeast
1   large egg white
1   Tbsp. water

**1.** In bread machine pan, place the water, eggs, oil, honey, ½ cup cheese, milk powder, salt, basil, flours and yeast in order suggested by manufacturer. Select dough setting (check dough after 5 minutes of mixing; add 1 to 2 Tbsp. of water or flour if needed).

**2.** When cycle is completed, turn dough onto a lightly floured surface. Shape into 12 balls. Push thumb through centers to form a 1½-in. hole. Stretch and shape dough to form an even ring. Cover and let rest for 10 minutes; flatten bagels slightly.

**3.** Fill a Dutch oven two-thirds full with water; bring to a boil. Drop bagels, 2 at a time, into boiling water. Cook for 45 seconds; turn and cook 45 seconds longer. Remove with a slotted spoon; drain well on paper towels.

**4.** In a small bowl, combine egg white and water; brush over bagels. Sprinkle with remaining cheese. Place 2 in. apart on greased baking sheets. Bake at 400° for 15-20 minutes or until golden brown. Remove to wire racks to cool.

**Note:** We recommend you do not use a bread machine's time-delay feature for this recipe.

**1 bagel:** 239 cal., 9g fat (2g sat. fat), 42mg chol., 342mg sod., 32g carb. (5g sugars, 3g fiber), 9g pro.

## TEST KITCHEN TIP

*You can still prepare these bagels even if you don't have a bread machine. Simply dissolve yeast in warm water. In a large bowl, whisk together flours. In another large bowl, combine oil, honey, eggs, salt, ½ cup cheese, milk powder, basil, yeast mixture and 2 cups flour mixture; beat on medium speed until smooth. Stir in enough remaining flour to form a soft dough (dough will be sticky). Turn onto a floured surface; knead until smooth and elastic, 6-8 minutes. Place in a greased bowl, turning once to grease top. Cover bowl and let dough rise in a warm place until doubled, about 1 hour. Preheat oven to 400°. Divide and shape dough into 12 balls. Push thumb through each center to form a 1½-in. hole, shaping dough to form an even ring. Flatten slightly; cover and let rest 10 minutes. Meanwhile, combine egg white and 1 Tbsp. water. Boil and bake as directed, brushing boiled bagels with egg white mixture and sprinkling with remaining cheese.*

# APRICOT, PINEAPPLE & ALMOND COFFEE CAKE

I created this recipe for a contest at the Los Angeles County Fair in the 1980s.
My kids were very proud of me when my name was called for first place.
—Marina Castle-Kelley, Canyon Country, CA

PREP: 30 MIN. • COOK: 1 HOUR + COOLING • MAKES: 12 SERVINGS

½ cup unsalted butter, softened
1 cup superfine sugar
2 large eggs, room temperature
½ tsp. almond extract
1½ cups all-purpose flour
½ cup almond flour
½ tsp. baking powder
½ tsp. baking soda
½ tsp. kosher salt
1 cup sour cream
¾ cup pineapple preserves
¾ cup apricot preserves
½ cup sliced almonds
Confectioners' sugar

1. Preheat oven to 350°. In a large bowl, beat butter and sugar until crumbly, about 2 minutes. Add eggs, 1 at a time, beating well after each addition. Beat in extract. In another bowl, whisk flour, almond flour, baking powder, baking soda and salt; add to creamed mixture alternately with sour cream, beating well after each addition.

2. Transfer half the batter to a greased 10-in. springform pan. Mix pineapple and apricot preserves; drop by tablespoonfuls over batter. Carefully top with remaining batter. Sprinkle with almonds. Bake until a toothpick inserted in center comes out clean, 60-65 minutes. Cool on a wire rack 10 minutes. Loosen side from pan with a knife. Cool completely. Remove rim from pan. Sprinkle with confectioners' sugar.

**1 piece:** 389 cal., 17g fat (8g sat. fat), 56mg chol., 182mg sod., 57g carb. (39g sugars, 1g fiber), 5g pro.

---

# OVERNIGHT YEAST ROLLS

It's easy to make light and flavorful rolls with this no-fuss recipe.
The dough can also be used for cinnamon rolls, herb bread or coffee cake.
—Trisha Kruse, Eagle, ID

PREP: 20 MIN. + CHILLING • BAKE: 15 MIN. • MAKES: 2 DOZEN

1 Tbsp. sugar
1 Tbsp. active dry yeast
1½ tsp. salt
5½ to 6 cups all-purpose flour
1 cup buttermilk
½ cup water
½ cup butter, cubed
3 large eggs, room temperature
2 Tbsp. butter, melted

1. In a large bowl, mix sugar, yeast, salt and 3 cups flour. In a small saucepan, heat buttermilk, water and ½ cup butter to 120°-130°. Add to dry ingredients; beat on medium speed 2 minutes. Add eggs; beat on high 2 minutes. Stir in enough remaining flour to form a soft dough (dough will be sticky).

2. Do not knead. Place dough in a large greased bowl. Cover; refrigerate overnight.

3. Punch down dough. Turn onto a lightly floured surface; divide and shape into 24 balls. Place 2 in. apart on greased baking sheets. Cover with kitchen towels; let rise in a warm place until almost doubled, about 1½ hours.

4. Preheat oven to 400°. Bake until golden brown, 15-20 minutes. Brush with melted butter. Remove from pans to wire racks; serve warm.

**1 roll:** 163 cal., 6g fat (3g sat. fat), 36mg chol., 215mg sod., 23g carb. (1g sugars, 1g fiber), 4g pro.

66
A delicious
homemade
coffee cake to
bring to a
potluck or family
gatherings. The
cake is soft and
not too sweet!
—JELLYBUG
TASTEOFHOME.COM

APRICOT, PINEAPPLE &
ALMOND COFFEE CAKE

# MAPLE-CHAI PUMPKIN MUFFINS

Why use ordinary pumpkin pie spice when you can up the ante with your own homemade chai spice? The maple syrup pairs so well with the pumpkin and this warming spice blend. If you do not want to make homemade chai spice, you can substitute pumpkin pie spice. If you prefer, you may substitute old-fashioned rolled oats, pecans, walnuts or even white chocolate chips for the pepitas topping.
—Debra Keil, Owasso, OK

**PREP:** 25 MIN. • **BAKE:** 20 MIN. • **MAKES:** 1 DOZEN

1   cup all-purpose flour
¾   cup whole wheat flour
1   tsp. baking soda
1   tsp. ground cardamom
½   tsp. salt
½   tsp. ground cinnamon
    Dash ground nutmeg
    Dash ground cloves
2   large eggs, room temperature
1   cup canned pumpkin
½   cup maple syrup
⅓   cup melted coconut oil
¼   cup 2% milk
1   tsp. vanilla extract
⅓   cup plus 1 Tbsp. pepitas, divided

1. Preheat oven to 325°. In a large bowl, whisk the first 8 ingredients. In another bowl, whisk eggs, pumpkin, syrup, coconut oil, milk and vanilla until blended. Add to flour mixture; stir just until moistened. Fold in ⅓ cup pepitas.

2. Fill greased or foil-lined muffin cups three-fourths full. Sprinkle with remaining 1 Tbsp. pepitas. Bake until a toothpick inserted in center comes out clean, 20-25 minutes. Cool 5 minutes before removing from pan to a wire rack. Serve warm.

**Freeze option:** Freeze cooled muffins in freezer containers. To use, thaw at room temperature or, if desired, microwave each muffin on high until heated through, 20-30 seconds.

**1 muffin:** 197 cal., 9g fat (6g sat. fat), 31mg chol., 230mg sod., 25g carb. (9g sugars, 2g fiber), 5g pro.

# SKILLET CORNBREAD

This skillet bread looks like a puffy pancake but has the easy-to-cut texture of conventional cornbread. It complements everything from chicken to chili.
—Kathy Teela, Tucson, AZ

**TAKES:** 15 MIN. • **MAKES:** 4 SERVINGS

¼   cup all-purpose flour
¼   cup cornmeal
½   tsp. baking powder
¼   tsp. salt
1   large egg
¼   cup 2% milk
4   tsp. vegetable oil,
    divided

1. In a small bowl, combine flour, cornmeal, baking powder and salt. In another small bowl, whisk the egg, milk and 3 tsp. oil; stir into dry ingredients just until moistened.

2. Heat remaining oil in a heavy 8-in. skillet over low heat. Pour batter into the hot skillet; cover and cook for 4-5 minutes. Turn and cook 4 minutes longer or until golden brown.

**1 piece:** 127 cal., 6g fat (1g sat. fat), 54mg chol., 222mg sod., 13g carb. (1g sugars, 1g fiber), 4g pro.

# SAGE FONTINA FOCACCIA

These rustic loaves have plenty of
sage flavor—a tasty addition to any feast.
—*Beth Dauenhauer, Pueblo, CO*

PREP: 30 MIN. + RISING • BAKE: 10 MIN. • MAKES: 1 LOAF (8 WEDGES)

1¼ tsp. active dry yeast
½ cup warm water (110° to 115°)
½ tsp. honey
¾ to 1 cup all-purpose flour
¼ cup whole wheat flour
1 Tbsp. olive oil
2 tsp. minced fresh sage
¼ tsp. salt

**TOPPING**
1½ tsp. olive oil, divided
8 fresh sage leaves
½ cup shredded fontina cheese

**1.** In a large bowl, dissolve yeast in warm water. Stir in honey; let stand for 5 minutes. Add ¾ cup all- purpose flour, whole wheat flour, oil, minced sage and salt. Beat on medium speed for 3 minutes or until smooth. Stir in enough remaining flour to form a soft dough (dough will be sticky).

**2.** Turn onto a lightly floured surface; knead until smooth and elastic, 6-8 minutes. Place in a greased bowl, turning once to grease the top. Cover and let rise in a warm place until doubled, about 1 hour.

**3.** Punch the dough down. Cover and let rest for 5 minutes. Place 1 Tbsp. olive oil in a 10-in. cast-iron or other ovenproof skillet; tilt pan to evenly coat. Add dough; shape to fit pan. Cover and let rise until doubled, about 30 minutes.

**4.** With fingertips, make several dimples over top of dough. For topping, brush dough with 1 tsp. oil. Top with sage leaves; brush leaves with remaining oil. Sprinkle with cheese. Bake at 400° until golden brown, 10-15 minutes. Remove to a wire rack. Serve warm.

**1 wedge:** 112 cal., 5g fat (2g sat. fat), 8mg chol., 131mg sod., 12g carb. (1g sugars, 1g fiber), 4g pro.

# DOUBLE CORN CORNBREAD

Looking for a moist bread to dunk in a bowl of chowder or chili? Try this tasty recipe. It's one of my faves! I could eat it for breakfast, lunch and dinner.
—*Silvana Nardone, Brooklyn, NY*

**PREP:** 15 MIN. • **BAKE:** 40 MIN. • **MAKES:** 1 LOAF (12 PIECES)

1 cup gluten-free all-purpose baking flour (without xanthan gum)
1 cup cornmeal
¼ cup sugar
1 Tbsp. baking powder
1 tsp. baking soda
1 tsp. salt
2 large eggs, lightly beaten
1 cup rice milk
¼ cup canola oil
1 Tbsp. cider vinegar
1 cup frozen corn, thawed

**1.** Preheat oven to 350°. In a large bowl, combine the flour, cornmeal, sugar, baking powder, baking soda and salt. In a small bowl, whisk the eggs, rice milk, oil and vinegar. Stir into dry ingredients just until moistened; stir in corn.

**2.** Transfer to a greased 8x4-in. loaf pan. Bake until top is lightly browned and a toothpick inserted in the center comes out clean, 40-45 minutes. Cool on a wire rack.

**Note:** Read all ingredient labels for possible gluten content prior to use. Ingredient formulas can change, and production facilities vary among brands. If you're concerned that your brand may contain gluten, contact the company.

**1 piece:** 334 cal., 13g fat (1g sat. fat), 71mg chol., 842mg sod., 51g carb. (10g sugars, 4g fiber), 7g pro.

## TEST KITCHEN TIP

*It's easy to make this gluten-free cornbread your own by switching up the mix-ins. Try herbs like sage, rosemary or thyme. You can also make a spicy cornbread with chili powder or red pepper flakes. To make this loaf vegan, use your favorite egg replacement.*
—MAGGIE KNOEBEL, *TASTE OF HOME* ASSOCIATE RECIPE EDITOR/TESTER

# MOM'S ITALIAN BREAD

I think Mom used to bake at least four of these tender loaves at once, and they never lasted long. She served the bread with every Italian meal. I love it toasted too.

—*Linda Harrington, Windham, NH*

**PREP:** 30 MIN. + RISING • **BAKE:** 20 MIN. • **MAKES:** 2 LOAVES (12 PIECES EACH)

1   pkg. (¼ oz.) active dry yeast
2   cups warm water (110° to 115°)
1   tsp. sugar
2   tsp. salt
5½  cups all-purpose flour

**1.** In a large bowl, dissolve yeast in warm water. Add the sugar, salt and 3 cups flour. Beat on medium speed for 3 minutes. Stir in remaining flour to form a soft dough.

**2.** Turn onto a floured surface; knead until smooth and elastic, 6-8 minutes. Place in a greased bowl, turning once to grease the top. Cover and let rise in a warm place until doubled, about 1 hour.

**3.** Punch dough down. Turn onto a floured surface; divide in half. Shape each portion into a loaf. Place each loaf seam side down on a greased baking sheet. Cover and let rise until doubled, about 30 minutes.

**4.** Meanwhile, preheat oven to 400°. With a sharp knife, make 4 shallow slashes across top of each loaf. Bake 20-25 minutes or until golden brown. Remove from pans to wire racks to cool.

**1 piece:** 106 cal., 0 fat (0 sat. fat), 0 chol., 197mg sod., 22g carb. (1g sugars, 1g fiber), 3g pro.

## TEST KITCHEN TIP

*It's important to always test yeast before you use it. To see if your yeast is still active, dissolve 1 tsp. of sugar into warm water and then mix in your active dry yeast. Allow to sit for 5-10 minutes. If the mixture becomes nice and foamy, you're good to go.*

“

My kids and I decided to try this one for pizza dough. It's the only dough we use for homemade pizza now.

—MARCIE
TASTEOFHOME.COM

PARMESAN GARLIC
BREADSTICKS

# PARMESAN GARLIC BREADSTICKS

These tender breadsticks fill the kitchen with a tempting aroma when they are baking,
and they're wonderful served warm. My family tells me I can't make them enough.
—Gaylene Anderson, Sandy, UT

PREP: 40 MIN. + RISING • BAKE: 10 MIN. • MAKES: 3 DOZEN

2 pkg. (¼ oz. each) active dry yeast
1½ cups warm water (110° to 115°)
½ cup warm 2% milk (110° to 115°)
3 Tbsp. sugar
3 Tbsp. plus ¼ cup butter, softened, divided
1 tsp. salt
4½ to 5½ cups all-purpose flour
¼ cup grated Parmesan cheese
½ tsp. garlic salt

1. In a large bowl, dissolve yeast in warm water. Add the milk, sugar, 3 Tbsp. butter, salt and 2 cups flour. Beat until smooth. Stir in enough remaining flour to form a soft dough.

2. Turn onto a floured surface; knead until smooth and elastic, 6-8 minutes. Place in a greased bowl, turning once to grease top. Cover and let rise in a warm place until doubled, about 45 minutes.

3. Punch the dough down. Turn onto a floured surface; divide into 36 pieces. Shape each piece into a 6-in. rope. Place 2 in. apart on greased baking sheets. Cover and let rise until doubled, about 25 minutes.

4. Melt remaining butter; brush over dough. Sprinkle with Parmesan cheese and garlic salt. Bake at 400° until golden brown, 8-10 minutes. Remove from pans to wire racks.

**1 breadstick:** 86 cal., 3g fat (2g sat. fat), 7mg chol., 126mg sod., 13g carb. (1g sugars, 0 fiber), 2g pro.

# GRANDMA'S BISCUITS

SHOWN ON PAGE 60

Homemade biscuits add a warm and comforting touch to any meal.
My grandmother makes these tender biscuits to go with her seafood chowder.
—Melissa Obernesser, Oriskany, NY

TAKES: 25 MIN. • MAKES: 10 BISCUITS

2 cups all-purpose flour
3 tsp. baking powder
1 tsp. salt
⅓ cup shortening
⅔ cup 2% milk
1 large egg, room temperature, lightly beaten

1. Preheat oven to 450°. In a large bowl, whisk flour, baking powder and salt. Cut in shortening until mixture resembles coarse crumbs. Add milk; stir just until moistened.

2. Turn onto a lightly floured surface; knead gently 8-10 times. Pat dough into a 10x4-in. rectangle. Cut rectangle lengthwise in half; cut crosswise to make 10 squares.

3. Place 1 in. apart on an ungreased baking sheet; brush tops with egg. Bake until golden brown, 8-10 minutes. Serve warm.

**1 biscuit:** 165 cal., 7g fat (2g sat. fat), 20mg chol., 371mg sod., 20g carb. (1g sugars, 1g fiber), 4g pro.

# LEMON POPOVERS WITH PECAN HONEY BUTTER

My mom passed this recipe down to me many years ago. We love the delicate lemon
flavor with the pecan honey butter. The popovers are a nice addition to any
dinner but they're especially delicious at breakfast with a bowl of fruit and yogurt.
—Joan Hallford, North Richland Hills, TX

**PREP: 10 MIN. • BAKE: 25 MIN. • MAKES: 6 SERVINGS**

2   large eggs, room temperature
1   cup 2% milk
1   cup all-purpose flour
½   tsp. salt
5   Tbsp. finely chopped toasted
    pecans, divided
¾   tsp. grated lemon zest
2   tsp. lemon juice
6   Tbsp. butter, softened
6   Tbsp. honey

1. Preheat oven to 450°. In a large bowl, whisk eggs and milk until blended. Whisk in flour and salt until smooth (do not overbeat). Stir in 3 Tbsp. pecans, lemon zest and lemon juice.

2. Generously grease a 6-cup popover pan with nonstick spray; fill cups half full with batter. Bake 15 minutes. Reduce oven setting to 350° (do not open oven door). Bake until deep golden brown, 10-15 minutes longer (do not underbake).

3. Meanwhile, combine butter, honey and remaining 2 Tbsp. pecans. Immediately remove popovers from pan to a wire rack. Pierce side of each popover with a sharp knife to let steam escape. Serve immediately with pecan honey butter.

**1 popover with about 2 Tbsp. honey butter:** 325 cal., 18g fat (9g sat. fat), 96mg chol., 332mg sod., 36g carb. (20g sugars, 1g fiber), 6g pro.

# BLUEBERRY BREAD

This is a simple quick bread recipe that I look forward to making when fresh
blueberries are in season. It's so good, though, that I end up making it year-round.
—Karen Scales, Waukesha, WI

**PREP: 10 MIN. • BAKE: 1 HOUR + COOLING • MAKES: 1 LOAF (12 PIECES)**

2   cups plus 2 Tbsp. all-purpose
    flour, divided
¾   cup sugar
1   tsp. baking powder
½   tsp. salt
¼   tsp. baking soda
1   large egg, room temperature
⅔   cup orange juice
2   Tbsp. butter, melted
1   cup fresh or frozen blueberries

1. Preheat oven to 325°. In a large bowl, combine 2 cups flour, sugar, baking powder, salt and baking soda. Whisk the egg, orange juice and butter. Stir into dry ingredients just until moistened. Toss blueberries with remaining flour; fold into batter.

2. Pour into a greased 8x4-in. loaf pan. Bake until a toothpick inserted in the center comes out clean, 60-65 minutes. Cool in pan for 10 minutes before removing to a wire rack to cool completely.

**Note:** If using frozen blueberries, use without thawing to avoid discoloring the batter.

**1 piece:** 165 cal., 3g fat (1g sat. fat), 21mg chol., 186mg sod., 33g carb. (15g sugars, 1g fiber), 3g pro. **Diabetic exchanges:** 2 starch, ½ fat.

LEMON POPOVERS
WITH PECAN
HONEY BUTTER

"
I shared
these with
company
and they
loved them!
—DEBPENNS
TASTEOFHOME.COM

# NO-KNEAD HARVEST BREAD

This loaf allows you to enjoy homemade bread without all the work. Fresh-baked slices are seriously irresistible.
—Taste of Home *Test Kitchen*

**PREP: 30 MIN. + RISING • BAKE: 30 MIN. • MAKES: 1 LOAF (16 PIECES)**

½ cup whole wheat flour
½ cup cornmeal
⅓ cup plus 2 Tbsp. assorted seeds, such as sesame seeds, flaxseed, sunflower kernels and poppy seeds, divided
1¾ tsp. salt
¼ tsp. active dry yeast
3 cups bread flour, divided
2¼ cups cool water (55° to 65°)
2 Tbsp. molasses
Additional cornmeal

**1.** In a large bowl, combine the whole wheat flour, cornmeal, ⅓ cup seeds, salt, yeast and 2½ cups bread flour. Stir in water and molasses until blended; dough will be wet and sticky.

**2.** Cover and let stand at room temperature until more than doubled in size and bubbles are present on surface, 12-18 hours. Stir in remaining bread flour.

**3.** Grease a baking sheet and sprinkle well with additional cornmeal; turn dough onto prepared pan. Gently shape with a spatula into a 9-in. round loaf. Cover and let rise at room temperature for 2 hours or until dough holds an indentation when gently pressed (loaf will slightly increase in size).

**4.** Arrange 1 oven rack at lowest rack setting; place second rack in middle of oven. Place an oven-safe skillet on bottom oven rack; preheat oven and skillet to 475°. Meanwhile, in a small saucepan, bring 2 cups water to a boil.

**5.** Gently press remaining seeds onto top of loaf. Wearing oven mitts, place bread on top rack. Pull bottom rack out by 6-8 in.; add boiling water to skillet. (Work quickly and carefully, pouring water away from you. Don't worry if some water is left in the saucepan.) Carefully slide bottom rack back into place; quickly close door to trap steam in oven.

**6.** Reduce heat to 425°; bake for 10 minutes. Remove skillet from oven; bake bread 20-25 minutes longer or until deep golden brown and bread sounds hollow when center is tapped. Cool on a wire rack.

**1 piece:** 134 cal., 2g fat (0 sat. fat), 0 chol., 265mg sod., 26g carb. (2g sugars, 2g fiber), 5g pro. **Diabetic exchanges:** 1½ starch.

**Dutch oven harvest bread:** After stirring in remaining bread flour, cover bowl again and let dough rise for 2 hours. Lightly oil an oven-safe 5-qt. round Dutch oven; cover and place in oven. Preheat oven to 425°. Carefully remove hot Dutch oven. Sprinkle a piece of parchment with cornmeal. With a spatula, transfer dough to prepared parchment. Using the parchment, immediately lower bread into heated Dutch oven. Sprinkle with remaining seeds. Cover and bake for 20 minutes. Uncover; bake until deep golden brown and bread sounds hollow when center is tapped, 15-20 minutes longer. Remove from pan to a wire rack. Bread may also be prepared in a clay bread baker; prepare baker according to manufacturer's directions.

# RIBBON PUMPKIN BREAD

No one will guess they're eating lighter when you serve moist slices of
this pretty pumpkin bread with a ribbon of cream cheese inside.
—*Beth Ask, Ulster, PA*

**PREP:** 15 MIN. • **BAKE:** 40 MIN. + COOLING • **MAKES:** 2 LOAVES (12 PIECES EACH)

6 oz. reduced-fat cream cheese
¼ cup sugar
1 Tbsp. all-purpose flour
2 large egg whites

## BATTER

1 cup canned pumpkin
½ cup unsweetened applesauce
1 large egg, room temperature
2 large egg whites, room temperature
1 Tbsp. canola oil
1⅔ cups all-purpose flour
1¼ cups sugar
1 tsp. baking soda
1 tsp. baking powder
½ tsp. salt
½ tsp. ground cinnamon
½ tsp. ground cloves
⅓ cup chopped walnuts

**1.** For filling, combine the cream cheese, sugar, flour and egg whites in a bowl; set aside.

**2.** In a bowl, beat the pumpkin, applesauce, egg, egg whites and oil. Combine the flour, sugar, baking soda, baking powder, salt, cinnamon and cloves; add to the pumpkin mixture. Stir in walnuts.

**3.** Divide half of the batter between two 8x4-in. loaf pans coated with cooking spray. Spread each with filling; top with remaining batter.

**4.** Bake at 350° for 40-45 minutes or until a toothpick inserted in the center comes out clean. Cool for 10 minutes before removing from pans to wire racks to cool completely. Refrigerate leftovers.

**1 piece:** 127 cal., 3g fat (1g sat. fat), 13mg chol., 165mg sod., 21g carb. (14g sugars, 1g fiber), 3g pro. **Diabetic exchanges:** 1½ starch, ½ fat.

BASIL CHICKEN
SANDWICHES, PAGE 99

"

This is a very
tasty sandwich
and so easy
to make. My
family loves it.
—CHRISSELLSCANDLES
TASTEOFHOME.COM

# CHAPTER 4

# SOUPS & SAMMIES

Don't settle for the same old soup and sandwich combo! Serving up something new, creative and tasty is a snap when you consider the finger-licking lip smackers found here. These are the family favorites home cooks are asked about most, and now they're sharing those secrets with you.

# TUNA CHEESE-WAFFLE SANDWICHES

I love cheddar chaffles and tuna salad sandwiches. Combining the two makes an incredible sandwich with a crunchy, cheesy element for the bread.
—Arlene Erlbach, Morton Grove, IL

**TAKES:** 30 MIN. • **MAKES:** 4 SANDWICHES

5 Tbsp. mayonnaise
2 Tbsp. cream cheese, softened
2 cans light tuna in water (5 oz. each), well drained
1 celery rib, finely chopped
¼ cup finely chopped red onion
2 Tbsp. minced fresh parsley
1 Tbsp. lemon juice
½ cup diced dill pickle, divided
4 large eggs, beaten
2 cups shredded extra sharp cheddar cheese
8 slices tomato
Lettuce leaves, optional

1. Preheat waffle maker. In a large bowl, whisk mayonnaise and cream cheese until smooth. Add tuna, celery, onion, parsley, lemon juice and 2 Tbsp. chopped pickles. Set aside.

2. In a separate bowl, whisk eggs. In the preheated waffle maker, sprinkle ½ cup cheese and half the remaining pickles. Pour half the whisked egg over the cheese. Top with ½ cup cheese. Close lid and bake according to manufacturer's directions until golden brown, 4-5 minutes. Repeat with remaining cheese, pickles and eggs.

3. Spread the tuna mixture evenly over half the waffle pieces; top with tomatoes, lettuce leaves if desired and remaining waffle pieces to make sandwiches.

**1 sandwich:** 515 cal., 39g fat (16g sat. fat), 281mg chol., 881mg sod., 6g carb. (3g sugars, 1g fiber), 34g pro.

# CHEDDAR BROCCOLI SOUP

Frozen broccoli speeds up the time it takes to prepare this creamy, comforting soup.
—Louise Beatty, Amherst, NY

**TAKES:** 30 MIN. • **MAKES:** 4 SERVINGS

1 small onion, chopped
2 garlic cloves, minced
2 Tbsp. butter
2 Tbsp. all-purpose flour
1 can (14½ oz.) beef broth
1½ cups 2% milk
1 pkg. (10 oz.) frozen chopped broccoli
1 tsp. ground mustard
1 tsp. Worcestershire sauce
¼ tsp. ground nutmeg
1 cup shredded cheddar cheese
Additional shredded cheddar cheese, optional

1. In a saucepan, saute onion and garlic in butter until tender. Stir in flour until blended. Gradually stir in broth; bring to a boil. Cook and stir for 2 minutes.

2. Stir in the milk, broccoli, mustard, Worcestershire sauce and nutmeg. Bring to a boil. Reduce heat; simmer, uncovered, for 6-8 minutes or until heated through. Stir in cheese until melted. If desired, serve with additional cheese.

**1 cup:** 252 cal., 16g fat (11g sat. fat), 52mg chol., 750mg sod., 15g carb. (7g sugars, 3g fiber), 13g pro.

> 66
> **This was a hit at a church benefit supper. Everyone just loved it!**
> —2124ARIZONA
> STAFF TITLE HERE

# LOUISIANA GUMBO

Gumbo is a stew-like dish made with meat or seafood, tomatoes, sweet bell peppers and okra.
You can serve it with hot pepper sauce on the side so guests can add their own heat.
—*Gloria Mason, Springhill, LA*

PREP: 20 MIN. • COOK: 1¾ HOURS + COOLING • MAKES: 12 SERVINGS

1 broiler/fryer chicken
(3 to 3½ lbs.), cut up
2 qt. water
¾ cup all-purpose flour
½ cup canola oil
½ cup sliced green onions
½ cup chopped onion
½ cup chopped green pepper
½ cup chopped sweet red pepper
½ cup chopped celery
2 garlic cloves, minced
½ lb. smoked sausage, cut into
1-in. cubes
½ lb. fully cooked ham, cut into
¾-in. cubes
½ lb. fresh or frozen uncooked
shrimp, peeled and deveined
1 cup fresh or frozen sliced okra
1 can (16 oz.) kidney beans,
rinsed and drained
½ tsp. salt
¼ tsp. pepper
¼ tsp. hot pepper sauce
Sliced green onions, optional

1. Place the chicken and water in a Dutch oven; bring to a boil. Reduce heat; cover and simmer until chicken is tender, 30-45 minutes.

2. Remove chicken; cool. Reserve 6 cups broth. Remove chicken from bones; cut into bite-size pieces.

3. In a Dutch oven or soup kettle, mix flour and oil until smooth; cook and stir over medium-low heat until browned, 2-3 minutes. Stir in onions, peppers, celery and garlic; cook until vegetables are tender, about 5 minutes. Stir in sausage, ham and reserved broth and chicken; cover and simmer for 45 minutes.

4. Add the shrimp, okra, beans, salt, pepper and hot pepper sauce; cover and simmer until shrimp turn pink, 2-4 minutes. If desired, serve with green onions and additional hot pepper sauce.

**1 cup:** 397 cal., 24g fat (5g sat. fat), 97mg chol., 643mg sod., 15g carb. (2g sugars, 3g fiber), 30g pro.

## TEST KITCHEN TIP

*If your Louisiana gumbo is thinner than you'd like, there are several methods you can use to thicken it. Try making a roux (a combination of equal parts fat and all-purpose flour) and whisk in 2 oz. for every cup of liquid in the recipe. Or you can add a bit of cornstarch or arrowroot—you'll need about 1 Tbsp. for every cup of liquid. Simply mix the cornstarch or arrowroot with equal parts water to create a slurry, then pour it into the pot.*
—SAMMI DIVITO, *TASTE OF HOME* ASSOCIATE EDITOR

# AIR-FRYER OLIVE BURGERS

My mom would reminisce about the olive burgers she would get at Coney Island when she was a girl. After a couple of attempts, I was able to make her one that was just like she remembered.
—*Lorraine Hickman, Lansing, MI*

**TAKES: 25 MIN. • MAKES: 4 SERVINGS**

- 1  lb. ground beef
- 2  tsp. reduced-sodium soy sauce
- 2  tsp. Worcestershire sauce
- ¼  tsp. garlic powder
- ¼  tsp. onion powder
- ½  cup sliced green olives with pimientos, drained
- ¼  cup Miracle Whip or mayonnaise
- 1  Tbsp. stone-ground mustard
- 4  hamburger buns, toasted
- ¼  cup crumbled feta cheese, optional Bibb lettuce leaves, optional

**1.** In a large bowl, combine beef, soy sauce, Worcestershire, garlic powder and onion powder, mixing lightly but thoroughly. Shape into four ½-in.-thick patties, indenting the center slightly.

**2.** Preheat air fryer to 350°. Arrange patties in a single layer in greased air fryer. Cook until a thermometer reads 160°, 8-10 minutes turning once.

**3.** Meanwhile, in a small bowl combine olives, Miracle Whip and mustard. Serve burgers on buns with olive mixture. If desired, top with feta cheese and lettuce.

**Note:** In our testing, we find cook times vary dramatically between brands of air fryers. As a result, we give wider than normal ranges on suggested cook times.

**1 burger with 2 Tbsp. olive mixture:** 400 cal., 21g fat (6g sat. fat), 75mg chol., 814mg sod., 26g carb. (5g sugars, 1g fiber), 25g pro.

---

# SPLIT PEA & SAUSAGE SOUP

A big bowl of satisfying soup is the perfect antidote to cold weather. Whether for a family meal or an informal get-together, I pull out my tried-and-true soup recipe and simply relax.
—*Trisha Kruse, Eagle, ID*

**PREP: 25 MIN. • COOK: 7 HOURS • MAKES: 6 SERVINGS (2¼ QT.)**

- 1  lb. smoked sausage, sliced
- 1  medium potato, peeled and cubed
- 2  medium carrots, thinly sliced
- 2  celery ribs, thinly sliced
- 1  medium onion, chopped
- 2  Tbsp. butter
- 3  garlic cloves, minced
- ¼  tsp. dried oregano
- 1  cup dried green split peas
- 2½  tsp. chicken bouillon granules
- 1  bay leaf
- 5  cups water

**1.** Saute the sausage, potato, carrots, celery and onion in butter in a skillet until vegetables are crisp-tender. Add garlic and oregano; cook 2 minutes.

**2.** Transfer to a 5-qt. slow cooker. Add the peas, bouillon, bay leaf and water. Cover and cook on low for 7-8 hours or until peas are tender. Discard bay leaf.

**1½ cups:** 429 cal., 25g fat (11g sat. fat), 61mg chol., 1267mg sod., 33g carb. (7g sugars, 10g fiber), 20g pro.

The best stromboli I've ever had. My teenage son loves it so much that he has made the entire recipe himself some nights.
—SKOOTER941
TASTEOFHOME.COM

# PIZZA STROMBOLI

I used to own a bakery, and this bread was one of our customers' favorites. Once they smelled the aroma of pizza and sampled these tempting spiral slices, they just couldn't resist taking some home.

—*John Morcom, Oxford, MI*

**PREP: 25 MIN. + RISING • BAKE: 25 MIN. • MAKES: 1 LOAF (12 PIECES)**

1 pkg. (¼ oz.) active dry yeast
¾ cup warm water (110° to 115°)
4½ tsp. honey
1 Tbsp. nonfat dry milk powder
2 cups bread flour
½ cup whole wheat flour
2 tsp. Italian seasoning
1 tsp. salt
4½ tsp. pizza sauce
¾ cup chopped pepperoni
½ cup shredded cheddar cheese, divided
¼ cup shredded Parmesan cheese
¼ cup shredded part-skim mozzarella cheese, divided
2 Tbsp. finely chopped onion
1 Tbsp. each chopped ripe olives, chopped pimiento-stuffed olives and chopped canned mushrooms

1. In a large bowl, dissolve yeast in warm water. Stir in honey and milk powder until well blended. In a small bowl, combine 1 cup bread flour, whole wheat flour, seasoning and salt. Add to yeast mixture; beat until smooth. Stir in pizza sauce. Stir in enough remaining bread flour to form a soft dough.

2. Turn onto a floured surface; knead until smooth and elastic, 6-8 minutes. Place in a greased bowl, turning once to grease top. Cover; let rise in a warm place until doubled, about 1 hour.

3. Preheat oven to 350°. Punch dough down. Turn onto a lightly floured surface; roll into a 14x12-in. rectangle. Sprinkle pepperoni, ¼ cup cheddar cheese, Parmesan cheese, 2 Tbsp. mozzarella cheese, onion, olives and mushrooms to within ½ in. of edges.

4. Roll up jelly-roll style, starting with a long side; pinch seam to seal and tuck ends under. Place seam side down on a greased baking sheet. Cover and let rise for 45 minutes.

5. Sprinkle with remaining cheddar and mozzarella cheeses. Bake until golden brown, 25-30 minutes. Remove from pan to a wire rack. Serve warm. Refrigerate leftovers.

**1 piece:** 192 cal., 7g fat (3g sat. fat), 15mg chol., 478mg sod., 24g carb. (3g sugars, 1g fiber), 8g pro.

## TEST KITCHEN TIP

*When you roll your stromboli, be sure it's tight enough to hold the filling without stretching out the dough. If your dough is overly elastic when you're trying to roll it out, cover and let it stand for 10 minutes. If the dough is stretchy and wrapped too tight, the stromboli tends to break open during baking.*

# PULLED PORK SANDWICHES

You'll love the ease of this recipe—just throw everything in the slow cooker and get out of the kitchen. You hardly have to lift a finger for delicious results!
—*Terri McKitrick, Delafield, WI*

PREP: 15 MIN. • COOK: 7 HOURS • MAKES: 8 SERVINGS

1 can (8 oz.) tomato sauce
1 cup chopped onion
1 cup barbecue sauce
3 tsp. chili powder
1 tsp. ground cumin
½ tsp. ground cinnamon
1 boneless pork sirloin roast (2 lbs.)
8 seeded hamburger buns, split
   Optional: Sliced red onion, fresh cilantro leaves and dill pickle slices

**1.** In a 3-qt. slow cooker, combine the first 6 ingredients; add the pork. Spoon some of the sauce over pork. Cover and cook on low for 7 hours or until the meat is tender.

**2.** Remove meat; shred with 2 forks. Return to slow cooker and heat through. Spoon ½ cup onto each bun. Serve with desired toppings.

**1 serving:** 322 cal., 10g fat (3g sat. fat), 68mg chol., 681mg sod., 29g carb. (9g sugars, 3g fiber), 28g pro. **Diabetic exchanges:** 3 lean meat, 2 starch.

---

# PORTOBELLO MELTS

We're always looking for satisfying vegetarian meals, and this one tops the list. These melts are especially delicious in the summer when we have tons of homegrown tomatoes.
—*Amy Smalley, Morehead, KY*

TAKES: 20 MIN. • MAKES: 2 SERVINGS

2 large portobello mushrooms (4 oz. each), stems removed
¼ cup olive oil
2 Tbsp. balsamic vinegar
½ tsp. salt
½ tsp. dried basil
4 tomato slices
2 slices mozzarella cheese
2 slices Italian bread (1 in. thick)
   Chopped fresh basil

**1.** Preheat broiler. Place mushrooms in a shallow bowl. Mix oil, vinegar, salt and dried basil; brush onto both sides of mushrooms. Let stand 5 minutes. Reserve remaining marinade.

**2.** Place mushrooms on a greased rack of a broiler pan, stem side down. Broil mushrooms 4 in. from heat until tender, 3-4 minutes per side. Top stem sides with tomato and cheese. Broil until cheese is melted, about 1 minute.

**3.** Place bread on a baking sheet; brush with reserved marinade. Broil 4 in. from heat until lightly toasted, 45-60 seconds. Top with mushrooms. Sprinkle with chopped basil.

**1 open-faced sandwich:** 460 cal., 35g fat (7g sat. fat), 22mg chol., 934mg sod., 26g carb. (8g sugars, 3g fiber), 12g pro.

PRESSURE-COOKER
LAMB PITAS WITH
YOGURT SAUCE

# PRESSURE-COOKER LAMB PITAS WITH YOGURT SAUCE

The spiced lamb in these stuffed pita pockets goes perfectly with cool
cucumber and yogurt. It's like having your own Greek gyro stand in the kitchen!
—*Angela Leinenbach, Mechanicsville, VA*

**PREP: 25 MIN. • COOK: 15 MIN. + RELEASING • MAKES: 8 SERVINGS**

2 Tbsp. olive oil
2 lbs. lamb stew meat (¾-in. pieces)
½ cup dry red wine
1 large onion, chopped
1 garlic clove, minced
1¼ tsp. salt, divided
1 tsp. dried oregano
½ tsp. dried basil
⅓ cup tomato paste
1 medium cucumber
1 cup plain yogurt
16 pita pocket halves, warmed
4 plum tomatoes, sliced

1. Select saute or browning setting on a 6-qt. electric pressure cooker. Adjust for medium heat; add oil. When oil is hot, brown lamb in batches. Add wine to pressure cooker. Cook 30 seconds, stirring to loosen browned bits. Press cancel. Add onion, garlic, 1 tsp. salt, oregano and basil. Return lamb to pressure cooker.

2. Lock lid; close pressure-release valve. Adjust to pressure-cook on high for 15 minutes. Let pressure release naturally for 10 minutes; quick-release any remaining pressure.

3. Select saute setting; adjust for low heat. Add tomato paste; simmer, uncovered, until mixture is thickened, 8-10 minutes, stirring occasionally. Press cancel.

4. To serve, dice enough cucumber to measure 1 cup; thinly slice remaining cucumber. Combine diced cucumber with yogurt and remaining salt. Fill pitas with lamb mixture, tomatoes, sliced cucumbers and yogurt mixture.

**2 filled pita halves:** 383 cal., 11g fat (3g sat. fat), 78mg chol., 766mg sod., 39g carb. (5g sugars, 3g fiber), 31g pro. **Diabetic exchanges:** 3 lean meat, 2½ starch, 1 fat.

# BASIL CHICKEN SANDWICHES

SHOWN ON PAGE 86

I created this recipe when family members with food allergies were coming to see our new home.
—*Kerry Durgin Krebs, New Market, MD*

**TAKES: 15 MIN. • MAKES: 6 SANDWICHES**

½ tsp. pepper
¼ tsp. salt
Dash paprika
1 lb. boneless skinless chicken breasts, cut into ½-in. slices
6 Tbsp. prepared olive oil vinaigrette salad dressing, divided
6 ciabatta rolls, split
18 basil leaves
1 jar (7 oz.) roasted sweet red peppers, drained
¼ cup shredded Romano cheese

1. In a bowl, combine the pepper, salt and paprika; sprinkle over chicken slices. In a nonstick skillet over medium-high heat, cook chicken in 2 Tbsp. salad dressing for 4-5 minutes on each side or until chicken is no longer pink.

2. Brush remaining 4 Tbsp. salad dressing on rolls. Place basil leaves on rolls; top with chicken and red peppers. Sprinkle with Romano cheese.

**1 sandwich:** 308 cal., 8g fat (2g sat. fat), 45mg chol., 824mg sod., 33g carb. (3g sugars, 2g fiber), 22g pro. **Diabetic exchanges:** 2 starch, 2 lean meat, 1 fat.

# CHEESY ROAST BEEF PINWHEELS

Take lunch to the next level with these savory pinwheels. Rolled in crescent dough,
cut into spirals and baked, they're a tasty twist on the traditional roast beef sandwich.
—*Holley Grainger, Brimingham, AL*

**TAKES: 30 MIN. • MAKES: 8 SERVINGS**

1  tube (8 oz.) refrigerated
   crescent rolls
2  Tbsp. honey mustard
   or Dijon mustard
8  slices provolone cheese
8  slices deli roast beef
½  cup finely chopped sweet
   red pepper, optional

**1.** Preheat oven to 375°. Unroll crescent dough and separate into 2 rectangles; press perforations to seal.

**2.** Spread rectangles with mustard. Top with cheese and roast beef, overlapping if needed, and, if desired, red pepper. Roll up jelly-roll style, starting with a short side; pinch seam to seal. Cut each roll crosswise into 4 slices; place on parchment-lined baking sheets, cut side down. Bake until pinwheels are golden brown and cheese is melted, 15-18 minutes. Serve warm.

**Freeze option:** Cover and freeze cooled pinwheels on parchment-lined baking sheets until firm. Transfer to freezer containers; return to freezer. To use, bake at 375° until heated through.

**1 pinwheel:** 203 cal., 12g fat (4g sat. fat), 27mg chol., 502mg sod., 14g carb. (4g sugars, 0 fiber), 11g pro.

# CHRISTMAS TORTELLINI & SPINACH SOUP

I originally made this tasty soup in the summer, but when
I saw its bright red and green colors, I knew it would
make a perfect first course for Christmas dinner.
—*Marietta Slater, Justin, TX*

**TAKES: 25 MIN. • MAKES: 6 SERVINGS**

2  cans (14½ oz. each) vegetable broth
1  pkg. (9 oz.) refrigerated cheese
   tortellini or tortellini of your choice
1  can (15 oz.) cannellini beans,
   rinsed and drained
1  can (14½ oz.) Italian diced
   tomatoes, undrained
¼  tsp. salt
⅛  tsp. pepper
3  cups fresh baby spinach
3  Tbsp. minced fresh basil
¼  cup shredded Asiago cheese

**1.** In a large saucepan, bring broth to a boil. Add tortellini; reduce heat. Simmer, uncovered, for 5 minutes. Stir in the beans, tomatoes, salt and pepper; return to a simmer. Cook until tortellini are tender, 4-5 minutes longer.

**2.** Stir in spinach and basil; cook until spinach is wilted. Top servings with cheese.

**1 cup:** 239 cal., 5g fat (3g sat. fat), 23mg chol., 1135mg sod., 38g carb. (7g sugars, 5g fiber), 11g pro.

# MUSTARD BARBECUE SHAVED HAM

This recipe makes enough ham sandwiches to feed a crowd and is so quick and easy. Have your butcher slice the ham very thin. I like to make this on the stovetop and serve it from my slow cooker.
—*Joyce Moynihan, Lakeville, MN*

**TAKES: 30 MIN. • MAKES: 20 SERVINGS**

| | |
|---|---|
| 1 | cup cider vinegar |
| 1 | cup yellow mustard |
| 1 | cup ketchup |
| ⅓ | cup packed brown sugar |
| ¼ | cup butter, cubed |
| 1 | Tbsp. Worcestershire sauce |
| 2 | tsp. onion powder |
| 1 | tsp. garlic powder |
| ½ | tsp. cayenne pepper |
| ½ | tsp. pepper |
| 5 | lbs. shaved deli ham |
| 20 | sandwich rolls, split |

In a Dutch oven, combine the first 10 ingredients. Cook and stir over medium heat until butter is melted. Bring to a boil; reduce heat. Simmer, covered, for 15 minutes. Add ham; heat through. Serve on rolls.

**1 sandwich:** 382 cal., 10g fat (2g sat. fat), 57mg chol., 1761mg sod., 46g carb. (15g sugars, 2g fiber), 29g pro.

---

# TOUCHDOWN BRAT SLIDERS

It's game time when these minis make an appearance. Two things my husband loves—beer and brats—get stepped up a notch with crunchy flavored chips.
—*Kirsten Shabaz, Lakeville, MN*

**PREP: 20 MIN. • COOK: 30 MIN. • MAKES: 16 SLIDERS**

| | |
|---|---|
| 5 | thick-sliced bacon strips, chopped |
| 1 | lb. uncooked bratwurst links, casings removed |
| 1 | large onion, finely chopped |
| 2 | garlic cloves, minced |
| 1 | pkg. (8 oz.) cream cheese, cubed |
| 1 | cup dark beer or nonalcoholic beer |
| 1 | Tbsp. Dijon mustard |
| ¼ | tsp. pepper |
| 16 | dinner rolls, split and toasted |
| 2 | cups cheddar and sour cream potato chips, crushed |

**1.** In a large cast-iron or other heavy skillet, cook bacon over medium heat until crisp. Remove to paper towels with a slotted spoon; drain, reserving drippings. Cook bratwurst and onion in drippings over medium heat until meat is no longer pink, breaking into crumbles. Add garlic; cook 1 minute longer. Drain well.

**2.** Stir in the cream cheese, beer, mustard and pepper. Bring to a boil. Reduce heat; simmer, uncovered, until thickened, 15-20 minutes, stirring occasionally. Stir in bacon. Spoon ¼ cup onto each roll; sprinkle with chips. Replace tops.

**1 slider:** 354 cal., 24g fat (10g sat. fat), 62mg chol., 617mg sod., 23g carb. (2g sugars, 2g fiber), 10g pro.

# CASHEW CHICKEN SALAD SANDWICHES

I think this is the best chicken salad recipe around! It's good for you and quick to make, and it has wonderful flavor.
—*Peggi Kelly, Fairbury, NE*

**TAKES: 15 MIN. • MAKES: 6 SERVINGS**

2 cups diced cooked chicken
½ cup chopped salted cashews
½ cup chopped red apple
½ cup chopped peeled cucumber
½ cup mayonnaise
½ tsp. sugar
½ tsp. salt
   Dash pepper
6 kaiser rolls or croissants, split
6 lettuce leaves, optional

In a large bowl, combine chicken, cashews, apple and cucumber. In a small bowl, combine mayonnaise, sugar, salt and pepper. Stir into chicken mixture. Serve on rolls, with lettuce if desired.

**1 sandwich:** 463 cal., 26g fat (4g sat. fat), 48mg chol., 720mg sod., 36g carb. (3g sugars, 2g fiber), 21g pro.

**Peanut Chicken Salad Sandwiches:** Substitute ½ chopped salted peanuts for the cashews.

# BACON GRILLED CHEESE SANDWICH

Bacon lovers, this one's for you! Overflowing with cheese and crispy bacon, this grilled cheese recipe is so hearty, you won't even need a side of tomato soup.
—*Josh Rink, Milwaukee, WI*

**TAKES: 25 MIN. • MAKES: 4 SERVINGS**

6 Tbsp. butter, softened, divided
8 slices sourdough bread
½ cup shredded sharp white cheddar cheese
½ cup shredded Monterey Jack cheese
½ cup shredded Gruyere cheese
3 Tbsp. mayonnaise
   3 Tbsp. finely shredded Manchego or Parmesan cheese
⅛ tsp. onion powder
4 oz. Brie cheese, rind removed and sliced
8 cooked bacon strips

1. Spread 3 Tbsp. butter on 1 side of each slice of bread. Place bread, butter side down, in a large skillet or electric griddle over medium-low heat until golden brown, 2-3 minutes; remove. In a small bowl, combine cheddar, Monterey Jack and Gruyere. In another bowl, mix together remaining 3 Tbsp. butter, mayonnaise, Manchego cheese and onion powder.

2. To assemble sandwiches, top toasted side of 4 bread slices with sliced Brie. Sprinkle cheddar cheese mixture evenly over Brie; add bacon. Top with remaining bread slices, toasted side facing inward. Spread the butter-mayonnaise mixture on the outsides of each sandwich. Place in same skillet and cook until golden brown and cheese is melted, 5-6 minutes on each side. Serve immediately.

**1 sandwich:** 767 cal., 57g fat (29g sat. fat), 145mg chol., 1405mg sod., 31g carb. (3g sugars, 1g fiber), 32g pro.

> " This is one of the best chicken salads ever. I take it to friends' houses and always come home with an empty bowl.
> —LYNN CASHMANN
> TASTEOFHOME.COM

"Love this chili. Won cook-offs with it. Absolutely delicious. My son would eat it every day if I let him.
—CINDY DUNCAN
TASTEOFHOME.COM

# CORNY CHILI

Loaded with corn, this southwestern chili is so delicious and fuss-free,
I love to share the recipe. Busy moms really appreciate its simplicity.
—*Marlene Olson, Hoople, ND*

PREP: 20 MIN. • COOK: 3 HOURS • MAKES: 6 SERVINGS

1 lb. ground beef
1 small onion, chopped
1 can (16 oz.) kidney beans,
  rinsed and drained
2 cans (14½ oz. each) diced
  tomatoes, undrained
1 can (11 oz.) whole kernel
  corn, drained
¾ cup picante sauce
1 Tbsp. chili powder
¼ to ½ tsp. garlic powder
  Optional: Corn chips, sour cream
  and shredded cheddar cheese

1. In a large skillet, cook beef and onion over medium heat until meat is no longer pink, breaking into crumbles; drain.

2. Transfer to a 3-qt. slow cooker. Stir in beans, tomatoes, corn, picante sauce, chili powder and garlic powder. Cover and cook on low for 3-4 hours or until heated through. If desired, serve with corn chips, sour cream and cheese.

**1 cup:** 274 cal., 9g fat (3g sat. fat), 47mg chol., 790mg sod., 27g carb. (10g sugars, 8g fiber), 20g pro. **Diabetic exchanges:** 3 lean meat, 2 starch.

## TEST KITCHEN TIP

*This chili will last up to 4 days in the fridge, but 4 to 6 months when stored in the freezer. Just put leftovers in freezer-safe containers, and when you're ready to eat it, let it thaw overnight in the fridge before simmering in a saucepan to heat through.*
—SAMMI DIVITO, *TASTE OF HOME* ASSOCIATE EDITOR

# DELI BEEF SANDWICHES WITH HORSERADISH MAYONNAISE

Sweet cherry preserves balance bold horseradish in this hearty sandwich. What a delicious noontime treat!
—*Greg Fontenot, The Woodlands, TX*

TAKES: 10 MIN. • MAKES: 4 SERVINGS

½ cup mayonnaise
2 Tbsp. cherry preserves
4 tsp. prepared horseradish
8 slices whole wheat bread
¾ lb. sliced deli roast beef
4 lettuce leaves
1 large tomato, thinly sliced
  Dash each salt and pepper

In a small bowl, combine mayonnaise, preserves and horseradish. Spread 1 Tbsp. over each of 4 bread slices. Layer with roast beef, lettuce and tomato; sprinkle with salt and pepper. Spread remaining mayonnaise mixture over remaining bread; place over top.

**1 sandwich:** 471 cal., 27g fat (4g sat. fat), 57mg chol., 947mg sod., 33g carb. (11g sugars, 5g fiber), 25g pro.

# ROASTED VEGGIE QUESADILLAS

I am always looking for recipes that will encourage children to eat vegetables and this one has been a huge success. Just remember to roast your vegetables before making the quesadillas.
—*Kathy Carlan, Canton, GA*

PREP: 40 MIN. • COOK: 5 MIN./BATCH • MAKES: 8 SERVINGS

2  medium red potatoes, quartered and sliced
1  medium zucchini, quartered and sliced
1  medium sweet red pepper, sliced
1  small onion, chopped
2  Tbsp. olive oil
1  garlic clove, minced
½  tsp. salt
½  tsp. dried oregano
¼  tsp. pepper
1  cup shredded part-skim mozzarella cheese
1  cup shredded reduced-fat cheddar cheese
8  whole wheat tortillas (8 in.)

**1.** In a large bowl, combine the first 9 ingredients. Transfer to a 15x10x1-in. baking pan. Bake at 425°until potatoes are tender, 24-28 minutes.

**2.** In a small bowl, combine cheeses. Spread ⅓ cup vegetable mixture over half of each tortilla. Sprinkle with ¼ cup cheese; fold tortillas to close. Cook in a greased cast-iron skillet or griddle over low heat until cheese is melted, 1-2 minutes on each side.

**1 quesadilla:** 279 cal., 12g fat (4g sat. fat), 18mg chol., 479mg sod., 30g carb. (4g sugars, 3g fiber), 12g pro. **Diabetic exchanges:** 2 starch, 1 medium-fat meat, 1 fat.

# PRESSURE-COOKER FRENCH DIP SANDWICHES

Beef chuck roast gives this classic sandwich and its rich broth a hearty flavor. Add a crusty roll and you have a filling meal.
—*Taste of Home Test Kitchen*

PREP: 20 MIN. • COOK: 1¼ HOURS + RELEASING • MAKES: 8 SERVINGS

1  boneless beef chuck roast (about 3 lbs.)
1  tsp. dried oregano
1  tsp. dried rosemary, crushed
½  tsp. seasoned salt
¼  tsp. pepper
3  cups beef broth
1  bay leaf
1  garlic clove, peeled
   French bread, sliced lengthwise
   Optional: Sliced provolone cheese or Swiss cheese

**1.** Place roast on a trivet in a 6-qt. electric pressure cooker; sprinkle with oregano, rosemary, seasoned salt and pepper. Add broth, bay leaf and garlic. Lock lid; close pressure-release valve. Adjust to pressure-cook on high for 1¼ hours.

**2.** Let pressure release naturally for 10 minutes; quick-release any remaining pressure. A thermometer inserted in beef should read at least 145°.

**3.** Remove beef; thinly slice or shred with 2 forks. Discard bay leaf and garlic from cooking juices. Serve beef with French bread. If desired, top with sliced cheese. Serve with cooking juices for dipping.

**4 oz. cooked beef:** 237 cal., 13g fat (5g sat. fat), 88mg chol., 378mg sod., 1g carb. (0 sugars, 0 fiber), 27g pro.

ROASTED VEGGIE
QUESADILLAS

CLUB ROLL-UPS

# CLUB ROLL-UPS

Packed with meat, cheese and olives, these roll-ups are always a hit at parties.
Experiment with different lunch meats and salad dressing flavors.
—*Linda Searl, Pampa, TX*

TAKES: 25 MIN. • MAKES: 8 SERVINGS

3 oz. cream cheese, softened
½ cup ranch salad dressing
2 Tbsp. ranch salad dressing mix
8 bacon strips, cooked and crumbled
½ cup finely chopped onion
1 can (2¼ oz.) sliced ripe olives, drained
1 jar (2 oz.) diced pimientos, drained
¼ cup diced canned jalapeno peppers
8 flour tortillas (10 in.), room temperature
8 thin slices deli ham
8 thin slices deli turkey
8 thin slices deli roast beef
2 cups shredded cheddar cheese

1. In a small bowl, beat the cream cheese, ranch dressing and dressing mix until well blended. In another bowl, combine the bacon, onion, olives, pimientos and jalapenos.

2. Spread cream cheese mixture over tortillas; layer with ham, turkey and roast beef. Sprinkle with bacon mixture and cheddar cheese; roll up.

**1 roll-up:** 554 cal., 29g fat (12g sat. fat), 80mg chol., 1802mg sod., 39g carb. (2g sugars, 7g fiber), 27g pro.

# SHREDDED BEEF AU JUS

My mom found this recipe in a farm journal soon after she and my dad got married.
The tender beef has been a family favorite for years, and my dad often requests it.
—*Danielle Brandt, Ruthton, MN*

PREP: 10 MIN. • COOK: 6 HOURS • MAKES: 8 SERVINGS

1 boneless beef chuck roast (3 lbs.)
2 cups water
2 tsp. beef bouillon granules
1½ tsp. dried oregano
1 tsp. garlic salt
1 tsp. seasoned salt
¼ tsp. dried rosemary, crushed
8 hamburger buns, split

1. Cut roast in half; place in a 4- or 5-qt. slow cooker. In a small bowl, mix water, bouillon granules and seasonings; pour over meat.

2. Cook, covered, on low 6-8 hours or until tender. Remove beef; cool slightly. Meanwhile, skim fat from the cooking liquid.

3. Shred meat with 2 forks; return to slow cooker. Using a slotted spoon, place meat on bun bottoms. Replace tops. Serve with additional cooking liquid on the side.

**1 sandwich with ¼ cup cooking liquid:** 411 cal., 18g fat (7g sat. fat), 111mg chol., 889mg sod., 22g carb. (3g sugars, 1g fiber), 37g pro.

# TUNA PATTY

My husband likes to top his sandwich with melted Swiss cheese and Dijon mustard.
—*Joann Brasington, Sumter, SC*

TAKES: 20 MIN. • MAKES: 4 SERVINGS

1 can (6 oz.) tuna, drained and flaked
1 large egg
½ cup Italian-seasoned bread crumbs
⅓ cup finely chopped onion
¼ cup chopped celery
¼ cup chopped sweet red pepper
¼ cup mayonnaise
2 Tbsp. chili sauce
½ tsp. dill weed
¼ tsp. salt
⅛ tsp. pepper
  Dash hot pepper sauce
  Dash Worcestershire sauce
1 tsp. olive oil
4 hamburger buns, split
  Tomato slices and lettuce
  leaves, optional

1. In a large bowl, combine tuna and next 12 ingredients; mix well. Shape into 4 patties (mixture will be soft).

2. In a nonstick skillet, cook patties in oil over medium-high heat until golden brown and cooked through, 3-4 minutes per side. Serve on buns. If desired, add tomato and lettuce.

**1 sandwich:** 363 cal., 16g fat (3g sat. fat), 71mg chol., 962mg sod., 36g carb. (6g sugars, 2g fiber), 18g pro.

## TEST KITCHEN TIP

*When making these patties, your choice of tuna is completely up to you, but maybe lean a little more toward albacore tuna. Albacore has a milder, less fishy taste, which plays terrifically with the seasonings in this tuna recipe.*

# CREAMY POTATO SOUP

This is one of my favorite recipes that uses wholesome milk—an important product we produce on our dairy farm. It's so rich and delicious, even the kids gobble it up!
—*Janis Plagerman, Ephrata, WA*

PREP: 40 MIN. • COOK: 20 MIN. • MAKES: 10 SERVINGS (2¾ QT.)

7 medium potatoes, peeled and cubed
2 celery ribs, diced
1 medium onion, chopped
1 qt. water
4 tsp. chicken bouillon granules
¼ cup butter
¼ cup all-purpose flour
1 qt. whole milk
2 tsp. salt
½ tsp. pepper
  Optional: Minced fresh parsley,
  chopped cooked bacon,
  shredded cheddar cheese

1. In a large saucepan, combine potatoes, celery, onion, water and bouillon; bring to a boil. Reduce heat; cover and simmer until potatoes are tender, 20-25 minutes.

2. In a Dutch oven, melt butter. Stir in flour until smooth. Gradually add the milk; bring to a boil. Cook and stir until thickened, 1-2 minutes. Add the potato mixture (with cooking liquid) to saucepan. Stir in salt and pepper. Mash until soup reaches desired consistency. If desired, garnish with parsley, bacon and cheese.

**1 cup:** 207 cal., 8g fat (5g sat. fat), 22mg chol., 896mg sod., 29g carb. (7g sugars, 2g fiber), 6g pro.

"
This is a great
alternative to
hamburgers.
A delicious,
healthy and
low-cost meal!
—JBDUPUIS
TASTEOFHOME.COM

This recipe
is awesome!
It's the bomb!
—EILEEN614
TASTEOFHOME.COM

# CHICKEN PESTO WRAPS

This makes a really quick meal for us. Using prepared pesto makes it so easy
to put together. My wife likes to put a little dollop of sour cream in hers.
—Gary Phile, Ravenna, OH

TAKES: 20 MIN. • MAKES: 2 SERVINGS

½ lb. ground chicken
1 Tbsp. canola oil
¼ cup sun-dried tomato pesto
2 flour tortillas (8 in.), warmed
½ cup shredded part-skim
  mozzarella cheese
8 grape tomatoes, cut in half
2 slices red onion, separated into rings
1 cup shredded lettuce

1. In a large skillet, cook chicken in oil over medium heat for 5-6 minutes or until
no longer pink; drain.

2. In a small bowl, combine the chicken and pesto. Spoon chicken mixture over
each tortilla; layer with cheese, tomatoes, onion and lettuce; roll up.

**1 wrap:** 323 cal., 15g fat (4g sat. fat), 46mg chol., 512mg sod., 30g carb. (2g sugars,
1g fiber), 18g pro. **Diabetic exchanges:** 2 starch, 2 lean meat, 1½ fat.

# JALAPENO SLOPPY JOES

My husband loves jalapenos—and I just love any and all heat.
This savory meal with some spice is a perfect make-ahead
solution for busy weeknights. Serve with your favorite chips.
—Julie Herrera-Lemler, Rochester, MN

PREP: 20 MIN. • COOK: 15 MIN. • MAKES: 8 SERVINGS

1 Tbsp. butter
1½ lbs. ground turkey
1 small onion, chopped
1 jalapeno pepper, seeded and
  finely chopped
4 garlic cloves, minced
1 cup ketchup
½ cup juice from pickled
  jalapeno slices
2 tsp. minced pickled jalapeno slices
2 Tbsp. brown sugar
2 Tbsp. Worcestershire sauce
1½ tsp. chili powder
½ tsp. crushed red pepper flakes
¼ tsp. salt
8 sesame seed hamburger buns, split

1. Heat butter in a large skillet over
medium heat. Add turkey, onion, fresh
jalapeno and garlic; cook until turkey
is no longer pink and vegetables are
tender, 8-10 minutes, breaking up
turkey into crumbles.

2. Stir in ketchup, jalapeno juice, pickled jalapenos, brown sugar, Worcestershire
sauce and seasonings. Bring to a boil. Reduce heat; simmer, uncovered,
15-20 minutes to allow flavors to blend, stirring occasionally. Serve on buns.

**Freeze option:** Freeze cooled meat mixture in freezer containers. To use, partially
thaw in refrigerator overnight. Heat through in a saucepan, stirring occasionally;
add broth or water if necessary.

**Note:** Wear disposable gloves when cutting hot peppers; the oils can burn skin.
Avoid touching your face.

**1 sandwich:** 322 cal., 11g fat (4g sat. fat), 60mg chol., 888mg sod., 37g carb.
(15g sugars, 1g fiber), 22g pro.

# EASY CREAMY TOMATO SOUP

One spoonful of this classic will take you back to your childhood, sipping warm tomato soup on a cold day. Pair it with a sandwich for a hearty lunch. We suggest grilled cheese!

—Taste of Home *Test Kitchen*

PREP: 20 MIN. • COOK: 30 MIN. • MAKES: 4 SERVINGS

2 Tbsp. butter
1 Tbsp. olive oil
1 medium onion, chopped
2 garlic cloves, minced
1 can (28 oz.) whole tomatoes, undrained
1 cup chicken stock
2 Tbsp. tomato paste
1 tsp. dried basil
½ tsp. salt
½ tsp. sugar
¼ tsp. dried thyme
¼ tsp. pepper
½ cup heavy whipping cream
  Fresh basil leaves, optional

**1.** In a large saucepan, heat butter and oil over medium heat until butter is melted. Add onion; cook and stir until tender, 5-7 minutes. Add garlic; cook 1 minute longer. Stir in the tomatoes, chicken stock, tomato paste, basil, salt, sugar, thyme and pepper. Bring to a boil. Reduce heat; simmer, uncovered, for 20-25 minutes to let flavors blend.

**2.** Remove pan from heat. Using a blender, puree soup until smooth. Return to pan. Slowly stir in cream. Cook and stir over low heat until heated through. If desired, garnish with basil and additional cream.

**1 cup:** 252 cal., 20g fat (11g sat. fat), 49mg chol., 778mg sod., 15g carb. (8g sugars, 4g fiber), 5g pro.

## TEST KITCHEN TIP

*Canned tomatoes withstand heat better and have a higher concentration of flavor than fresh tomatoes; however, fresh tomatoes can work in this recipe. You would need about 4 cups of fresh tomatoes to replace one 28-oz. can. This recipe calls for whole canned tomatoes, so you will need to peel the fresh tomatoes before adding them to the soup.*

SPRING PEA & RADISH
SALAD, PAGE 132

66
This is a
superior recipe!
It's easy to
make, and
the flavors
are uniquely
delicious.
—ANNRMS
TASTEOFHOME.COM

CHAPTER 5

# POPULAR SIDES & SALADS

It's easy to round out menus when you have a stable of family-approved add-ons at hand. This chapter serves up 34 ideas that complement everything from weeknight meals to special-occasion buffets.

# THREE-PEPPER COLESLAW

There are never any leftovers when I make this dish
for a picnic, barbecue or any social gathering.
—*Priscilla Gilbert, Indian Harbour Beach, FL*

PREP: 20 MIN. + CHILLING • MAKES: 8 SERVINGS

1  pkg. (10 oz.) angel hair
   coleslaw mix
1  medium sweet red pepper,
   finely chopped
1  medium green pepper,
   finely chopped
1  to 2 jalapeno peppers,
   seeded and finely chopped
3  green onions, chopped
¼  cup white wine vinegar
2  Tbsp. lime juice
2  tsp. canola oil
1  tsp. sugar
½  tsp. salt
¼  tsp. pepper

Place the first 5 ingredients in a large serving bowl. In a small bowl, whisk the remaining ingredients. Pour over coleslaw mixture; toss to coat. Cover and refrigerate for at least 30 minutes before serving.

**Note:** Wear disposable gloves when cutting hot peppers; the oils can burn skin. Avoid touching your face.

**¾ cup:** 36 cal., 1g fat (0 sat. fat), 0 chol., 158mg sod., 6g carb. (3g sugars, 2g fiber), 1g pro. **Diabetic exchanges:** 1 vegetable.

## TEST KITCHEN TIP

*If your family doesn't like things on the spicy side, simply use only 1 jalapeno pepper or leave it out altogether.*

# BERRY NECTARINE SALAD

I've been making this recipe for years. Whenever my family has a summer get-together, everyone requests it. The nectarines and berries look beautiful together, and the topping is the perfect accent.
—*Mindee Myers, Lincoln, NE*

PREP: 15 MIN. + CHILLING • MAKES: 8 SERVINGS

4  medium nectarines, sliced
¼  cup sugar
1  tsp. lemon juice
½  tsp. ground ginger
3  oz. reduced-fat cream cheese
2  cups fresh raspberries
1  cup fresh blueberries

**1.** In a large bowl, toss nectarines with sugar, lemon juice and ginger. Refrigerate, covered, 1 hour, stirring mixture once.

**2.** Drain nectarines, reserving juices. Gradually beat reserved juices into cream cheese. Gently combine nectarines and berries; serve with cream cheese mixture.

**1 serving:** 109 cal., 3g fat (2g sat. fat), 8mg chol., 46mg sod., 21g carb. (15g sugars, 4g fiber), 2g pro. **Diabetic exchanges:** 1 fruit, ½ starch, ½ fat.

66
I've made this for family gatherings and gotten nothing but raves about it. It is one of the best coleslaws I've ever tasted.
—DEB1856
TASTEOFHOME.COM

BUTTERY
WHISKEY-GLAZED
PEARL ONIONS

# BUTTERY WHISKEY-GLAZED PEARL ONIONS

I always have pearl onions on hand to add to stews and vegetable dishes—they're great pickled too. Every Thanksgiving, I make this glazed onion dish. It can easily be made ahead and reheated the day of.
—Ann Sheehy, Lawrence, MA

**TAKES: 30 MIN. • MAKES: 10 SERVINGS**

2   pkg. (14.4 oz. each) pearl onions
⅓   cup cider vinegar
¼   cup butter, cubed
¼   cup whiskey or apple cider
¼   cup maple syrup
½   tsp. dried thyme
½   tsp. kosher salt
¼   tsp. pepper
1⅓  cups water

1. Place all ingredients in a large nonstick skillet; bring to a boil. Reduce heat to medium-low; cook, covered, until onions are tender, 6-8 minutes.

2. Increase heat to medium-high; cook, uncovered, until liquid is almost evaporated and onions are glazed, 10-12 minutes, stirring occasionally. Remove from heat.

**¼ cup:** 100 cal., 5g fat (3g sat. fat), 12mg chol., 147mg sod., 13g carb. (9g sugars, 1g fiber), 1g pro.

# GRANDMA'S CLASSIC POTATO SALAD

When I asked my grandmother how old this recipe was, she told me that her mom used to make it when she was a little girl. It has definitely stood the test of time.
—Kimberly Wallace, Dennison, OH

**PREP: 25 MIN. • COOK: 20 MIN. + COOLING • MAKES: 10 SERVINGS**

6    medium potatoes, peeled and cubed
¼    cup all-purpose flour
1    Tbsp. sugar
1½   tsp. salt
1    tsp. ground mustard
1    tsp. pepper
¾    cup water
2    large eggs, beaten
¼    cup white vinegar
4    hard-boiled large eggs, divided use
2    celery ribs, chopped
1    medium onion, chopped
     Sliced green onions, optional

1. Place potatoes in a large saucepan and cover with water. Bring to a boil. Reduce heat; cover and cook until tender, 15-20 minutes. Drain and cool to room temperature.

2. Meanwhile, in a small heavy saucepan, combine flour, sugar, salt, mustard and pepper. Gradually stir in water until smooth. Cook and stir over medium-high heat until thickened and bubbly. Reduce heat; cook and stir 2 minutes longer.

3. Remove from the heat. Stir a small amount of hot mixture into beaten eggs; return all to the pan, stirring constantly. Bring to a gentle boil; cook and stir 2 minutes longer. Remove from the heat and cool completely. Gently stir in vinegar.

4. Chop and refrigerate 1 hard-boiled egg; chop the remaining 3 hard-boiled eggs. In a large bowl, combine the potatoes, celery, chopped onion and eggs; add dressing and stir until blended. Refrigerate until chilled. Garnish with reserved chopped egg and, if desired, sliced green onions.

**¾ cup:** 144 cal., 3g fat (1g sat. fat), 112mg chol., 402mg sod., 23g carb. (3g sugars, 2g fiber), 6g pro. **Diabetic exchanges:** 1½ starch, ½ fat.

# CHILI VERDE ESQUITES (MEXICAN CORN SALAD)

The sausages add a wallop of flavor in this kicked-up corn salad! We leave half the kernels raw for crunch, and quickly pickle shallots and serrano pepper in lime juice for brightness. Half the Cotija cheese gets added for creaminess while the mixture is hot, and the other half is added as a topping once it's cooled.
—*Cara Nicoletti, Wellesley, MA*

**PREP:** 20 MIN. • **COOK:** 10 MIN. + COOLING • **MAKES:** 8 SERVINGS

5   Tbsp. lime juice
3   Tbsp. olive oil
6   medium ears sweet corn, husked
2   shallots, sliced into rings
1   serrano pepper, sliced into rings, optional
1   pkg. (12 oz.) Seemore Fully Cooked Chicken Chili Verde Sausages
1   Tbsp. canola oil
½   cup Cotija cheese, crumbled and divided
1   cup roughly chopped fresh cilantro leaves

**1.** In a large serving bowl, whisk together lime juice and olive oil. Cut kernels off corn cobs. Add half to the serving bowl; stir in shallots and, if desired, serrano pepper. Set aside.

**2.** Crumble sausages into small pieces. In a large cast-iron or stainless steel skillet over medium-high heat, cook and stir sausage in canola oil until golden brown, about 5 minutes. With a slotted spoon, transfer sausage to paper towel.

**3.** In same pan, add remaining corn to drippings; cook over high heat, not stirring, until lightly charred on 1 side, 2-3 minutes. Transfer corn to shallot mixture; add sausage and ¼ cup Cotija cheese. Toss to combine; let stand until cooled to room temperature, 15-20 minutes. Stir in ½ cup cilantro. Top with remaining ½ cup cilantro and ¼ cup Cotija cheese.

**¾ cup:** 229 cal., 14g fat (3g sat. fat), 40mg chol., 364mg sod., 18g carb. (6g sugars, 2g fiber), 12g pro. **Diabetic exchanges:** 2 lean meat, 2 fat, 1 starch.

## TEST KITCHEN TIP

*While fresh corn is best for this salad, you can use frozen corn in a pinch. You'll want to thaw the corn completely and make sure it's as dry as possible, then proceed with the recipe as directed.*

"Boy, were these good! I served them with a side of ranch dressing and a side of cocktail sauce.
—JELLYBUG
TASTEOFHOME.COM

# ZUCCHINI-CORNBREAD FRITTERS

Over 40 years ago a friend gave me this basic recipe. Over time, I have adjusted the ingredients for my family's taste. I pan-fry these fritters so they don't get too greasy but you can deep-fry them if you'd like.
—*Marietta Slater, Justin, TX*

**TAKES: 25 MIN. • MAKES: 2 DOZEN**

1 pkg. (8½ oz.) corn bread/muffin mix
1 large egg, beaten
1 cup shredded zucchini
1 cup shredded cheddar cheese
¼ cup finely chopped onion
1 tsp. minced garlic
1 tsp. Old Bay Seasoning
   Oil for deep-fat frying

In a large bowl, stir together the first 7 ingredients. In a deep-fat fryer or skillet, heat 2 in. of oil to 375°. Drop batter by rounded tablespoonfuls into skillet. Fry until golden brown, about 2 minutes on each side. Drain on paper towels; keep warm.

**1 fritter:** 102 cal., 7g fat (2g sat. fat), 13mg chol., 144mg sod., 7g carb. (2g sugars, 1g fiber), 2g pro.

## TEST KITCHEN TIP

*Don't have Old Bay Seasoning on hand? Flavor the batter with a teaspoon of whatever spices or seasoning blend your family enjoys.*

# LEMON-BUTTER BRUSSELS SPROUTS

Kick up those sprouts. Lots of folks claim to dislike them, but this recipe charms even my toddler.
—*Jenn Tidwell, Fair Oaks, CA*

**TAKES: 25 MIN. • MAKES: 4 SERVINGS**

1 lb. fresh or frozen Brussels
   sprouts, thawed
3 Tbsp. olive oil
2 garlic cloves, minced
¼ cup white wine
½ cup chicken broth
4 tsp. lemon juice
½ tsp. dried thyme
¼ tsp. salt
¼ tsp. pepper
2 Tbsp. butter
1 tsp. grated lemon zest
   Minced fresh parsley, optional

1. Cut Brussels sprouts in half. In a large skillet, heat oil over medium heat. Add Brussels sprouts and garlic; cook and stir 5 minutes or until sprouts begin to brown.

2. Add wine, stirring to loosen browned bits from pan. Stir in broth, lemon juice, thyme, salt and pepper. Bring to a boil. Reduce heat; simmer, covered, until sprouts are tender, 8-10 minutes.

3. Stir in butter and lemon zest until butter is melted. Sprinkle with parsley if desired.

**1 serving:** 207 cal., 16g fat (5g sat. fat), 16mg chol., 340mg sod., 12g carb. (3g sugars, 5g fiber), 4g pro.

# GRILLED CORN WITH LIME BUTTER

I've always made herb butter and garlic butter to go with my corn on the cob. Once, I put a little lime juice in the butter and have done that ever since. My family loves it and asks for it every time we have corn!
—*Lynn Caruso, Gilroy, CA*

PREP: 20 MIN. + CHILLING • GRILL: 25 MIN. • MAKES: 8 SERVINGS

⅓ cup butter, softened
1 Tbsp. lime juice
2 tsp. minced fresh parsley
¼ tsp. garlic powder
¼ tsp. grated lime zest
¼ tsp. cayenne pepper
8 large ears sweet corn in husks

1. In a small bowl, mix the first 6 ingredients. Shape into a log; wrap and refrigerate 30 minutes or until firm.

2. Meanwhile, carefully peel back corn husks to within 1 in. of bottoms; remove silk. Rewrap corn in husks and secure with kitchen string. Place in a stockpot; cover with cold water. Soak 20 minutes.

3. Drain corn. Grill, covered, over medium heat until tender, 25-30 minutes, turning often. Cut lime butter into slices; serve with corn. If desired, serve with lime wedges.

**1 ear of corn with 2 tsp. butter:** 214 cal., 12g fat (7g sat. fat), 27mg chol., 93mg sod., 28g carb. (5g sugars, 4g fiber), 5g pro.

# CARROT, PARSNIP & POTATO GRATIN

Thanks to a challenge in the *Taste of Home* community a few years back, my husband and I tried parsnips and discovered that we liked them! In fact, I started growing them in my garden and trying new things with them. This recipe is one of my experiments, and it turned out to be something we really enjoy.
—*Sue Gronholz, Beaver Dam, WI*

PREP: 20 MIN. • BAKE: 50 MIN. • MAKES: 8 SERVINGS

1 lb. medium carrots, thinly sliced
½ lb. medium parsnips, peeled and thinly sliced
½ lb. Yukon Gold potatoes, peeled and thinly sliced
1 small onion, halved and sliced
2 garlic cloves, minced
1½ tsp. minced fresh rosemary
½ tsp. salt
½ tsp. ground nutmeg
1 cup half-and-half cream
¼ cup heavy whipping cream

Preheat oven to 400°. In a large bowl, combine all ingredients. Transfer to a greased 13x9-in. or 3-qt. baking dish. Cover and bake until the vegetables are tender, 40-45 minutes. Uncover and bake until cream has thickened and is beginning to turn golden brown, 10-15 minutes longer. Let stand 5-10 minutes before serving.

**¾ cup:** 141 cal., 6g fat (4g sat. fat), 23mg chol., 208mg sod., 19g carb. (6g sugars, 3g fiber), 3g pro.

> **We made this while camping and everyone loved it! I made the butter early so it was ready when we were. Easy and delicious!**
> —XXCSKIER
> TASTEOFHOME.COM

# SMOKY CAULIFLOWER BITES

These healthy little treats work well as a side or as a fun appetizer.
Roasting the cauliflower adds deep flavor and gives it an irresistible crunch.

*—Courtney Stultz, Weir, KS*

**TAKES:** 20 MIN. • **MAKES:** 4 SERVINGS

3   lbsp. olive oil
¾   tsp. sea salt
1   tsp. paprika
½   tsp. ground cumin
¼   tsp. ground turmeric
⅛   tsp. chili powder
1   medium head cauliflower,
    broken into florets

Preheat oven to 450°. Mix first 6 ingredients. Add cauliflower florets; toss to coat. Transfer to a 15x10x1-in. baking pan. Roast until tender, 15-20 minutes, stirring halfway.

**1 cup:** 129 cal., 11g fat (2g sat. fat), 0 chol., 408mg sod., 8g carb. (3g sugars, 3g fiber), 3g pro. **Diabetic exchanges:** 2 fat, 1 vegetable.

## TEST KITCHEN TIP

*Give these bites even more smoky, spicy flavor by dipping them in chipotle mayo, and if you really like smoky flavors, use smoked Spanish-style paprika.*

# SWEET PEPPER PESTO PASTA

What's a family gathering or potluck without at least one pasta salad?
This one's great freshly made or for several days after.

*—Karen Hentges, Bakersfield, CA*

**TAKES:** 30 MIN. • **MAKES:** 8 SERVINGS

20  miniature sweet peppers,
    seeded and cut into rings
2   tsp. olive oil
½   tsp. garlic powder
4½  cups uncooked bow tie pasta
1   cup prepared pesto
1   can (2¼ oz.) sliced ripe
    olives, drained
⅓   cup grated Parmesan cheese

**1.** Preheat oven to 350°. Toss peppers with oil and garlic powder; spread evenly in a greased 15x10x1-in. pan. Roast until tender, 10-15 minutes.

**2.** Cook pasta according to package directions. Drain; rinse with cold water and drain. Place in a large bowl.

**3.** Stir in pesto, olives and peppers. Refrigerate, covered, until serving. Sprinkle with cheese.

**1 cup:** 308 cal., 14g fat (3g sat. fat), 3mg chol., 493mg sod., 37g carb. (3g sugars, 3g fiber), 9g pro.

# PRESSURE-COOKER ORANGE SPICE CARROTS

To get my son to eat veggies, I mix and match flavors and spices.
My carrots with orange and cinnamon won him over.
—*Christy Addison, Clarksville, OH*

PREP: 10 MIN. • COOK: 5 MIN. • MAKES: 6 SERVINGS

- 2 lbs. medium carrots or baby carrots, cut into ¾-in. pieces
- ½ cup packed brown sugar
- ½ cup orange juice
- 2 Tbsp. butter
- ¾ tsp. ground cinnamon
- ½ tsp. salt
- ¼ tsp. ground nutmeg
- 1 Tbsp. cornstarch
- ¼ cup cold water

1. In a 6-qt. electric pressure cooker, combine the first 7 ingredients. Lock lid; close pressure-release valve. Adjust to pressure-cook on low for 3 minutes. Quick-release pressure.

2. Select saute setting, and adjust for high heat; bring liquid to a boil. In a small bowl, mix cornstarch and water until smooth; gradually stir into carrot mixture. Cook and stir until sauce is thickened, 1-2 minutes.

**⅔ cup:** 187 cal., 4g fat (3g sat. fat), 10mg chol., 339mg sod., 38g carb. (27g sugars, 4g fiber), 2g pro.

---

# BROWN RICE WITH ALMONDS & CRANBERRIES

I'm always looking to switch things up during the holiday season. This rice salad
fits the bill, as it's on the lighter side and it uses ingredients I always have on hand.
—*Joan Hallford, North Richland Hills, TX*

PREP: 35 MIN. • BAKE: 1¼ HOURS • MAKES: 10 SERVINGS

- 3 cans (14½ oz. each) beef broth
- ¼ cup butter, cubed
- 1 large onion, chopped
- 1 cup uncooked long grain brown rice
- ½ cup bulgur
- ½ cup slivered almonds
- ½ cup dried cranberries
- ¾ cup minced fresh parsley, divided
- ¼ cup chopped green onions
- ¼ tsp. salt
- ¼ tsp. pepper

1. Preheat oven to 375°. In a large saucepan, bring the broth to a simmer; reduce heat to low and keep hot. In a large skillet, heat butter over medium heat. Add onion; cook and stir until tender, 3-4 minutes. Add brown rice, bulgur and slivered almonds; cook and stir until rice is lightly browned and has a nutty aroma, 2-3 minutes.

2. Transfer to a greased 13x9-in. baking dish. Stir in cranberries, ½ cup fresh parsley, green onions, salt and pepper. Stir in the hot broth. Bake, covered, 45 minutes. Uncover and continue to cook until liquid is absorbed and rice is tender, 30-35 minutes longer. Remove from oven and fluff with a fork. Cover; let stand 5-10 minutes. Sprinkle with remaining parsley before serving.

**¾ cup:** 207 cal., 8g fat (3g sat. fat), 12mg chol., 658mg sod., 29g carb. (7g sugars, 4g fiber), 5g pro. **Diabetic exchanges:** 2 starch, 1½ fat.

GRILLED LEBANESE SALAD

# GRILLED LEBANESE SALAD

Amazingly, even our kids eat their greens, herbs and garden veggies when
they're prepared this way. Fresh and healthy never tasted more delicious.
—*Trisha Kruse, Eagle, ID*

PREP: 30 MIN. • GRILL: 10 MIN. • MAKES: 13 SERVINGS (¾ CUP EACH)

8 plum tomatoes
½ lb. whole fresh mushrooms
2 medium red onions
2 medium green peppers
6 Tbsp. olive oil, divided
½ tsp. garlic salt
4 cups cubed French bread
  (¾-in. cubes)
2 tsp. dried thyme
1 tsp. dried oregano
½ tsp. salt
½ tsp. pepper
1 medium cucumber, peeled,
  seeded and sliced
½ cup fresh basil leaves, thinly sliced
3 Tbsp. balsamic vinegar

1. Cut tomatoes and mushrooms in half; place in a large bowl. Cut onions and peppers into ½-in.-thick slices; add to bowl. Drizzle with 4 Tbsp. oil and sprinkle with garlic salt; toss to coat.

2. Place bread cubes in another large bowl. Drizzle with remaining oil. Sprinkle with thyme, oregano, salt and pepper; toss to coat. Thread on metal or soaked wooden skewers.

3. Transfer vegetables to a grill wok or basket. Grill, uncovered, over medium heat for 8-12 minutes or until tender, stirring frequently. Grill bread cubes, covered, over medium heat for 1 to 2 minutes or until toasted, turning occasionally.

4. Coarsely chop the tomatoes, onions and peppers; place in a large bowl. Add the mushrooms, bread cubes, cucumber and basil; drizzle with vinegar and gently toss to coat.

**¾ cup:** 113 cal., 7g fat (1g sat. fat), 0 chol., 239mg sod., 12g carb. (4g sugars, 2g fiber), 2g pro. **Diabetic exchanges:** 1 starch, 1 fat.

# OVEN-DRIED TOMATOES

We owned an organic greenhouse and business where we taught classes. I had 100 tomato
varieties to work with, so I started oven-drying them and taught my students how to do it as well.
—*Sue Gronholz, Beaver Dam, WI*

PREP: 15 MIN. • BAKE: 5 HOURS • MAKES: 4 SERVINGS

8 plum tomatoes
  Ice water
¼ cup olive oil
¼ cup minced fresh basil
4 garlic cloves, minced
½ tsp. salt
¼ tsp. pepper

1. Preheat oven to 250°. Fill a large saucepan two-thirds with water; bring to a boil. Cut a shallow "X" on the bottom of each tomato. Place tomatoes, a few at a time, in boiling water just until skin at the "X"s begins to loosen, about 30 seconds. Remove and immediately drop into ice water. Pull off and discard skins.

2. Cut tomatoes in half lengthwise. Combine tomatoes, oil, basil, garlic, salt and pepper; toss to coat. Transfer tomatoes, cut side up, to a greased 15x10x1-in. baking pan. Roast until tomatoes are soft and slightly shriveled, about 5 hours. Cool completely; store in the refrigerator.

**4 tomato halves:** 147 cal., 14g fat (2g sat. fat), 0 chol., 302mg sod., 6g carb. (3g sugars, 2g fiber), 1g pro. **Diabetic exchanges:** 3 fat, 1 vegetable.

# SPICED SQUASH & FRUIT CRUMBLE

This sweet and savory dish is a perfect side for cold weather and would be amazing with any meal. It is versatile and perfect for potlucks or family dinners.
—Joan Hallford, North Richland Hills, TX

**PREP:** 25 MIN. • **BAKE:** 45 MIN. • **MAKES:** 12 SERVINGS

6 thick-sliced bacon strips, cut into ½-in. pieces
1¼ lbs. cubed peeled butternut squash (1-in. cubes)
3 medium Granny Smith apples, peeled and cut into wedges (about 4 cups)
2 medium pears, peeled and cut into 1-in. cubes
½ cup packed brown sugar
1 Tbsp. all-purpose flour
1 tsp. salt
¼ tsp. ground cinnamon
¼ tsp. ground mace
¼ cup cold butter
½ cup chopped pecans, toasted

1. Preheat oven to 350°. In a large skillet, cook bacon over medium heat until almost crisp, stirring occasionally. Drain on paper towels.

2. Combine squash, apples and pears in an ungreased 13x9-in. baking dish. In a small bowl, mix brown sugar, flour, salt, cinnamon and mace. Cut in butter until mixture resembles coarse crumbs. Fold in pecans and bacon. Sprinkle over squash mixture.

3. Bake until squash and fruit are tender, 45-50 minutes.

**¾ cup:** 187 cal., 10g fat (4g sat. fat), 15mg chol., 357mg sod., 24g carb. (16g sugars, 3g fiber), 3g pro.

## TEST KITCHEN TIP

*This combo of squash and fruit is ideal, but if you don't have the pears called for, replace them with additional apples.*

# SPRING PEA & RADISH SALAD

SHOWN ON PAGE 116

Winters can be very long here in New Hampshire. I always look forward to the first veggies of spring so I can make some lighter dishes like this fresh salad.
—Jolene Martinelli, Fremont, NH

**TAKES:** 20 MIN. • **MAKES:** 6 SERVINGS

½ lb. fresh wax or green beans
½ lb. fresh sugar snap peas
2 cups water
6 large radishes, thinly sliced
2 Tbsp. honey
1 tsp. dried tarragon
¼ tsp. kosher salt
¼ tsp. coarsely ground pepper

1. Snip ends off beans and sugar snap peas; remove strings from snap peas. In a large saucepan, bring water to a boil over high heat. Add beans and reduce heat; simmer, covered, 4-5 minutes. Add sugar snap peas; simmer, covered, until both beans and peas are crisp-tender, another 2-3 minutes. Drain.

2. Toss beans and peas with radishes. Stir together honey, tarragon, salt and pepper. Drizzle over vegetables.

**⅔ cup:** 50 cal., 0 fat (0 sat. fat), 0 chol., 86mg sod., 11g carb. (8g sugars, 2g fiber), 2g pro. **Diabetic exchanges:** 1 vegetable, ½ starch.

SPICED SQUASH
& FRUIT CRUMBLE

> **"**
> What a refreshing salad. My husband and daughter loved it! I've never seen them so excited about a salad.
> —PDARWIN
> TASTEOFHOME.COM

# MEDITERRANEAN COBB SALAD

I'm a huge fan of taking classic dishes and adding some flair to them.
I also like to change up heavier dishes, like the classic Cobb salad.
I've traded out typical chicken for crunchy falafel that's just as satisfying.
—*Jenn Tidwell, Fair Oaks, CA*

**PREP: 1 HOUR • COOK: 5 MIN./BATCH • MAKES: 10 SERVINGS**

1   pkg. (6 oz.) falafel mix
½   cup sour cream or plain yogurt
¼   cup chopped seeded
    peeled cucumber
¼   cup 2% milk
1   tsp. minced fresh parsley
¼   tsp. salt
4   cups torn romaine
4   cups fresh baby spinach
3   hard-boiled large eggs, chopped
2   medium tomatoes, seeded
    and finely chopped
1   medium ripe avocado,
    peeled and finely chopped
¾   cup crumbled feta cheese
8   bacon strips, cooked and crumbled
½   cup pitted Greek olives,
    finely chopped

**1.** Prepare and cook falafel according to package directions. When cool enough to handle, crumble or coarsely chop falafel.

**2.** In a small bowl, mix sour cream, cucumber, milk, parsley and salt. In a large bowl, combine romaine and spinach; transfer to a platter. Arrange crumbled falafel and remaining ingredients over greens. Drizzle with dressing.

**1 cup:** 258 cal., 18g fat (5g sat. fat), 83mg chol., 687mg sod., 15g carb. (3g sugars, 5g fiber), 13g pro.

## TEST KITCHEN TIP

*Lighten up this dish by using reduced-fat sour cream or yogurt in the dressing. You can also forgo the salt and decrease the bacon.*

# MASHED POTATOES WITH CHEDDAR

Everybody loves fluffy homemade mashed potatoes,
and they're even better with sharp cheddar cheese.
—*Darlene Brenden, Salem, OR*

**PREP: 15 MIN. • COOK: 30 MIN. • MAKES: 8 SERVINGS**

3   lbs. potatoes, peeled
    and cubed (about 6 cups)
1   to 1¼ cups half-and-half cream
3   Tbsp. butter
1   tsp. salt
3   cups shredded extra-sharp
    cheddar cheese

**1.** Place peeled potatoes in a 6-qt. stockpot; add water to cover. Bring to a boil. Reduce heat; cook, uncovered, 15-20 minutes or until tender. Meanwhile, in a saucepan, heat cream, butter and salt until butter is melted.

**2.** Drain potatoes; return to pot. Mash potatoes, gradually adding cream mixture. Stir in cheddar cheese.

**¾ cup:** 348 cal., 21g fat (14g sat. fat), 71mg chol., 614mg sod., 25g carb. (3g sugars, 2g fiber), 14g pro.

# EASY FRIED RICE

This easy recipe really captures the flavor of fried rice served in restaurants.
Use leftover chicken for a satisfying dish that's simple to put together.
—*Lori Schweer, Mapleton, MN*

**TAKES: 30 MIN. • MAKES: 4 SERVINGS**

2 large eggs, beaten
¼ tsp. salt
3 Tbsp. canola oil, divided
4 cups cooked rice
1½ cups frozen stir-fry vegetable blend
½ cup sliced green onions
1 garlic clove, minced
1 cup diced cooked chicken
3 Tbsp. soy sauce
1 Tbsp. chicken broth
½ tsp. pepper
¼ tsp. ground ginger
4 bacon strips, cooked and crumbled

1. Combine eggs and salt. In a large skillet or wok over medium heat, scramble eggs in 1 tsp. oil, breaking eggs into small pieces. Remove from skillet and set aside.

2. Add remaining 2 Tbsp. plus 2 tsp. canola oil to skillet. Stir-fry cooked rice over medium-high heat for 5 minutes. Add vegetables, onions and garlic; stir-fry for 5 minutes. Add chicken; stir-fry until heated through, 3-5 minutes. Combine soy sauce, broth, pepper and ginger. Add to rice; stir to coat. Add bacon and eggs; heat through.

**1½ cups:** 476 cal., 19g fat (4g sat. fat), 133mg chol., 1077mg sod., 51g carb. (2g sugars, 2g fiber), 23g pro.

# JEN'S BAKED BEANS

My daughters wanted baked beans, so I gave this homemade version a shot.
With mustard, molasses and a dash of heat, I made these beans irresistible.
—*Jennifer Heasley, York, PA*

**PREP: 20 MIN. • BAKE: 50 MIN. • MAKES: 8 SERVINGS**

6 bacon strips, chopped
4 cans (15½ oz. each) great northern beans, rinsed and drained
1⅓ cups ketchup
⅔ cup packed brown sugar
⅓ cup molasses
3 Tbsp. yellow mustard
2½ tsp. garlic powder
1½ tsp. hot pepper sauce
¼ tsp. crushed red pepper flakes

1. Preheat oven to 325°. In an ovenproof Dutch oven, cook bacon over medium heat until crisp, stirring occasionally. Remove with a slotted spoon; drain on paper towels. Discard drippings.

2. Return bacon to pan. Stir in the remaining ingredients; bring to a boil. Place in oven; bake, covered, to allow flavors to blend, 50-60 minutes.

**Freeze option:** Freeze cooled baked beans in freezer containers. To use, partially thaw in refrigerator overnight. Heat through in a saucepan, stirring occasionally; add broth or water if necessary.

**¾ cup:** 362 cal., 3g fat (1g sat. fat), 6mg chol., 1000mg sod., 71g carb. (39g sugars, 11g fiber), 13g pro.

“
Made this for
my fiance and
he absolutely
loved it! Very
easy to make.
Now I make it
all the time.
—HAIRDOC
TASTEOFHOME.COM

GREEN BEAN &
CAULIFLOWER
CASSEROLE

# GREEN BEAN & CAULIFLOWER CASSEROLE

I like to make a savory homemade cream sauce for the timeless green bean casserole.
This time I added another vegetable for a delicious twist that sets my casserole apart from the rest!
You can omit the vermouth if you'd like by substituting another half cup of chicken broth.
—*Ann Sheehy, Lawrence, MA*

PREP: 45 MIN. • BAKE: 30 MIN. • MAKES: 10 SERVINGS

1 lb. fresh cauliflowerets, cut into 1-in. pieces
1 lb. fresh green beans, trimmed and cut into 2-in. pieces
4 tsp. olive oil, divided
1 cup panko bread crumbs
1 cup french-fried onions, crumbled
2 Tbsp. butter
8 oz. thinly sliced fresh mushrooms
1 shallot, finely chopped
2 garlic cloves, minced
¼ cup all-purpose flour
½ cup dry vermouth or reduced-sodium chicken broth
1½ cups reduced-sodium chicken broth
1 tsp. salt
1 tsp. dried thyme
½ tsp. pepper
¼ tsp. ground nutmeg
½ cup cubed fully cooked ham
½ cup sour cream
1 cup plain Greek yogurt

1. Preheat oven to 375°. In a Dutch oven, bring 12 cups water to a boil. Add cauliflower and beans; cook, uncovered, just until beans turn bright green, 1-2 minutes. Drain and immediately drop into ice water. Drain and pat dry.

2. In a large skillet, heat 1 tsp. oil over medium-high heat. Add panko bread crumbs; cook and stir until lightly browned, 2-3 minutes. Stir in french-fried onions; set aside.

3. In the same skillet, heat butter and remaining oil over medium heat. Add mushrooms and shallot; cook and stir until tender, 8-10 minutes. Add garlic; cook 1 minute longer. Stir in flour until blended. Gradually whisk in vermouth; cook, stirring until most of the liquid is gone. Whisk in broth and seasonings. Stirring constantly, bring to a boil; cook and stir until thickened, 6-8 minutes. Remove from heat; stir in ham, sour cream, yogurt and reserved vegetables. Transfer to a greased 13x9-in. baking dish.

4. Bake, uncovered, until bubbly, 30-40 minutes. Sprinkle with bread crumb mixture before serving.

**1 cup:** 217 cal., 13g fat (6g sat. fat), 19mg chol., 539mg sod., 19g carb. (5g sugars, 3g fiber), 7g pro.

---

# APRICOT-GINGER ACORN SQUASH

It's a real treat digging into tender baked squash with a buttery apricot sauce. Natural fruit preserves add sweetness, and ginger makes it savory without loading on unwanted calories.
—*Trisha Kruse, Eagle, ID*

PREP: 10 MIN. • BAKE: 1 HOUR • MAKES: 2 SERVINGS

1 small acorn squash
2 Tbsp. apricot preserves
4 tsp. butter, melted
1½ tsp. reduced-sodium soy sauce
¼ tsp. ground ginger
¼ tsp. pepper

1. Preheat oven to 350°. Cut squash lengthwise in half; remove seeds. Cut a thin slice from bottoms to level if desired. Place in a greased 11x7-in. baking dish, cut side up.

2. Mix remaining ingredients; spoon over squash. Bake, covered, 45 minutes. Uncover; bake until tender, 15-20 minutes.

**½ squash:** 234 cal., 8g fat (5g sat. fat), 20mg chol., 221mg sod., 43g carb. (15g sugars, 4g fiber), 3g pro.

# SUPER ITALIAN CHOPPED SALAD

Antipasto ingredients are sliced and diced to make this substantial salad. I like to buy sliced meat from the deli and chop it all so we can get a bit of everything in each bite.

—*Kim Molina, Duarte, CA*

**TAKES:** 25 MIN. • **MAKES:** 10 SERVINGS

- 3  cups torn romaine
- 1  can (15 oz.) garbanzo beans or chickpeas, rinsed and drained
- 1  jar (6½ oz.) marinated artichoke hearts, drained and chopped
- 1  medium green pepper, chopped
- 2  medium tomatoes, chopped
- 1  can (2¼ oz.) sliced ripe olives, drained
- 5  slices deli ham, chopped
- 5  thin slices hard salami, chopped
- 5  slices pepperoni, chopped
- 3  slices provolone cheese, chopped
- 2  green onions, chopped
- ¼  cup olive oil
- 2  Tbsp. red wine vinegar
- ¼  tsp. salt
- ⅛  tsp. pepper
- 2  Tbsp. grated Parmesan cheese
   Pepperoncini, optional

In a large bowl, combine the first 11 ingredients. For dressing, in a small bowl, whisk oil, vinegar, salt and pepper. Pour over salad; toss to coat. Sprinkle with cheese. Top with pepperoncini if desired.

**Note** Look for pepperoncini (pickled peppers) in the pickle and olive section of your grocery store.

**¾ cup:** 185 cal., 13g fat (3g sat. fat), 12mg chol., 444mg sod., 11g carb. (3g sugars, 3g fiber), 7g pro.

# CRANBERRY PECAN STUFFING

I love stuffing, but my family wasn't that fond of it—that is, until I found this recipe. I added a few extras and now they gobble it up. I think the cranberries give it that something special.
—Robin Lang, Muskegon, MI

**PREP:** 30 MIN. • **BAKE:** 40 MIN. • **MAKES:** 13 SERVINGS

1 cup orange juice
½ cup dried cranberries
½ lb. bulk pork sausage
¼ cup butter, cubed
3 celery ribs, chopped
1 large onion, chopped
1 tsp. poultry seasoning
6 cups seasoned stuffing cubes
1 medium tart apple, peeled and finely chopped
½ cup chopped pecans
¼ tsp. salt
⅛ tsp. pepper
¾ to 1 cup chicken broth

1. In a small saucepan, bring orange juice and cranberries to a boil. Remove from the heat; let stand for 5 minutes. Meanwhile, in a large skillet, cook sausage until no longer pink; drain. Transfer to a large bowl.

2. In the same skillet, melt butter. Add celery and onion; saute until tender. Stir in poultry seasoning.

3. Add to sausage mixture. Stir in the stuffing cubes, orange juice mixture, apple, pecans, salt, pepper and enough broth to reach desired moistness.

4. Transfer to a greased 13x9-in. baking dish. Cover and bake at 325° for 30 minutes. Uncover; bake until lightly browned, 10-15 minutes longer.

**NOTE:** This recipe makes enough to stuff a 14-lb. turkey. If you are cooking it inside the bird, bake until a meat thermometer reads at least 170° for turkey and 165° for stuffing.

**¾ cup:** 219 cal., 11g fat (4g sat. fat), 16mg chol., 532mg sod., 27g carb. (8g sugars, 2g fiber), 4g pro.

# ROSEMARY ROASTED POTATOES & ASPARAGUS

Showcase asparagus when you dress it in fresh rosemary and red potatoes for an earthy counterpoint to the fresh, green spears. Add minced garlic and you get a gorgeous, flavorful side dish.
—*Trisha Kruse, Eagle, ID*

PREP: 10 MIN. • BAKE: 35 MIN. • MAKES: 4 SERVINGS

½  lb. fingerling potatoes,
    cut into 1-in. pieces
¼  cup olive oil, divided
2  Tbsp. minced fresh rosemary or
    2 tsp. dried rosemary, crushed
2  garlic cloves, minced
1  lb. fresh asparagus, trimmed
¼  tsp. salt
¼  tsp. freshly ground pepper

**1.** In a small bowl, combine the potatoes, 2 Tbsp. oil, rosemary and garlic; toss to coat. Transfer to a greased 15x10x1-in. baking pan. Roast at 400° for 20 minutes, stirring once.

**2.** Drizzle asparagus with remaining oil; add to the pan. Roast 15-20 minutes longer or until tender, stirring occasionally. Sprinkle with salt and pepper.

**1 serving:** 175 cal., 14g fat (2g sat. fat), 0 chol., 156mg sod., 11g carb. (1g sugars, 2g fiber), 3g pro. **Diabetic exchanges:** 3 fat, 1 vegetable, ½ starch.

## TEST KITCHEN TIP

*Dress up this cooked side dish with a sprinkling of cooked and crumbled bacon, a little feta or Parmesan cheese, pine nuts or a simple drizzle of melted butter.*

# APPLE WALNUT SLAW

After a co-worker shared this recipe with me, it became a family favorite of my own. Apples, walnuts and raisins are a fun way to dress up coleslaw.
—*Joan Hallford, North Richland Hills, TX*

TAKES: 15 MIN. • MAKES: 12 SERVINGS

¾   cup mayonnaise
¾   cup buttermilk
4   to 5 Tbsp. sugar
4½  tsp. lemon juice
¾   tsp. salt
¼   to ½ tsp. pepper
6   cups shredded cabbage
1½  cups shredded carrots
⅓   cup finely chopped red onion
1   cup coarsely chopped
     walnuts, toasted
¾   cup raisins
2   medium apples, chopped

**1.** Whisk together first 6 ingredients. In a large bowl, combine vegetables, walnuts and raisins; toss with dressing. Fold in apples.

**2.** Refrigerate, covered, until serving.

**Note:** To toast nuts, bake in a shallow pan in a 350°; oven for 5-10 minutes or cook in a skillet over low heat until lightly browned, stirring occasionally.

**¾ cup:** 233 cal., 17g fat (2g sat. fat), 2mg chol., 264mg sod., 21g carb. (14g sugars, 3g fiber), 3g pro.

66

The aroma was wonderful and so was the taste. Perfect side for salmon. I highly endorse it for flavor and ease. Presentation is nice too.
—APPY_GIRL
TASTEOFHOME.COM

# RUTABAGA CARROT CASSEROLE

This scoopable side with its sweet, crunchy topping makes a
delightful alternative to the traditional sweet potato casserole.

—*Joan Hallford, North Richland Hills, TX*

PREP: 30 MIN. • BAKE: 30 MIN. • MAKES: 8 SERVINGS

1 large rutabaga, peeled and cubed
3 large carrots, shredded
1 large egg, beaten
2 Tbsp. brown sugar
1 Tbsp. butter
½ tsp. salt
¼ tsp. ground nutmeg
   Dash pepper
1 cup cooked brown rice
1 cup fat-free evaporated milk

### TOPPING
¼ cup all-purpose flour
¼ cup packed brown sugar
2 Tbsp. cold butter
½ cup chopped pecans

1. Place rutabaga in a Dutch oven and cover with water. Bring to a boil. Cook, uncovered, until tender, 15-20 minutes, adding the carrots during the last 5 minutes of cooking; drain.

2. In a large bowl, mash the rutabaga mixture with egg, brown sugar, butter, salt, nutmeg and pepper. Stir in rice and milk. Transfer to an 11x7-in. baking dish coated with cooking spray.

3. For topping, in a small bowl, combine flour and brown sugar; cut in butter until crumbly. Stir in pecans. Sprinkle over top. Bake, uncovered, at 350° until bubbly, 30-35 minutes.

**½ cup:** 249 cal., 11g fat (3g sat. fat), 39mg chol., 267mg sod., 34g carb. (21g sugars, 4g fiber), 6g pro. **Diabetic exchanges:** 2 starch, 2 fat.

---

# CHARD WITH BACON-CITRUS SAUCE

Chard is a leafy veggie often used in Mediterranean cooking.
I dress it with orange juice and bacon, and my family gobbles it up.

—*Teri Rasey, Cadillac, MI*

TAKES: 25 MIN. • MAKES: 6 SERVINGS

½ lb. thick-sliced
   peppered
   bacon strips
2 lbs. rainbow Swiss
   chard, chopped
1 cup orange juice
2 Tbsp. butter
4 tsp. grated
   orange zest
⅛ tsp. salt
⅛ tsp. pepper

1. In a large cast-iron or other heavy skillet, cook bacon over medium heat until crisp; drain on paper towels. Discard all but 1 Tbsp. drippings. Cut bacon into small pieces.

2. Add chard to drippings; cook and stir just until wilted, 5-6 minutes. Add remaining ingredients; cook 1-2 minutes, stirring occasionally. Top with bacon.

**½ cup:** 162 cal., 11g fat (5g sat. fat), 22mg chol., 655mg sod., 10g carb. (5g sugars, 3g fiber), 7g pro.

# GRANNY'S APPLE SCALLOPED POTATOES

I created this dish because I love scalloped potatoes and apples. It is delicious with baked
breaded pork chops, which you could cook at the same time in another cast-iron pan.
—*Shirley Rickis, The Villages, FL*

PREP: 25 MIN. • BAKE: 55 MIN. + STANDING • MAKES: 4 SERVINGS

1 medium Granny Smith apple,
  peeled and thinly sliced
1 tsp. sugar
1 tsp. lemon juice
2 Tbsp. butter
½ cup sliced sweet onion
4 medium red potatoes, thinly sliced
¾ cup plus 2 Tbsp. shredded
  Parmesan cheese, divided
½ cup heavy whipping cream
½ tsp. minced fresh thyme or
  ¼ tsp. dried thyme
¼ tsp. salt
¼ tsp. pepper
4 bacon strips, cooked and crumbled
  Chopped fresh parsley, optional

1. Preheat oven to 350°. In a small bowl, combine apple slices, sugar and lemon juice; toss to coat. Set aside. In an 8- or 9-in. cast-iron or other ovenproof skillet, heat butter over medium heat. Add onion; cook and stir until crisp-tender, about 3 minutes. Remove from the heat.

2. Alternately arrange potato and apple slices in a single layer in same skillet. Combine ¾ cup Parmesan cheese with cream, thyme, salt and pepper; pour over top.

3. Bake, uncovered, 50 minutes. Top with bacon and remaining 2 Tbsp. Parmesan cheese. Bake until potatoes are tender and top is lightly browned, 5-10 minutes longer. Let stand 10 minutes before serving. If desired, sprinkle with parsley.

**1 serving:** 376 cal., 25g fat (15g sat. fat), 70mg chol., 651mg sod., 27g carb. (7g sugars, 3g fiber), 13g pro.

---

# LAYERED BROCCOLI SALAD

Everyone enjoys this simple salad with dinner. The layers look festive, and the crisp broccoli,
sunflower seeds and bacon are a nice contrast to the chewy bits of dried cranberries.
—*Darlene Brenden, Salem, OR*

TAKES: 20 MIN. • MAKES: 8 SERVINGS

6 cups chopped fresh broccoli florets
1 small red onion, thinly sliced
⅔ cup dried cranberries
½ cup plain yogurt
2 Tbsp. mayonnaise
2 Tbsp. honey
2 Tbsp. cider vinegar
1½ cups shredded cheddar cheese
¼ cup sunflower kernels
2 bacon strips, cooked and crumbled

In a large glass bowl, layer the broccoli, onion and cranberries. Combine the yogurt, mayonnaise, honey and vinegar; drizzle over salad. Sprinkle with cheese, sunflower kernels and bacon.

**¾ cup:** 209 cal., 12g fat (6g sat. fat), 27mg chol., 222mg sod., 19g carb. (13g sugars, 3g fiber), 8g pro.

GRANNY'S
APPLE
SCALLOPED
POTATOES

> "This recipe was awesome. Love the aioli with this. I also made roasted potatoes and used the aioli.
> —AUG95
> TASTEOFHOME.COM

# ROASTED BRUSSELS SPROUTS WITH SRIRACHA AIOLI

This dish constantly surprises you—it's crispy, easy to eat, totally sharable and yet it's a vegetable! This recipe is also gluten-free, dairy-free and paleo, and it can be vegan if you use vegan mayo.
—*Molly Winsten, Medford, MA*

**PREP: 20 MIN. • COOK: 20 MIN. • MAKES: 8 SERVINGS**

16  fresh Brussels sprouts (about 1 lb.), trimmed and halved
2   Tbsp. olive oil
2   to 4 tsp. Sriracha chili sauce, divided
½   tsp. salt, divided
½   tsp. pepper, divided
½   cup mayonnaise
2   tsp. lime juice
1   Tbsp. lemon juice

1. Preheat oven to 425°. Place Brussels sprouts on a rimmed baking sheet. Drizzle with oil and 1 tsp. chili sauce; sprinkle with ¼ tsp. salt and ¼ tsp. pepper. Toss to coat. Roast until crispy, 20-25 minutes.

2. Meanwhile, mix mayonnaise and lime juice and the remaining 1-3 tsp. chili sauce, ¼ tsp. salt and ¼ tsp. pepper. Drizzle lemon juice over Brussels sprouts before serving with the aioli.

**4 pieces with 1 Tbsp. sauce:** 146 cal., 14g fat (2g sat. fat), 1mg chol., 310mg sod., 6g carb. (2g sugars, 2g fiber), 2g pro.

# TEXAS PECAN RICE

For a special holiday side dish, I dressed up an old recipe to give it a little more Texas character. Everyone loved the savory flavor and crunchy pecans.
—*Joan Hallford, North Richland Hills, TX*

**PREP: 30 MIN. • BAKE: 1 HOUR • MAKES: 10 SERVINGS**

½   cup unsalted butter, cubed
1½  cups sliced fresh mushrooms
3   green onions, sliced
2   cups uncooked long grain brown rice
1   garlic clove, minced
1½  cups chopped pecans, toasted
½   tsp. salt
½   tsp. dried thyme
½   tsp. pepper
¼   tsp. ground cumin
3   cans (10½ oz. each) condensed beef consomme, undiluted
2¼  cups water
5   bacon strips, cooked and crumbled Toasted pecan halves, optional

1. Preheat oven to 400°. In a Dutch oven, heat butter over medium-high heat. Add mushrooms and green onions; cook and stir until tender, 3-5 minutes. Add rice and garlic; cook and stir 3 minutes. Stir in pecans, salt, thyme, pepper and cumin. Add consomme and water; bring to a boil.

2. Bake, covered, 1-1¼ hours or until liquid is absorbed and rice is tender. Transfer to a serving bowl. Top with bacon and, if desired, pecan halves.

**¾ cup:** 372 cal., 24g fat (8g sat. fat), 29mg chol., 783mg sod., 32g carb. (2g sugars, 4g fiber), 10g pro.

# BACON CAESAR SALAD

Family and friends always say my Caesar salad rivals any restaurant version. The addition of bacon is a little untraditional, but it lends a slightly smoky flavor and makes it unique.

—*Sharon Tipton, Casselberry, FL*

**TAKES:** 20 MIN. • **MAKES:** 12 SERVINGS

2 Tbsp. olive oil
2 cups cubed day-old bread
3 garlic cloves, sliced

**DRESSING**
½ cup olive oil
¼ cup lemon juice
1 Tbsp. Dijon mustard
3 garlic cloves, minced
1½ tsp. anchovy paste
Dash pepper

**SALAD**
1 large bunch romaine, torn
4 bacon strips, cooked and crumbled
½ cup shredded Parmesan cheese

**1.** For croutons, in a large skillet, heat oil over medium heat. Add bread cubes; cook and stir until golden brown, 4-5 minutes. Add garlic; cook 1 minute longer. Remove to paper towels; cool.

**2.** For dressing, in a small bowl, whisk oil, lemon juice, mustard, garlic, anchovy paste and pepper.

**3.** In a serving bowl, combine romaine and bacon. Drizzle with dressing; toss to coat. Sprinkle with croutons and cheese.

**To make ahead:** Prepare the croutons a few days before. Store in an airtight container.

**¾ cup:** 58 cal., 14g fat (3g sat. fat), 8mg chol., 229mg sod., 6g carb. (1g sugars, 1g fiber), 3g pro.

**Chicken Caesar Salad:** Top salad with slices of grilled chicken breast.

PRESSURE-COOKER
SESAME CHICKEN, PAGE 168

"

I have made
this so many
times now,
and I've shared
it with all
my friends.
It's so good!
—LINDSEY718
TASTEOFHOME.COM

# CHAPTER 6

# BEEF & POULTRY DINNERS

When it comes to hearty main courses that everyone can agree on, beef, chicken and turkey entrees sit at the top of the list. Turn here for satisfying meals that fit the bill for any occasion and promise thumbs-up approval from your family.

# CHICKEN & RICE DINNER

The chicken in this recipe bakes up to a beautiful golden brown while
the moist rice is packed with flavor. The taste is simply unbeatable!
—Denise Baumert, Dalhart, TX

PREP: 15 MIN. • BAKE: 50 MIN. • MAKES: 6 SERVINGS

¼ to ⅓ cup all-purpose flour
1 broiler/fryer chicken
  (3½ to 4 lbs.), cut up
2 Tbsp. canola oil
2⅓ cups water
1½ cups uncooked long grain rice
1 cup 2% milk
1 tsp. salt
1 tsp. poultry seasoning
½ tsp. pepper
  Minced fresh parsley

1. Preheat oven to 350°. Place flour in a shallow bowl. Dredge chicken in flour. Dip chicken in flour to coat all sides, shaking off excess. In a large skillet, heat oil over medium heat; brown chicken in batches.

2. In a large bowl, combine water, rice, milk, salt, poultry seasoning and pepper. Pour into a greased 13x9-in. baking dish. Top with chicken.

3. Cover and bake until chicken juices run clear, 50-55 minutes. Sprinkle with parsley.

**5 oz. cooked chicken with ¾ cup rice:** 604 cal., 26g fat (6g sat. fat), 125mg chol., 519mg sod., 45g carb. (2g sugars, 1g fiber), 44g pro.

---

# EASY GROUND BEEF STROGANOFF

This ground beef Stroganoff is one of the dishes my family requests
most often whenever I ask what they'd like for dinner. It takes
only minutes and it tastes great, so I always honor the request.
—Julie Curfman, Chehalis, WA

TAKES: 25 MIN. • MAKES: 3 SERVINGS

½ lb. ground beef
1 cup sliced fresh mushrooms
1 medium onion, chopped
1 garlic clove, minced
1 can (10¾ oz.) condensed cream
  of mushroom or cream of
  chicken soup, undiluted
¼ tsp. pepper
1 cup sour cream
3 cups cooked egg noodles
  Chopped fresh parsley, optional

In a skillet, cook beef, mushrooms, onion and garlic over medium heat until meat is crumbly and no longer pink; drain. Stir in soup and pepper. Cook 2-3 minutes or until heated through. Reduce heat. Stir in sour cream; cook until heated through. Serve with noodles. If desired, top with chopped fresh parsley.

**1 serving:** 554 cal., 28g fat (14g sat. fat), 141mg chol., 797mg sod., 44g carb. (7g sugars, 3g fiber), 26g pro.

## TEST KITCHEN TIP

*To make your ground beef Stroganoff dairy-free, skip the sour cream and mix in coconut milk or unsweetened almond milk instead. Add a little lemon juice and mustard to taste.*

> " My kids love
> this dish. It is
> so easy to put
> together. Just
> pop it into
> the oven and
> dinner is
> ready soon.
> —OBXGOER
> TASTEOFHOME.COM

> "
> Very easy to make with great results. I have made this many times and it pleases even picky eaters.
>
> —CAITLIN4978
> TASTEOFHOME.COM

SPAGHETTI
CHICKEN
PARMESAN

# SPAGHETTI CHICKEN PARMESAN

I like to make this yummy recipe when I have extra spaghetti sauce on hand. The herbed coating on the tender chicken gets nice and golden.
—*Margie Eddy, Ann Arbor, MI*

**TAKES: 20 MIN. • MAKES: 4 SERVINGS**

½  cup seasoned bread crumbs
½  cup grated Parmesan cheese, divided
1½ tsp. dried oregano, divided
½  tsp. dried basil
½  tsp. salt
¼  tsp. pepper
1  large egg
1  Tbsp. water
4  boneless skinless chicken breast halves (6 oz. each)
2  Tbsp. butter
2  cups meatless spaghetti sauce
½  tsp. garlic salt
1  cup shredded part-skim mozzarella cheese
   Hot cooked spaghetti

**1.** In a shallow bowl, combine bread crumbs, ¼ cup Parmesan cheese, 1 tsp. oregano, basil, salt and pepper. In another shallow bowl, combine egg and water. Dip chicken into egg mixture, then coat with crumb mixture.

**2.** In a large skillet, melt butter over medium heat. Add chicken; cook 5-7 minutes on each side or until a thermometer reads 165°.

**3.** Meanwhile, in a large saucepan, combine spaghetti sauce, garlic salt and remaining ½ tsp. oregano. Cook over medium heat until heated through. Spoon over chicken; sprinkle with mozzarella cheese and remaining Parmesan cheese. Serve with pasta.

**1 chicken breast half:** 479 cal., 20g fat (10g sat. fat), 182mg chol., 1818mg sod., 24g carb. (10g sugars, 3g fiber), 50g pro.

## TEST KITCHEN TIP

*Use your favorite pasta when preparing this recipe. Try it with angel hair or rigatoni.*

# CONTEST-WINNING TACO CASSEROLE

My preschooler doesn't eat ground beef unless it's taco flavored, so I came up with this casserole we all like. To make assembly easy, I prepare the taco meat and freeze several bags at a time.
—*Kathy Wilson, Romeoville, IL*

**PREP: 15 MIN. • BAKE: 30 MIN. • MAKES: 6 SERVINGS**

3  cups uncooked bow tie pasta
1  lb. ground beef
¼  cup chopped onion
2  cups shredded cheddar cheese
1  jar (16 oz.) salsa
1  can (14½ oz.) diced tomatoes, undrained
1  envelope taco seasoning
2  cups nacho tortilla chips, crushed

**1.** Preheat oven to 350°. Cook pasta according to package directions. In a skillet, cook beef and onion over medium heat until meat is no longer pink, crumbling beef; drain. Add cheese, salsa, tomatoes and seasoning. Drain pasta; stir into beef.

**2.** Transfer to a greased 11x7-in. baking dish. Cover and bake for 20 minutes. Uncover; sprinkle with chips. Bake until heated through, about 10 minutes longer.

**1 cup:** 578 cal., 28g fat (11g sat. fat), 84mg chol., 1377mg sod., 53g carb. (6g sugars, 3g fiber), 29g pro.

# SHEET-PAN STEAK DINNER

Asparagus and steak form a classic combination for a delicious dinner.
Cooking them together makes for easy prep and cleanup. In our house, any meal that
can be put in the oven while we get a few more things done for the day is a win!
—Pamela Forrest, Springfield, OR

**PREP: 15 MIN. • BAKE: 25 MIN. • MAKES: 4 SERVINGS**

1 tsp. minced fresh rosemary
½ tsp. each salt, pepper, paprika
  and garlic powder
1½ lbs. beef flank steak
1 lb. fresh asparagus, trimmed
2 Tbsp. avocado oil
2 Tbsp. butter, melted
1 garlic clove, minced

**1.** Preheat oven to 400°. In a small bowl, combine rosemary and seasonings; set aside.

**2.** Place steak on 1 side of a 15x10x1-in. baking pan; place asparagus on the other side in a single layer. Brush steak with oil and sprinkle with seasoning mix. Combine butter and garlic; pour over asparagus.

**3.** Cover with foil; bake 25-30 minutes or until meat reaches desired doneness (for medium-rare, a thermometer should read 135°; medium, 140°; medium-well, 145°). Let steak stand 5-10 minutes before slicing. Serve with asparagus.

**5 oz. cooked beef with 8 asparagus spears:** 380 cal., 25g fat (10g sat. fat), 96mg chol., 448mg sod., 3g carb. (1g sugars, 1g fiber), 34g pro.

# COLA BBQ CHICKEN

My dad has been making a basic version of this family favorite for years.
I've made it my own by spicing it up a bit with hoisin sauce and red pepper
flakes. Sometimes I let the chicken and sauce simmer in my slow cooker.
—Brigette Schroeder, Yorkville, IL

**TAKES: 30 MIN. • MAKES: 6 SERVINGS**

1 cup cola
⅓ cup finely chopped onion
⅓ cup barbecue sauce
2 tsp. hoisin sauce
1 garlic clove, minced
⅛ tsp. salt
⅛ tsp. pepper
⅛ tsp. crushed red pepper flakes
6 boneless skinless chicken thighs
  (about 1½ lbs.)
  Hot cooked rice

**1.** In a large saucepan, combine first 8 ingredients; bring to a boil. Reduce heat; simmer, uncovered, until slightly thickened, stirring occasionally, 10-15 minutes. Reserve ¾ cup for serving.

**2.** Grill chicken, covered, over medium heat or broil 4 in. from heat 5-7 minutes on each side or until a thermometer reads 165°, basting occasionally with the remaining sauce during the last 5 minutes of cooking. Serve chicken with rice and reserved sauce.

**1 chicken thigh with 2 Tbsp. sauce:** 213 cal., 8g fat (2g sat. fat), 76mg chol., 298mg sod., 12g carb. (10g sugars, 0 fiber), 21g pro.

> **This is a fantastic new version of sloppy joes! My family really likes it!**
> —ERINSHEA1982
> TASTEOFHOME.COM

# SLOPPY JOE TATER TOT CASSEROLE

This simple casserole is an easy dinner for both you and the kids.
Serve with carrot and celery sticks for a fuss-free feast. You can also
stir in some spicy brown mustard if the adults want more zing.
—*Laura Wilhelm, West Hollywood, CA*

**PREP: 20 MIN. • COOK: 4 HOURS + STANDING • MAKES: 10 SERVINGS**

1   bag (32 oz.) frozen
    Tater Tots, divided
2   lbs. ground beef or turkey
1   can (15 oz.) tomato sauce
1   bottle (8 oz.) sweet chili sauce
2   Tbsp. packed brown sugar
1   Tbsp. Worcestershire sauce
1   Tbsp. dried minced garlic
1   Tbsp. dried minced onion
½   tsp. salt
½   tsp. pepper
1¼  cups shredded Colby-
    Monterey Jack cheese
¼   tsp. paprika

**1.** Place half of the Tater Tots in the bottom of a 5-qt. slow cooker.

**2.** In a large skillet, cook beef over medium-high heat until no longer pink, 5-6 minutes, breaking into crumbles; drain. Stir in the next 8 ingredients; reduce heat and simmer 2-3 minutes. Place beef mixture in slow cooker; top with remaining Tater Tots. Cook, covered, on low 4 hours.

**3.** Top with cheese. Sprinkle with paprika. Let stand, uncovered, 15 minutes before serving.

**1 cup:** 466 cal., 24g fat (9g sat. fat), 69mg chol., 1332mg sod., 41g carb. (18g sugars, 4g fiber), 22g pro.

## TEST KITCHEN TIP

*To bake this casserole, put the meat mixture in a greased 3½-qt. baking dish, lasagna pan or regular 13x9-in. dish. Place all the Tater Tots on top. (The baking dish will be full.) Bake the casserole at 400° until bubbly, 35-40 minutes.*
—CHRISTINE RUKAVENA, *TASTE OF HOME* SENIOR BOOK EDITOR

# AIR-FRYER CRISPY CURRY DRUMSTICKS

These air-fryer chicken drumsticks are flavorful, crispy on the outside and juicy on the inside.
Sometimes I'll add some red pepper flakes in addition to the curry powder if I want to spice them up.
—*Zena Furgason, Norman, OK*

PREP: 35 MIN. • COOK: 15 MIN./BATCH • MAKES: 4 SERVINGS

1 lb. chicken drumsticks
¾ tsp. salt, divided
2 Tbsp. olive oil
2 tsp. curry powder
½ tsp. onion salt
½ tsp. garlic powder
  Minced fresh cilantro, optional

1. Place chicken in a large bowl; add ½ tsp. salt and enough water to cover. Let stand 15 minutes at room temperature. Drain and pat dry.

2. Preheat air fryer to 375°. In another bowl, mix oil, curry powder, onion salt, garlic powder and remaining ¼ tsp. salt; add chicken and toss to coat. In batches, place chicken in a single layer on tray in air-fryer basket. Cook 15-17 minutes or until a thermometer inserted in chicken reads 170°-175°, turning halfway through. If desired, sprinkle with cilantro.

**2 oz. cooked chicken:** 180 cal., 13g fat (3g sat. fat), 47mg chol., 711mg sod., 1g carb. (0 sugars, 1g fiber), 15g pro.

---

# SLOW-COOKER BEEF & BROCCOLI

I love introducing my kids to all kinds of flavors. This Asian-inspired
slow-cooker meal is one of their favorites, so I serve it often.
—*Brandy Stansbury, Edna, TX*

PREP: 20 MIN. • COOK: 6½ HOURS • MAKES: 4 SERVINGS

2 cups beef broth
½ cup reduced-sodium soy sauce
⅓ cup packed brown sugar
1½ tsp. sesame oil
1 garlic cloves, minced
1 beef top sirloin steak (1½ lbs.), cut into ½-in.-thick strips
2 Tbsp. cornstarch
¼ cup cold water
4 cups fresh broccoli florets
  Hot cooked rice
  Optional: Sesame seeds and thinly sliced green onions

1. In a 5-qt. slow cooker, combine the first 5 ingredients. Add beef; stir to coat. Cover and cook on low until tender, about 6 hours.

2. In a small bowl, whisk cornstarch and cold water until smooth; stir into slow cooker. Cover and cook on high until thickened, about 30 minutes. Meanwhile, in a large saucepan, place a steamer basket over 1 in. water. Place broccoli in basket. Bring water to a boil. Reduce heat to maintain a simmer; steam, covered, until crisp-tender, 3-4 minutes. Stir broccoli into slow cooker. Serve over rice. If desired, garnish with sesame seeds and green onions.

**1 cup:** 366 cal., 9g fat (3g sat. fat), 69mg chol., 1696mg sod., 28g carb. (19g sugars, 2g fiber), 42g pro.

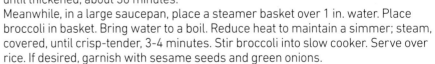

66
My son told me this is the best pasta he's ever had in his whole life.
—ANGELA901
TASTEOFHOME.COM

# COWBOY PASTA

This pasta combines ground beef, bacon, corn, tangy buttermilk and Monterey Jack cheese
for an easy but hearty weeknight dinner. Add more chili powder or
a chopped jalapeno to give this delicious pasta dish more of an Old West kick.
—Taste of Home *Test Kitchen*

**PREP:** 15 MIN. • **BAKE:** 20 MIN. • **MAKES:** 10 SERVINGS

8   oz. medium pasta shells
5   bacon strips, chopped
1   lb. ground beef
1   medium red onion, chopped
1   medium green or sweet red pepper, chopped
2   garlic cloves, minced
2   cups frozen corn, thawed
1   can (14½ oz.) diced tomatoes, drained
1¼ cups buttermilk
4   oz. cream cheese, cubed
1   tsp. chili powder
½   tsp. salt
¼   tsp. pepper
1   cup shredded Monterey Jack cheese

1. Cook pasta according to package directions. Drain; set aside.

2. Meanwhile, in a large skillet, cook bacon over medium heat until crisp, stirring occasionally. Remove with a slotted spoon; drain on paper towels. Discard all but 1 Tbsp. drippings.

3. In the same pan, cook beef, onion and green pepper over medium heat until meat is crumbly and no longer pink; drain. Add garlic; cook and stir until fragrant, 2 minutes. Add corn, tomatoes, buttermilk, cream cheese, chili powder, salt, pepper and the cooked pasta; stir to combine.

4. Stir in Monterey Jack cheese and bacon pieces. If desired, sprinkle with additional chopped cooked bacon.

**1 cup:** 333 cal., 16g fat (8g sat. fat), 56mg chol., 456mg sod., 29g carb. (5g sugars, 2g fiber), 18g pro.

## TEST KITCHEN TIP

*Top individual servings of cowboy pasta with a few Tots to make it reminiscent of traditional midwestern Tater Tot casserole—in our opinion, it's one of the best midwestern casseroles!*

# CREAMY CHICKEN ENCHILADA PIZZA

This is a twist on a family favorite. We wanted the taste of my chicken enchilada recipe, but we wanted it even faster. This kicked-up pizza is the fun creation we came up with.
—*Crystal Jo Bruns, Iliff, CO*

**TAKES: 30 MIN. • MAKES: 6 SERVINGS**

1 tube (11 oz.) refrigerated thin pizza crust
1 pkg. (8 oz.) cream cheese, softened, cubed
1 cup shredded Mexican cheese blend, divided
2 tsp. ground cumin
1½ tsp. garlic powder
½ tsp. salt
2 cups ready-to-use fajita chicken strips, cubed
½ cup salsa
¼ cup green enchilada sauce
Optional toppings: Shredded lettuce, chopped tomatoes and sliced olives

1. Preheat oven to 400°. Unroll and press pizza dough onto the bottom and ½ in. up the sides of a greased 15x10x1-in. baking pan. Bake 5 minutes.

2. Meanwhile, in a small saucepan, combine softened cream cheese, ½ cup Mexican cheese blend, cumin, garlic powder and salt over medium heat; cook and stir for 5 minutes or until blended. Remove from the heat. Add fajita chicken strips; toss to coat.

3. Spread over crust. Drizzle with salsa and enchilada sauce; sprinkle with remaining cheese. Bake 8-12 minutes longer or until crust is golden and cheese is melted. Serve with toppings of your choice.

**1 piece:** 428 cal., 25g fat (12g sat. fat), 83mg chol., 1061mg sod., 30g carb. (5g sugars, 1g fiber), 20g pro.

---

# SOUTHERN POT ROAST

Cajun seasoning adds kick to this tender beef roast that's served with a corn and tomato mixture. It is an unusual dish, but it's full of flavor.
—*Amber Zurbrugg, Alliance, OH*

**PREP: 10 MIN. • COOK: 5 HOURS • MAKES: 5 SERVINGS**

1 boneless beef chuck roast (2½ lbs.)
1 Tbsp. Cajun seasoning
1 pkg. (9 oz.) frozen corn, thawed
½ cup chopped onion
½ cup chopped green pepper
1 can (14½ oz.) diced tomatoes, undrained
½ tsp. pepper
½ tsp. hot pepper sauce

1. Cut roast in half; place in a 5-qt. slow cooker. Sprinkle with Cajun seasoning. Top with corn, onion and green pepper. Combine tomatoes, pepper and hot pepper sauce; pour over vegetables.

2. Cover and cook on low until meat is tender, 5-6 hours. Slice or shred meat; serve corn with a slotted spoon.

**Freeze option:** Freeze cooled meat and corn mixture in freezer containers. To use, thaw in refrigerator overnight. Microwave, covered, on high until heated through.

**1 serving:** 455 cal., 22g fat (8g sat. fat), 147mg chol., 601mg sod., 17g carb. (5g sugars, 3g fiber), 47g pro.

# PRESSURE-COOKER SESAME CHICKEN
### SHOWN ON PAGE 152

Your family will love the flavorful sauce that coats this chicken, and you'll love how quick and easy it is for a weeknight dinner! If you serve gluten-free meals, use tamari instead of soy sauce.
—*Karen Kelly, Germantown, MD*

**PREP: 10 MIN. • COOK: 10 MIN. • MAKES: 4 SERVINGS**

1    to 2 Tbsp. sesame oil
1½  lbs. boneless skinless chicken
      breasts, cut into 1-in. pieces
¼   cup honey
¼   cup soy sauce or gluten-free
      tamari soy sauce
¼   cup water
3    garlic cloves, minced
¼   tsp. crushed red pepper flakes
3    tsp. cornstarch
2    Tbsp. cold water
      Hot cooked rice
1    Tbsp. sesame seeds
      Thinly sliced green onions, optional

1. Select saute or browning setting on a 6-qt. electric pressure cooker. Adjust for medium heat; add 1 Tbsp. sesame oil. When oil is hot, brown chicken in batches using additional oil as necessary. Press cancel. Return all to pressure cooker. In a bowl, whisk honey, soy sauce, water, garlic and pepper flakes; stir into pressure cooker. Lock lid; close pressure-release valve. Adjust to pressure-cook on high 4 minutes.

2. Quick-release pressure. In a small bowl, mix cornstarch and water until smooth; stir into pressure cooker. Select saute setting and adjust for low heat. Simmer, stirring constantly, until thickened, 1-2 minutes. Serve with rice. Sprinkle with sesame seeds and, if desired, green onions.

**1 serving:** 311 cal., 9g fat (2g sat. fat), 94mg chol., 1004mg sod., 20g carb. (17g sugars, 0 fiber), 37g pro.

---

# TURKEY LEG POT ROAST

Well-seasoned turkey legs and tender veggies make an ideal dinner for a crisp fall day. And the recipe couldn't be easier!
—*Rick and Vegas Pearson, Cadillac, MI*

**PREP: 15 MIN. • COOK: 5 HOURS • MAKES: 3 SERVINGS**

3    medium potatoes, quartered
2    cups fresh baby carrots
2    celery ribs, cut into 2½-in. pieces
1    medium onion, peeled and quartered
3    garlic cloves, peeled and quartered
½   cup chicken broth
3    turkey drumsticks, skin removed
2    tsp. seasoned salt
1    tsp. dried thyme
1    tsp. dried parsley flakes
¼   tsp. pepper
      Chopped fresh parsley, optional

In a greased 5-qt. slow cooker, combine the first 6 ingredients. Place turkey drumsticks over vegetables. Sprinkle with the seasoned salt, thyme, dried parsley flakes and pepper. Cook, covered, on low heat 5-5½ hours or until turkey is tender. If desired, top with chopped fresh parsley just before serving.

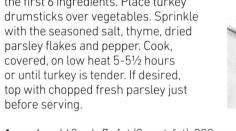

**1 serving:** 460 cal., 7g fat (2g sat. fat), 202mg chol., 1416mg sod., 44g carb. (10g sugars, 6g fiber), 54g pro.

# CHEESY FIESTA BEEF CASSEROLE

Over the years I've tweaked this recipe to end up with a delicious quick meal.
Feel free to spice it up with jalapenos if you prefer a little heat.
—*Joan Hallford, North Richland Hills, TX*

PREP: 25 MIN. • COOK: 15 MIN. • MAKES: 8 SERVINGS

- 1 lb. ground beef
- 1 medium onion, chopped
- 1 can (15 oz.) black beans, rinsed and drained
- 1 cup picante sauce
- ½ tsp. chili powder
- 1 can (10½ oz.) reduced-fat reduced-sodium condensed cream of chicken soup, undiluted
- 1 can (10 oz.) diced tomatoes and green chiles, undrained
- 1 can (4 oz.) chopped green chiles
- 1 pkg. (9¾ oz.) nacho-flavored tortilla chips or plain tortilla chips, crushed
- 1 cup shredded sharp cheddar cheese
- 1 cup shredded Monterey Jack cheese
  Optional: Avocado and sour cream

**1.** In a large skillet, cook beef and onion over medium heat until beef is no longer pink, 6-8 minutes, breaking up beef into crumbles; drain. Stir in beans, picante sauce and chili powder.

**2.** In a bowl, combine chicken soup, tomatoes and green chiles. In a lightly greased 2½-qt. baking dish, layer half the chips, beef mixture, soup mixture and cheeses. Repeat layers.

**3.** Microwave on medium high, uncovered, until heated through and cheese is melted, about 12 minutes. If desired, top with avocado and sour cream.

**1¼ cups:** 477 cal., 26g fat (9g sat. fat), 63mg chol., 1119mg sod., 37g carb. (4g sugars, 5g fiber), 23g pro.

# ROSEMARY-LEMON CHICKEN THIGHS

A cooking show inspired me to create this lemony chicken. Ask your butcher
to remove the bones from chicken thighs but leave the skin intact.
—*Jenn Tidwell, Fair Oaks, CA*

TAKES: 30 MIN. • MAKES: 4 SERVINGS

- 2 bacon strips, chopped
- 1 tsp. minced fresh rosemary or ¼ tsp. dried rosemary, crushed
- 4 boneless, skin-on chicken thighs
- ⅛ tsp. pepper
  Dash salt
- ⅓ cup chicken broth
- 3 Tbsp. lemon juice

**1.** In a large skillet, cook bacon and rosemary over medium heat until bacon is crisp, stirring occasionally. Using a slotted spoon, remove bacon to paper towels; reserve drippings in pan.

**2.** Sprinkle chicken with pepper and salt; brown in drippings on both sides. Cook, covered, skin side down, over medium heat 4-6 minutes or until a thermometer reads 170°. Remove from pan; keep warm. Pour off drippings from pan.

**3.** Add broth and lemon juice to skillet. Bring to a boil, scraping to loosen browned bits; cook until liquid is reduced by half. Spoon over chicken; sprinkle with bacon.

**1 chicken thigh with 1 Tbsp. sauce and 2 tsp. cooked bacon:** 286 cal., 20g fat (6g sat. fat), 91mg chol., 279mg sod., 1g carb. (1g sugars, 0 fiber), 24g pro.

# ROSEMARY ROASTED TURKEY

Perching a turkey on top of onions makes for a flavorful bird. The onions will cook down and caramelize in the pan drippings—and if you like, you can serve them alongside the turkey.
—Taste of Home *Test Kitchen*

PREP: 30 MIN. • BAKE: 3½ HOURS + STANDING • MAKES: 14 SERVINGS (2½ CUPS GRAVY)

3 whole garlic bulbs
6 large onions, halved
5 fresh rosemary sprigs
1 turkey (14 to 16 lbs.)
2 cups white wine
3 Tbsp. olive oil
1 Tbsp. minced fresh rosemary
¾ tsp. salt
¾ tsp. pepper
¼ cup butter, cubed
¼ cup all-purpose flour

1. Remove the papery outer skin from garlic (do not peel or separate cloves). Cut the tops off garlic bulbs. Place garlic, onions and rosemary sprigs in a shallow roasting pan. Pat turkey dry. Tuck wings under turkey; tie drumsticks together. Place breast side up over onion mixture. Pour wine into pan.

2. Brush turkey with oil and sprinkle with rosemary, salt and pepper. Bake at 325°, uncovered, 3½-4 hours or until a thermometer inserted in thickest part of thigh reads 170°-175°, basting occasionally with drippings. Cover loosely with foil if turkey browns too quickly. Cover and let stand 20 minutes before slicing.

3. For gravy, strain drippings into a small bowl. In a small saucepan, melt butter. Stir in flour until smooth; gradually add drippings. Bring to a boil; cook and stir until thickened, about 2 minutes. Serve with turkey.

**8 oz. cooked turkey with 2 Tbsp. gravy:** 658 cal., 31g fat (10g sat. fat), 254mg chol., 328mg sod., 12g carb. (3g sugars, 1g fiber), 74g pro.

# SAUCY PEACH-BALSAMIC CHICKEN

I throw this sweet and savory chicken dish together in no time on a weeknight. With a side of broccoli and rice, it's a healthy meal that my whole family enjoys.
—*Trisha Kruse, Eagle, ID*

TAKES: 30 MIN. • MAKES: 4 SERVINGS

4 boneless skinless chicken breast halves (4 oz. each)
½ tsp. salt
¼ tsp. pepper
2 Tbsp. butter
¼ cup reduced-sodium chicken broth
¼ cup sherry or additional reduced-sodium chicken broth
⅓ cup peach preserves
2 garlic cloves, thinly sliced
2 tsp. minced fresh tarragon
1 Tbsp. balsamic vinegar

1. Sprinkle chicken with salt and pepper. In a large skillet, brown chicken on both sides in butter. Remove from the skillet and keep warm.

2. Add broth and sherry to the skillet, stirring to loosen the browned bits from pan. Stir in preserves, garlic and tarragon. Bring to a boil. Reduce heat; simmer, uncovered, 5 minutes, stirring occasionally. Stir in vinegar. Return chicken to the skillet; cover and cook over medium heat 8-10 minutes or until a thermometer reads 165°.

**1 chicken breast half with 1 Tbsp. sauce:** 249 cal., 8g fat (4g sat. fat), 78mg chol., 427mg sod., 19g carb. (17g sugars, 0 fiber), 23g pro. **Diabetic exchanges:** 3 lean meat, 1½ fat, 1 starch.

# POTLUCK FRIED CHICKEN

This Sunday dinner staple is first fried and then baked to a crispy golden brown. Well-seasoned with oregano and sage, this classic is sure to satisfy diners at church potlucks or late-summer picnics too. I love fixing it for family and friends.
—*Donna Kuhaupt, Slinger, WI*

PREP: 40 MIN. • BAKE: 25 MIN. • MAKES: 12 SERVINGS

1½ cups all-purpose flour
½ cup cornmeal
¼ cup cornstarch
3 tsp. salt
2 tsp. paprika
1 tsp. dried oregano
1 tsp. rubbed sage
1 tsp. pepper
2 large eggs
¼ cup water
2 broiler/fryer chickens (3 to 4 lbs. each), cut up
 Oil for frying

1. In a large shallow dish, combine the flour, cornmeal, cornstarch, salt, paprika, oregano, sage and pepper. In a shallow bowl, beat eggs and water. Dip chicken into egg mixture; place in flour mixture, a few pieces at a time, and turn to coat.

2. In an electric skillet, heat 1 in. oil to 375°. Fry chicken, a few pieces at a time, until golden and crispy, 3-5 minutes on each side.

3. Place in 2 ungreased 15x10x1-in. baking pans. Bake, uncovered, at 350° until juices run clear, 25-30 minutes.

**5 oz. cooked chicken:** 497 cal., 29g fat (6g sat. fat), 135mg chol., 693mg sod., 20g carb. (0 sugars, 1g fiber), 36g pro.

# PEPPERY ROAST BEEF

With its spicy coating and creamy horseradish sauce, this tender roast is sure to be the star of any meal, whether it's a sit-down dinner or serve-yourself buffet.
—*Maureen Brand, Somers, IA*

PREP: 15 MIN. • BAKE: 2½ HOURS + STANDING • MAKES: 12 SERVINGS

1 Tbsp. olive oil
1 Tbsp. seasoned pepper
2 garlic cloves, minced
½ tsp. dried thyme
¼ tsp. salt

**HORSERADISH SAUCE**
1 boneless beef eye round or top round roast (4 to 5 lbs.)
1 cup sour cream
2 Tbsp. lemon juice
2 Tbsp. milk
2 Tbsp. prepared horseradish
1 Tbsp. Dijon mustard
¼ tsp. salt
⅛ tsp. pepper

1. Preheat oven to 325°. In a small bowl, combine oil, seasoned pepper, garlic, thyme and salt; rub over roast. Place fat side up on a rack in a shallow roasting pan.

2. Bake, uncovered, 2½-3 hours or until meat reaches desired doneness (for medium-rare, a thermometer should read 135°; medium, 140°; medium-well, 145°). Let stand for 10 minutes before slicing.

3. In a small bowl, combine the sauce ingredients. Serve with roast.

**4 oz. cooked beef with about 1 Tbsp. sauce:** 228 cal., 10g fat (4g sat. fat), 83mg chol., 211mg sod., 3g carb. (1g sugars, 0 fiber), 30g pro.

"
The best potpie
ever! Even my
picky 3-year-old
asks specifically
for this dish.
—AWINES
TASTEOFHOME.COM

# OLD-FASHIONED CHICKEN POTPIE

Although this uses leftover chicken, I serve it sometimes as a special company dinner.
Actually, my husband may enjoy it more than the original roasted bird with all the fixings!
—*Marilyn Hockey, Lisle, ON*

**PREP:** 30 MIN. • **BAKE:** 30 MIN. • **MAKES:** 6 SERVINGS

⅓ cup butter
⅓ cup all-purpose flour
1 garlic clove, minced
½ tsp. salt
¼ tsp. pepper
1½ cups water
⅔ cup 2% milk
2 tsp. chicken bouillon granules
2 cups cubed cooked chicken
1 cup frozen mixed vegetables

**CRUST**
1⅔ cups all-purpose flour
2 tsp. celery seed
1 pkg. (8 oz.) cream cheese, cubed
⅓ cup cold butter

**1.** Preheat oven to 425°. In a saucepan, melt butter over medium heat. Stir in flour, garlic, salt and pepper until blended. Gradually stir in water, milk and bouillon. Bring to a boil; cook and stir until thickened, 1-2 minutes. Remove from heat. Stir in chicken and vegetables; set aside.

**2.** For crust, in a large bowl, combine flour and celery seed. Cut in the cream cheese and butter until crumbly. Work the mixture by hand until dough forms a ball. On a lightly floured surface, roll two-thirds of dough into a 12-in. square. Transfer to an 8-in. square baking dish. Pour filling into crust. Roll the remaining dough into a 9-in. square; place over filling. Trim, seal and flute edges. Cut slits in the crust.

**3.** Bake until crust is golden brown and filling is bubbly, 30-35 minutes.

**1 serving:** 592 cal., 38g fat (22g sat. fat), 136mg chol., 823mg sod., 40g carb. (4g sugars, 3g fiber), 22g pro.

## TEST KITCHEN TIP

*You can store chicken potpie in an airtight container in the refrigerator for 3-4 days. To freeze it directly after baking, freeze it in its baking dish. Once it's frozen solid, remove the potpie from the baking dish and store it in an airtight container for up to 3 months.*
—ELLIE CROWLEY, *TASTE OF HOME* ASSISTANT CULINARY PRODUCER

# PRESSURE-COOKER BEEF BRISKET IN BEER

One bite of this super tender brisket and your family will be hooked!
The rich gravy is perfect for spooning over a side of creamy mashed potatoes.
—Eunice Stoen, Decorah, IA

**PREP:** 15 MIN. • **COOK:** 70 MIN. + RELEASING • **MAKES:** 6 SERVINGS

1  fresh beef brisket (2½ to 3 lbs.)
2  tsp. liquid smoke, optional
1  tsp. celery salt
½  tsp. pepper
¼  tsp. salt
1  large onion, sliced
1  can (12 oz.) beer or nonalcoholic beer
2  tsp. Worcestershire sauce
2  Tbsp. cornstarch
¼  cup cold water

**1.** Cut brisket in half; rub with liquid smoke if desired, celery salt, pepper and salt. Place the brisket fatty side up in a 6-qt. electric pressure cooker. Top with onion. Combine beer and Worcestershire sauce; pour over the meat. Lock the lid; close pressure-release valve. Adjust to pressure-cook on high 70 minutes. Allow for pressure to naturally release 10 minutes; quick-release any remaining pressure. If brisket isn't fork-tender, reseal cooker and cook for an additional 10-15 minutes.

**2.** Remove brisket, cover with foil and keep warm. Strain cooking juices, then return juices to pressure cooker. Select saute setting and adjust for medium heat; bring liquid to a boil. In a small bowl, mix cornstarch and water until smooth; gradually stir into juices. Cook and stir until sauce is thickened, about 2 minutes. Serve sauce with the beef.

**1 serving:** 285 cal., 8g fat (3g sat. fat), 80mg chol., 430mg sod., 7g carb. (3g sugars, 0 fiber), 39g pro.

# HEARTY CHICKEN SPAGHETTI CASSEROLE

This creamy, cheesy casserole is so hearty that second helpings are a must!
—Lynne German, Buford, GA

**PREP:** 25 MIN. • **BAKE:** 25 MIN. • **MAKES:** 6 SERVINGS

8  oz. uncooked spaghetti
3  cups cubed cooked chicken
1  can (10¾ oz.) condensed cream
   of chicken soup, undiluted
1  cup 2% milk
1  medium onion, chopped
1  cup shredded sharp cheddar
   cheese, divided
1  cup shredded Swiss cheese, divided
1  can (4 oz.) mushroom stems
   and pieces, drained
½  cup chopped roasted red peppers
3  Tbsp. mayonnaise
1½  tsp. steak seasoning
½  tsp. dried basil

**1.** Cook spaghetti according to package directions. Meanwhile, in a large bowl, combine the chicken, soup, milk, onion, ½ cup cheddar cheese, ½ cup Swiss cheese, mushrooms, peppers, mayonnaise, steak seasoning and basil.

**2.** Drain spaghetti. Add to chicken mixture; toss to coat. Transfer to a greased 13x9-in. baking dish. Cover and bake at 350° for 20 minutes. Uncover; sprinkle with remaining cheeses. Bake until heated through and cheese is melted, 5-10 minutes longer.

**1⅓ cups:** 549 cal., 25g fat (11g sat. fat), 109mg chol., 957mg sod., 40g carb. (6g sugars, 2g fiber), 38g pro.

66
**Made this
for dinner and
it was delicious!
My husband
loved it.
Thanks for this
easy and really
good recipe!**

—DMKINSEY
TASTEOFHOME.COM

# BAKED CHICKEN & ZUCCHINI

Because I love zucchini, this colorful dish is one of my favorites, and I make it often in summer. It's especially good with tomatoes fresh from the garden.
—*Sheryl Goodnough, Eliot, ME*

**PREP:** 20 MIN. • **BAKE:** 35 MIN. • **MAKES:** 4 SERVINGS

1 large egg
1 Tbsp. water
¾ tsp. salt, divided
⅛ tsp. pepper
1 cup dry bread crumbs
4 boneless skinless chicken breast halves (6 oz. each)
4 Tbsp. olive oil, divided
5 medium zucchini, sliced
4 medium tomatoes, sliced
1 cup shredded part-skim mozzarella cheese, divided
2 tsp. minced fresh basil

**1.** In a shallow bowl, beat egg, water, ½ tsp. salt and pepper. Reserve 2 Tbsp. bread crumbs. Place the remaining crumbs in a large shallow dish. Dip chicken into egg mixture, then place in crumbs and turn to coat.

**2.** In a large skillet, cook chicken in 2 Tbsp. oil until golden brown, 2-3 minutes on each side; remove and set aside. In the same skillet, saute zucchini in the remaining oil until crisp-tender; drain. Transfer to a greased 13x9-in. dish.

**3.** Sprinkle the reserved bread crumbs over zucchini. Top with tomato slices; sprinkle with ⅔ cup mozzarella cheese, basil and remaining salt. Top with chicken. Cover and bake at 400° for 25 minutes or until a thermometer reads 170°. Uncover; sprinkle with remaining cheese. Bake until cheese is melted, about 10 minutes longer.

**1 serving:** 572 cal., 27g fat (7g sat. fat), 169mg chol., 898mg sod., 34g carb. (9g sugars, 5g fiber), 49g pro.

## TEST KITCHEN TIP

*Coatings, brines, marinades and rubs usually prevent dry chicken, so this chicken dish shouldn't be dry. If you want to add extra moisture, try spooning a sauce over the chicken.*

# SPICE-CRUSTED STEAKS WITH CHERRY SAUCE

If you're hosting meat lovers, these impressive cast-iron skillet steaks are guaranteed
to please. They're perfect for a special-occasion dinner without too much fuss.
—Taste of Home *Test Kitchen*

PREP: 20 MIN. + CHILLING • COOK: 45 MIN. • MAKES: 4 SERVINGS

½ cup dried cherries
¼ cup port wine, warmed
3½ tsp. coarsely ground pepper
1 tsp. brown sugar
¾ tsp. garlic powder
¾ tsp. paprika
¾ tsp. ground coffee
½ tsp. kosher salt
¼ tsp. ground cinnamon
¼ tsp. ground cumin
⅛ tsp. ground mustard
4 beef tenderloin steaks (6 oz. each)
1 Tbsp. canola oil
1 large shallot, finely chopped
1 Tbsp. butter
1 cup reduced-sodium beef broth
1 tsp. minced fresh thyme
½ cup heavy whipping cream
 Crumbled blue cheese, optional

**1.** Preheat the oven to 350°. In a small bowl, combine cherries and wine; set aside. In a shallow dish, combine pepper, brown sugar, garlic powder, paprika, coffee, salt, cinnamon, cumin and mustard. Add steak, 1 at a time, and turn to coat. Cover and refrigerate 30 minutes.

**2.** Place oil in a 10-in. cast-iron or other ovenproof skillet; tilt to coat bottom. Heat oil over medium-high heat; sear steaks, 2 minutes on each side. Bake, uncovered, until meat reaches desired doneness (for medium rare, a thermometer should read 135°; medium, 140°; medium well, 145°), about 15 minutes. Remove steaks and keep warm.

**3.** For sauce, wipe skillet clean; saute shallot in butter until crisp-tender. Add broth and thyme. Bring to a boil; cook 8 minutes or until liquid is reduced by half. Stir in cream; bring to a boil. Cook until thickened, stirring occasionally, about 8 minutes.

**4.** Stir in the cherry mixture. Serve sauce with steaks and, if desired, blue cheese.

**1 steak with 3 Tbsp. sauce:** 506 cal., 28g fat (13g sat. fat), 124mg chol., 381mg sod., 20g carb. (13g sugars, 1g fiber), 39g pro.

# ARUGULA PESTO CHICKEN

We had an abundance of arugula in our garden, so I turned it into pesto.
The bold green color reminds my son of something the Hulk would eat.
—Courtney Stultz, Weir, KS

TAKES: 25 MIN. • MAKES: 4 SERVINGS

4 cups fresh arugula or spinach
1 cup fresh basil leaves
¼ cup pine nuts
1 garlic clove, minced
1½ tsp. sea salt, divided
¼ cup plus 1 Tbsp. olive oil, divided
4 medium zucchini
1 rotisserie chicken, skin removed, shredded
2 plum tomatoes, chopped
¼ tsp. pepper
 Grated Parmesan cheese, optional

**1.** Pulse arugula, basil, pine nuts, garlic and 1 tsp. salt in a food processor until chopped. While processing, gradually add ¼ cup oil in a steady stream until mixture is smooth. Using a shredder or spiralizer, shred zucchini lengthwise into long strands.

**2.** In a large skillet, heat remaining oil over medium heat. Add zucchini strands and chicken. Cook and stir until zucchini is crisp-tender, about 4 minutes.

**3.** Remove from heat. Add tomatoes, pesto, pepper and remaining salt; toss to coat. If desired, sprinkle with Parmesan cheese. Serve using a slotted spoon.

**1½ cups:** 488 cal., 32g fat (5g sat. fat), 110mg chol., 836mg sod., 10g carb. (6g sugars, 3g fiber), 41g pro.

SPICE-CRUSTED STEAKS
WITH CHERRY SAUCE

# CITRUS-MUSTARD ROASTED CHICKEN

Tender roast chicken is a snap to make and elegant to serve. We love
the tang of orange and lemon slices and the subtle heat from mustard.

*—Debra Keil, Owasso, OK*

**PREP:** 20 MIN. + CHILLING • **BAKE:** 1¼ HOURS + STANDING • **MAKES:** 4 SERVINGS

3 Tbsp. mustard seed
¼ cup olive oil
1 Tbsp. minced fresh chervil or
   1 tsp. dried chervil
1 Tbsp. champagne vinegar
1 Tbsp. Worcestershire sauce
½ tsp. pepper
1 broiler/fryer chicken (3 to 4 lbs.)
2 orange slices
2 lemon slices
2 onion slices
3 sprigs fresh parsley, stems removed

**1.** Using a spice grinder or a mortar and pestle, grind mustard seed to a powder; transfer to a small bowl. Stir in oil, chervil, vinegar, Worcestershire sauce and pepper. Rub over outside and inside of chicken; place on a large plate. Refrigerate, covered, overnight.

**2.** Preheat oven to 350°. Place chicken in a shallow roasting pan, breast side up. Loosely stuff chicken with orange, lemon, onion and parsley. Tuck wings under chicken; tie drumsticks together.

**3.** Roast 1¼-1¾ hours or until a thermometer inserted in thickest part of thigh reads 170°-175°. (Cover loosely with foil if chicken browns too quickly.) Remove chicken from oven; tent with foil. Let stand 15 minutes before carving.

**1 serving:** 537 cal., 37g fat (8g sat. fat), 131mg chol., 156mg sod., 6g carb. (2g sugars, 2g fiber), 44g pro.

# SPICY LASAGNA SKILLET DINNER

Shortcut lasagna bails me out when I'm in a frenzy to serve dinner.
A leafy salad and buttery garlic toast round out the meal.
—Donna Booth, Tomahawk, KY

**TAKES:** 30 MIN. • **MAKES:** 6 SERVINGS

1  pkg. (6.4 oz.) lasagna dinner mix
1  lb. lean ground beef (90% lean)
1  large onion, chopped
1  medium green pepper, chopped
1  garlic clove, minced
1  jar (14 oz.) meatless spaghetti sauce
½  cup chunky salsa
1  tsp. garlic powder
1  tsp. Italian seasoning
½  tsp. dried thyme
½  tsp. ground cumin
¼  tsp. salt
¼  tsp. crushed red pepper flakes
1  cup shredded mozzarella and
   provolone cheese blend

**1.** Fill a large saucepan three-fourths full with water; bring to a boil. Add pasta from lasagna dinner; cook, uncovered, 10-12 minutes or until tender.

**2.** Meanwhile, in a large skillet, cook beef, onion, green pepper and garlic over medium heat 6-8 minutes or until beef is no longer pink and vegetables are tender, breaking the beef into crumbles; drain.

**3.** Stir in the spaghetti sauce, salsa, seasonings and contents of seasoning packet from lasagna dinner. Bring to a boil. Reduce heat; simmer, uncovered, 5 minutes. Remove from heat.

**4.** Drain pasta. Add to tomato mixture; toss to coat. Sprinkle with cheese; let stand, covered, until cheese is melted.

**Freeze option:** Freeze cooled pasta mixture and cheese in separate freezer containers. To use, partially thaw in refrigerator overnight. Heat through in a skillet, stirring occasionally; add water if necessary. Remove from heat. Sprinkle with cheese; let stand, covered, until cheese is melted.

**1 cup:** 319 cal., 11g fat (5g sat. fat), 60mg chol., 1403mg sod., 31g carb. (7g sugars, 3g fiber), 24g pro.

# MY MOM'S BEST MEAT LOAF

The Rice Krispies used in this recipe are my mom's secret ingredient. While they may seem odd or out of place, they help hold the meat loaf together. And once they are cooked, no one realizes they're even there.

*—Kelly Simmons, Hopkinsville, KY*

**PREP:** 10 MIN. • **BAKE:** 1 HOUR + STANDING • **MAKES:** 8 SERVINGS

½ cup chili sauce
¼ cup ketchup
2 cups Rice Krispies
1 medium onion, finely chopped
1 small green or sweet red pepper, finely chopped
¾ cup shredded part-skim mozzarella cheese
1 large egg, lightly beaten
½ tsp. salt
¼ tsp. pepper
2 lbs. ground beef

1. Preheat oven to 350°. In a small bowl, mix chili sauce and ketchup. In a large bowl, combine Rice Krispies, onion, green pepper, cheese, egg, salt and pepper; stir in half of the chili sauce mixture. Add the beef; mix lightly but thoroughly.

2. Transfer beef mixture to an ungreased 9x5-in. loaf pan. Make a shallow indentation down center of loaf. Spread remaining chili sauce mixture over loaf, being sure to fill indentation.

3. Bake 60-70 minutes or until a thermometer reads 160°; use a turkey baster to remove drippings every 20 minutes. Let stand 10 minutes before slicing.

**1 piece:** 303 cal., 16g fat (6g sat. fat), 100mg chol., 654mg sod., 15g carb. (7g sugars, 0 fiber), 24g pro.

66

Very easy to make and so tasty. This whips up very quickly. Simple, tasty meal for weeknights or for special occasions.

—CONNIEK
TASTEOFHOME.COM

PORK CHOPS WITH
PARMESAN SAUCE, PAGE 191

# CHAPTER 7

# PORK & OTHER ENTREES

Mix up your meal plan with a savory specialty that turns ham,
sausage and pork into a much-loved moment. From quick, easy dinners
perfect for busy work nights to memory-making holiday menus,
the ideal entree is always at hand with the following recipes.

# HABANERO RASPBERRY RIBS

Roasting these tender, fall-off-the-bone ribs in the oven means you can enjoy them any time of year—no waiting for grilling season. The heat from the habanero pepper and the sweetness of the raspberry jam complement each other perfectly.

—Yvonne Roat, Linden, MI

**PREP:** 10 MIN. • **BAKE:** 3 HOURS 10 MIN. • **MAKES:** 5 SERVINGS

2 racks pork baby back ribs (about 4½ lbs.)
2½ cups barbecue sauce, divided
2 cups seedless raspberry jam
1 habanero pepper, finely chopped

**1.** Place each rack of ribs on a double thickness of heavy-duty foil (about 28x18 in.). Combine 2 cups barbecue sauce, jam and habanero pepper; pour over ribs. Wrap foil tightly around ribs.

**2.** Place in a shallow roasting pan. Bake at 325° until meat is tender, about 3 hours.

**3.** Carefully unwrap ribs. Place on baking sheets. Brush with remaining barbecue sauce. Broil 4 in. from the heat until bubbly, 8-10 minutes. If desired, serve with additional barbecue sauce.

**1 serving:** 1067 cal., 38g fat (14g sat. fat), 147mg chol., 1562mg sod., 139g carb. (122g sugars, 1g fiber), 41g pro.

---

# MOSTACCIOLI

Even though we're not Italian, this rich, cheesy pasta dish is a family tradition for holidays and other special occasions. It tastes just like lasagna without the layering work.

—Nancy Mundhenke, Kinsley, KS

**PREP:** 15 MIN. • **BAKE:** 45 MIN. • **MAKES:** 12 SERVINGS

1 lb. uncooked mostaccioli
1½ lbs. bulk Italian sausage
1 jar (28 oz.) meatless spaghetti sauce
1 large egg, lightly beaten
1 carton (15 oz.) ricotta cheese
2 cups shredded part-skim mozzarella cheese
½ cup grated Romano cheese

**1.** Cook pasta according to the package directions; drain. Crumble sausage into a Dutch oven. Cook over medium heat until no longer pink; drain. Stir in the spaghetti sauce and pasta. In a large bowl, combine egg, ricotta cheese and mozzarella cheese.

**2.** Spoon half the pasta mixture into a greased shallow 3-qt. baking dish; layer with cheese mixture and the remaining pasta mixture.

**3.** Cover and bake at 375° until a thermometer reads 160°, about 40 minutes. Uncover; top with Romano cheese. Bake 5 minutes longer or until heated through.

**1 cup:** 386 cal., 18g fat (9g sat. fat), 74mg chol., 747mg sod., 36g carb. (8g sugars, 2g fiber), 22g pro.

> "
> This is an excellent recipe. The pork was tender, juicy and flavorful. My husband says it's a keeper.
> —SUSANRIGHTNOUR
> TASTEOFHOME.COM

# MARINATED PORK KABOBS

This recipe was originally for lamb, but I adapted it to pork and adjusted the spices. It's always requested when the grill comes out for the season.
—*Bobbie Jo Miller, Fallon, NV*

**PREP:** 15 MIN. + MARINATING • **GRILL:** 15 MIN. • **MAKES:** 8 SERVINGS

2 cups plain yogurt
2 Tbsp. lemon juice
4 garlic cloves, minced
½ tsp. ground cumin
¼ tsp. ground coriander
2 lbs. pork tenderloin, cut into 1½-in. cubes
8 small white onions, halved
8 cherry tomatoes
1 medium sweet red pepper, cut into 1½-in. pieces
1 medium green pepper, cut into 1½-in. pieces
Salt and pepper to taste

1. In a shallow dish, combine yogurt, lemon juice, garlic, cumin and coriander. Add pork and turn to coat; cover and refrigerate 6 hours or overnight.

2. Alternate pork, onions, tomatoes and peppers on 8 metal or soaked wooden skewers. Season to taste with salt and pepper. Grill, covered, over medium heat until meat juices run clear, 15-20 minutes, turning occasionally.

**1 kabob:** 190 cal., 5g fat (2g sat. fat), 67mg chol., 63mg sod., 11g carb. (7g sugars, 2g fiber), 25g pro. **Diabetic exchanges:** 3 lean meat, 1 vegetable, ½ fat.

## TEST KITCHEN TIP

*Feel free to try this recipe with chicken instead of pork, and add some mushrooms to the skewers if you'd like.*

---

# PORK CHOPS WITH PARMESAN SAUCE

Tender skillet chops make a speedy weeknight meal. These are finished with a creamy and flavorful Parmesan sauce. Here's a new family favorite!
—*Taste of Home Test Kitchen*

**TAKES:** 20 MIN. • **MAKES:** 4 SERVINGS

4 boneless pork loin chops (4 oz. each)
½ tsp. salt
¼ tsp. pepper
1 Tbsp. butter
2 Tbsp. all-purpose flour
1 cup fat-free milk
⅓ cup grated Parmesan cheese
2 Tbsp. grated onion
3 tsp. minced fresh parsley
¼ tsp. minced fresh or dried thyme
¼ tsp. ground nutmeg

1. Sprinkle pork chops with salt and pepper. In a large nonstick skillet, cook the chops in butter over medium heat until meat juices run clear; remove and keep warm.

2. Combine flour and milk until smooth; stir into pan. Bring to a boil; cook and stir 2 minutes or until thickened. Stir in remaining ingredients; heat through. Serve with chops. If desired, top with additional fresh thyme.

**1 pork chop with ¼ cup sauce:** 244 cal., 11g fat (5g sat. fat), 69mg chol., 475mg sod., 7g carb. (3g sugars, 0 fiber), 27g pro. **Diabetic exchanges:** 3 lean meat, ½ starch, ½ fat.

# MOTHER'S HAM CASSEROLE

This ham casserole recipe was one of my mother's favorite dishes, and it always brings back fond memories of her when I prepare it. It's a terrific use of leftover ham from a holiday dinner.

—*Linda Childers, Murfreesboro, TN*

**PREP:** 35 MIN. • **BAKE:** 25 MIN. • **MAKES:** 6 SERVINGS

- 2 cups cubed peeled potatoes
- 1 large carrot, sliced
- 2 celery ribs, chopped
- 3 cups water
- 2 cups cubed fully cooked ham
- 2 Tbsp. chopped green pepper
- 2 tsp. finely chopped onion
- 7 Tbsp. butter, divided
- 3 Tbsp. all-purpose flour
- 1½ cups 2% milk
- ¾ tsp. salt
- ⅛ tsp. pepper
- 1 cup shredded cheddar cheese
- ½ cup soft bread crumbs

**1.** Preheat oven to 375°. In a saucepan, bring potatoes, carrot, celery and water to a boil. Reduce heat; cover and cook until tender, about 15 minutes. Drain.

**2.** In a large skillet, saute ham, green pepper and onion in 3 Tbsp. butter until tender. Add the potato mixture. Transfer to a greased 1½-qt. baking dish.

**3.** In a large saucepan, melt the remaining 4 Tbsp. butter; stir in flour until smooth. Gradually whisk in milk, salt and pepper. Bring to a boil; cook and stir 2 minutes or until thickened. Reduce heat; add cheddar cheese and stir until melted.

**4.** Pour over ham mixture. Sprinkle with bread crumbs. Bake until heated through, 25-30 minutes.

**Note:** To make soft bread crumbs, tear bread into pieces and place in a food processor or blender. Cover and pulse until crumbs form. One slice of bread yields ½-¾ cup crumbs.

**1 cup:** 360 cal., 23g fat (14g sat. fat), 87mg chol., 1157mg sod., 21g carb. (5g sugars, 2g fiber), 18g pro.

## TEST KITCHEN TIP

*Get creative with this casserole's topping. Use crushed butter-flavored crackers, french-fried onions or sliced almonds. If you love amazing Tex-Mex recipes, add chopped green chiles, sub pepper jack cheese for cheddar and top the casserole with crushed tortilla chips.*

—CHRISTINE RUKAVENA, *TASTE OF HOME* BOOK EDITOR

“

This was the best ham casserole I've ever tasted. My family agreed by eating the whole thing up and asking for more.
—SCRAPPY16
TASTEOFHOME.COM

# SAUSAGE FETTUCCINE BAKE

This family-pleasing dish, rich and loaded with sausage, veggies and cheese, will become a favorite.
—Lisa Varner, El Paso, TX

PREP: 25 MIN. • BAKE: 25 MIN. + STANDING • MAKES: 2 CASSEROLES (6 SERVINGS EACH)

1½ lbs. uncooked fettuccine
2 lbs. bulk Italian sausage
2 large onions, chopped
1 medium green pepper, chopped
2 cans (28 oz. each) diced tomatoes, undrained
2 jars (4½ oz. each) sliced mushrooms, drained
4 tsp. Italian seasoning
4 cups (1 lb.) shredded part-skim mozzarella cheese, divided
2 cans (10¾ oz. each) condensed cream of mushroom soup, undiluted
½ cup beef broth
1 cup grated Parmesan cheese

1. Cook fettuccine according to package directions. Meanwhile, in a Dutch oven, cook sausage, onions and green pepper over medium heat until meat is crumbly and no longer pink; drain. Add tomatoes, mushrooms and Italian seasoning. Bring to a boil. Reduce heat; simmer, uncovered, about 5 minutes.

2. Drain fettuccine; stir into meat mixture. Transfer half of the sausage mixture to 2 greased 13x9-in. baking dishes. Sprinkle each with 1 cup mozzarella cheese; top with remaining sausage mixture.

3. In a small bowl, whisk soup and broth; spread over casseroles. Sprinkle with Parmesan cheese and remaining mozzarella cheese.

4. Cover and bake at 350°, about 20 minutes. Uncover; bake 5-10 minutes longer or until bubbly and cheese is melted. Let stand 10 minutes before serving.

**1½ cups:** 531 cal., 22g fat (9g sat. fat), 60mg chol., 1311mg sod., 55g carb. (10g sugars, 6g fiber), 30g pro.

# SMOKED PORK CHOPS WITH SWEET POTATOES

Apple and sweet potato flavors combine so nicely with pork. My family enjoys simple dinners like this one.
—Helen Sanders, Fort Myers, FL

PREP: 15 MIN. • COOK: 45 MIN. • MAKES: 6 SERVINGS

6 smoked boneless pork chops (7 oz. each)
1 Tbsp. canola oil
4 large sweet potatoes, cooked, peeled and cut lengthwise into thirds
½ cup packed brown sugar
⅛ tsp. pepper
2 large tart apples, peeled and thinly sliced
¼ cup apple juice or water

1. Preheat oven to 325°. In a large skillet, cook chops in oil over medium heat 2-3 minutes on each side or until lightly browned; drain.

2. Transfer to a greased 13x9-in. baking dish. Top with sweet potatoes. Combine brown sugar and pepper; sprinkle over sweet potatoes. Top with apples; drizzle with apple juice.

3. Cover and bake 30 minutes. Uncover; bake 10-15 minutes longer or until meat is tender.

**1 serving:** 584 cal., 16g fat (5g sat. fat), 95mg chol., 2462mg sod., 56g carb. (37g sugars, 4g fiber), 52g pro.

# SLOPPY JOE DOGS

There are so many different ways to top a hot dog, but this tasty sloppy joe version beats them all!
—*Kimberly Wallace, Dennison, OH*

**PREP: 20 MIN. • COOK: 15 MIN. • MAKES: 16 SERVINGS**

## SLOPPY JOE TOPPING
- 2  lbs. ground beef
- 2  celery ribs, chopped
- 1  small green pepper, finely chopped
- 1  small onion, chopped
- 1  can (10¾ oz.) condensed tomato soup
- ¼  cup packed brown sugar
- ¼  cup ketchup
- 1  Tbsp. cider vinegar
- 1  Tbsp. prepared mustard
- 1½  tsp. Worcestershire sauce
- 1  tsp. pepper
- ½  tsp. salt
- ¼  tsp. garlic powder

## DOGS
- 16  hot dogs
- 16  hot dog buns, split
   Optional: Warmed cheese dip and grilled onions

1. In a Dutch oven, cook beef, celery, green pepper and onion over medium heat 5-7 minutes or until meat is no longer pink, breaking into crumbles; drain. Stir in the tomato soup, brown sugar, ketchup, vinegar, mustard, Worcestershire sauce, pepper, salt and garlic powder; heat through.

2. Grill hot dogs, covered, over medium heat until heated through, 6-10 minutes, turning occasionally. Serve on buns. Top each with ¼ cup beef mixture. If desired, top with warmed cheese dip and grilled onions.

**1 hot dog:** 422 cal., 23g fat (9g sat. fat), 68mg chol., 959mg sod., 31g carb. (10g sugars, 1g fiber), 22g pro.

## TEST KITCHEN TIP

*While this recipe is ideal on hot dogs, you might just want to prepare the sloppy joe alone for sandwiches.*

TAILGATE
SAUSAGES

# TAILGATE SAUSAGES

You'll need just a handful of ingredients to fix these tasty sandwiches. Fully cooked sausages are placed in buns with cheese and topped with giardiniera, then wrapped in foil so they're easy to transport and grill.
—*Matthew Hass, Ellison Bay, WI*

**TAKES: 20 MIN. • MAKES: 4 SERVINGS**

½ cup giardiniera, drained
½ tsp. sugar
4 slices provolone cheese
4 brat buns or hot dog buns, split
4 cooked Italian sausage links
  Additional giardiniera, optional

1. In a bowl, combine giardiniera and sugar; set aside.

2. Place cheese in buns; top with sausages and giardiniera mixture. Wrap individually in a double thickness of heavy-duty foil (about 12x10 in.). Grill, uncovered, over medium heat 8-10 minutes or until heated through and cheese is melted. Open foil carefully to allow steam to escape. If desired, serve with additional giardiniera.

**1 sausage:** 584 cal., 33g fat (15g sat. fat), 84mg chol., 1401mg sod., 39g carb. (9g sugars, 2g fiber), 31g pro.

---

# ITALIAN PORK STEW

Don't skip the anchovy paste in this stew! It gives a savory, salty flavor but doesn't taste fishy at all. Add a salad and artisan bread for a wholesome meal.
—*Lynne German, Buford, GA*

**PREP: 30 MIN. • COOK: 2¼ HOURS • MAKES: 8 SERVINGS (2 QT.)**

⅔ cup all-purpose flour
2 lbs. boneless pork loin, cut into 1-in. pieces
4 Tbsp. olive oil, divided
1 large onion, chopped
5 garlic cloves, crushed
1 can (28 oz.) diced tomatoes, undrained
1 cup dry red wine or beef broth
3 bay leaves
1 cinnamon stick (3 in.)
1 Tbsp. tomato paste
1 Tbsp. red wine vinegar
1 tsp. anchovy paste
1 tsp. each dried oregano, basil and sage leaves
½ tsp. salt
½ tsp. crushed red pepper flakes
¼ tsp. pepper
¼ cup minced fresh parsley
  Hot cooked bow tie pasta
  Grated Parmesan cheese

1. Place flour in a shallow dish. Add pork loin, a few pieces at a time, and turn to coat. In a Dutch oven, brown pork loin in 3 Tbsp. oil in batches. Remove and keep warm.

2. In the same pan, saute onion in remaining oil until crisp-tender. Add garlic; cook 1 minute longer. Stir in tomatoes, wine, bay leaves, cinnamon, tomato paste, vinegar, anchovy paste, oregano, basil, sage, salt, red pepper flakes, pepper and pork; bring to a boil.

3. Reduce heat; cover and simmer 1½ hours, stirring occasionally. Stir in parsley. Cover and cook 30-40 minutes longer or until meat is tender. Skim fat; discard the bay leaves and cinnamon stick.

4. Serve with pasta; sprinkle with Parmesan cheese.

**Freeze option:** Place individual portions of cooled stew in freezer containers and freeze. To use, partially thaw in refrigerator overnight. Heat through in a saucepan, stirring occasionally; add water if necessary.

**1 cup:** 256 cal., 12g fat (3g sat. fat), 59mg chol., 349mg sod., 12g carb. (4g sugars, 2g fiber), 24g pro. **Diabetic exchanges:** 3 lean meat, 1 vegetable, 1 fat.

# PROSCIUTTO PASTA TOSS

I love quick, simple pasta dishes, and this is one of my favorites. I prepare a tossed green salad while the pasta cooks and serve up a lovely light supper in minutes!
—*Laura Murphy-Ogden, Charlotte, NC*

**TAKES:** 20 MIN. • **MAKES:** 6 SERVINGS

1   pkg. (16 oz.) linguine
½   cup fresh or frozen peas, thawed
2   Tbsp. minced garlic
1   Tbsp. Italian seasoning
1   tsp. pepper
¼   cup olive oil
½   lb. thinly sliced prosciutto
    or deli ham, chopped
¼   cup shredded Parmesan cheese

1. Cook linguine according to package directions, adding peas in the last 3 minutes. Meanwhile, in a large cast-iron or other heavy skillet, saute garlic, Italian seasoning and pepper in oil until garlic is tender, about 1 minute. Stir in prosciutto.

2. Drain linguine and peas; add to skillet and toss to coat. Sprinkle with cheese.

**1⅓ cups:** 461 cal., 16g fat (4g sat. fat), 36mg chol., 802mg sod., 58g carb. (3g sugars, 3g fiber), 22g pro.

# AIR-FRYER APRICOT-ROSEMARY PORK MEDALLIONS

I needed to use a pork tenderloin from my fridge, but I didn't want to wait for it to roast. I tried this, and not only was it quick, but my family loved it. You can play with different preserves to make your favorite flavors.
—*Lynn Caruso, Gilroy, CA*

**PREP:** 10 MIN. • **COOK:** 30 MIN. • **MAKES:** 4 SERVINGS

1   pork tenderloin (1 lb.)
¼   cup seasoned bread crumbs
    Cooking spray
3   cups fresh broccoli florets
⅓   cup apricot preserves
2   Tbsp. white wine or chicken broth
1   tsp. minced fresh rosemary or
    ¼ tsp. dried rosemary, crushed
¼   tsp. salt
    Dash pepper
2⅔  cups hot cooked brown rice

1. Preheat air fryer to 375°. Cut pork tenderloin crosswise into 8 slices. Place seasoned bread crumbs in a shallow bowl. Dip pork tenderloin slices into crumbs, patting to help coating adhere. In batches, place pork on greased tray in air-fryer basket; spritz with cooking spray. Cook 4-5 minutes per side or until a thermometer reads 145°. Remove and keep warm.

2. Place broccoli in air-fryer basket. Cook until tender, 4-6 minutes, stirring once.

3. In a small saucepan, mix apricot preserves, white wine, rosemary, salt and pepper. Cook and stir over medium-low heat until apricot preserves are melted, 3-5 minutes. Serve with pork, broccoli and rice.

**1 serving:** 405 cal., 6g fat (2g sat. fat), 64mg chol., 289mg sod., 58g carb. (13g sugars, 4g fiber), 29g pro.

# PRESSURE-COOKER TERIYAKI PORK ROAST

I'm always looking for no-fuss recipes, so I was thrilled to find this one.
The tender teriyaki pork has become a family favorite.
—*Roxanne Hulsey, Gainesville, GA*

PREP: 10 MIN. • COOK: 30 MIN. + RELEASING • MAKES: 10 SERVINGS

¾ cup unsweetened apple juice
2 Tbsp. sugar
2 Tbsp. reduced-sodium soy sauce
1 Tbsp. white vinegar
1 tsp. ground ginger
¼ tsp. garlic powder
⅛ tsp. pepper
1 boneless pork loin roast
   (about 3 lbs.), halved
8 tsp. cornstarch
3 Tbsp. cold water
   Chopped green onions
   and sesame seeds, optional

1. Combine the first 7 ingredients in a 6-qt. electric pressure cooker. Add roast and turn to coat. Lock lid; close pressure-release valve. Adjust to pressure-cook on high for 25 minutes. Let pressure release naturally 10 minutes; quick-release any remaining pressure. Press cancel. A thermometer inserted in pork should read at least 145°.

2. Remove pork to a serving platter; keep warm. In a small bowl, mix cornstarch and water until smooth; stir into pressure cooker. Select saute setting and adjust for low heat. Simmer, stirring until thickened, 1-2 minutes. Serve with pork. If desired, sprinkle with green onions and sesame seeds.

**4 oz. cooked pork:** 198 cal., 6g fat (2g sat. fat), 68mg chol., 155mg sod., 7g carb. (4g sugars, 0 fiber), 27g pro. **Diabetic exchanges:** 4 lean meat, ½ starch.

# HAM RAVIOLI BAKE

I based this recipe on a dish my husband likes to order when we go out for Italian food. Not only does he love it, my young daughter does too!
—*Jennifer Berger, Eau Claire, WI*

PREP: 20 MIN. • BAKE: 20 MIN. • MAKES: 4 SERVINGS

1 pkg. (25 oz.) frozen cheese ravioli
1½ cups cubed fully cooked ham
1⅓ cups sliced fresh mushrooms
¼ cup chopped onion
¼ cup chopped green pepper
1 Tbsp. canola oil
1 jar (15 oz.) Alfredo sauce

1. Cook ravioli according to package directions. In a large skillet, cook ham, mushrooms, onion and green pepper in oil over medium heat 4-5 minutes or until vegetables are crisp-tender.

2. Spread 2 Tbsp. Alfredo sauce into a greased 8-in. square baking dish. Stir the remaining Alfredo sauce into ham mixture; cook 3-4 minutes or until heated through.

3. Drain ravioli; place half in the prepared baking dish. Top with half the ham mixture. Repeat layers. Cover and bake at 375° until bubbly, 20-25 minutes.

**1 serving:** 653 cal., 31g fat (16g sat. fat), 137mg chol., 1496mg sod., 61g carb. (5g sugars, 3g fiber), 35g pro.

# GRILLED PORK TENDERLOIN WITH CHERRY SALSA MOLE

The combination of pork and cherries has long been a favorite of mine. The hint of spice and chocolate in the salsa mole makes the combination even more special.

—Roxanne Chan, Albany, CA

PREP: 25 MIN. • GRILL: 15 MIN. + STANDING • MAKES: 6 SERVINGS

2 pork tenderloins (¾ lb. each)
1 Tbsp. canola oil
½ tsp. salt
¼ tsp. ground cumin
¼ tsp. chili powder
1 cup pitted fresh or frozen dark sweet cherries, thawed, chopped
1 jalapeno pepper, seeded and minced
½ cup finely chopped peeled jicama
1 oz. semisweet chocolate, grated
2 Tbsp. minced fresh cilantro
1 green onion, thinly sliced
1 Tbsp. lime juice
1 tsp. honey
Salted pumpkin seeds or pepitas

**1.** Brush tenderloins with oil; sprinkle with salt, cumin and chili powder. Grill, covered, over medium heat 15-20 minutes or until a thermometer reads 145°, turning occasionally. Let stand 10-15 minutes.

**2.** Meanwhile, combine cherries, jalapeno, jicama, chocolate, cilantro, green onion, lime juice and honey. Slice pork; serve with cherry salsa and pumpkin seeds.

**3 oz. cooked pork with ¼ cup salsa:** 218 cal., 8g fat (3g sat. fat), 64mg chol., 248mg sod., 11g carb. (9g sugars, 2g fiber), 23g pro. **Diabetic exchanges:** 3 lean meat, ½ starch, ½ fat.

## TEST KITCHEN TIP

*Not everyone has jicama on hand. Skip a trip to the grocery store and replace it with chopped apple, pear or even celery.*

SLOW-COOKED
PORK ROAST

# SLOW-COOKED PORK ROAST

This tasty meal is wonderful for summer because it doesn't heat up the kitchen!
—*Marion Lowery, Medford, OR*

**PREP: 20 MIN. • COOK: 6 HOURS + STANDING • MAKES: 12 SERVINGS**

2 cans (8 oz. each) unsweetened crushed pineapple, undrained
1 cup barbecue sauce
2 Tbsp. unsweetened apple juice
1 Tbsp. minced fresh rosemary or 1 tsp. dried rosemary, crushed
1 tsp. minced garlic
2 tsp. grated lemon zest
1 tsp. liquid smoke, optional
½ tsp. salt
¼ tsp. pepper
2 Tbsp. olive oil
1 boneless pork loin roast (3 to 4 lbs.)

**1.** For the sauce, in a large saucepan, combine first 9 ingredients. Bring to a boil. Reduce heat; simmer, uncovered, about 3 minutes.

**2.** Meanwhile, cut roast in half. In a nonstick skillet, heat oil over medium heat; add roast and brown on all sides.

**3.** Place pork roast in a 5-qt. slow cooker; pour sauce over pork and turn to coat. Cover and cook on low 6-7 hours or until meat is tender. Let stand 10 minutes before slicing.

**3 oz. cooked pork:** 205 cal., 5g fat (2g sat. fat), 57mg chol., 364mg sod., 16g carb. (13g sugars, 1g fiber), 22g pro.

---

# TENDER PORK CHOPS WITH MANGO SALSA

To save time, I make the salsa and season the pork in the morning so it's ready to throw on the grill later. For a spicier topping, I add jalapenos to the salsa.
—*Andrea Rivera, Westbury, NY*

**PREP: 15 MIN. + MARINATING • GRILL: 10 MIN. • MAKES: 4 SERVINGS**

3 Tbsp. cider vinegar
1 Tbsp. salt-free steak grilling blend
1 Tbsp. olive oil
4 bone-in pork loin chops (7 oz. each)

**SALSA**
2 medium mangoes, peeled and chopped
1 cup chopped sweet onion
1 jalapeno pepper, seeded and finely chopped
1 Tbsp. lemon juice
2 tsp. honey

**1.** In a large shallow dish, combine the vinegar, grilling blend and oil. Add the pork; turn to coat. Cover and refrigerate for at least 2 hours.

**2.** Drain pork, discarding marinade. Grill chops, covered, over medium heat or broil 4-5 in. from the heat for 4-5 minutes on each side or until a thermometer reads 145°. Let stand for 5 minutes before serving.

**3.** Meanwhile, in a small bowl, combine the salsa ingredients. Serve with chops.

**Note:** Wear disposable gloves when cutting hot peppers; the oils can burn skin. Avoid touching your face.

**1 pork chop with ¾ cup salsa:** 330 cal., 12g fat (4g sat. fat), 86mg chol., 67mg sod., 25g carb. (20g sugars, 3g fiber), 31g pro. **Diabetic exchanges:** 4 lean meat, 1 fruit, ½ starch, ½ fat.

# CAJUN PORK & RICE

I created this recipe after returning home from my travels and discovering I had little food in the house. I used ingredients that were already available in the refrigerator and pantry.
—Allison Gapinski, Cary, NC

**PREP:** 20 MIN. • **COOK:** 4¼ HOURS • **MAKES:** 4 SERVINGS

1½ tsp. ground cumin
1½ tsp. chili powder
1½ lbs. boneless pork loin chops
1 can (14½ oz.) petite diced tomatoes, undrained
1 small onion, finely chopped
1 celery rib, finely chopped
1 small carrot, julienned
1 garlic clove, minced
½ tsp. Louisiana-style hot sauce
¼ tsp. salt
1½ cups uncooked instant rice
1 cup reduced-sodium chicken broth
1 tsp. olive oil
1 medium green pepper, julienned

1. Mix cumin and chili powder; sprinkle pork chops with 2 tsp. spice mixture. Transfer to a 4-qt. slow cooker.

2. In a bowl, mix tomatoes, onion, celery, carrot, garlic, hot sauce, salt and the remaining spice mixture; pour over chops. Cook, covered, on low 4-5 hours.

3. Stir in rice and chicken broth, breaking up pork into pieces. Cook, covered, on low until rice is tender, 12-15 minutes longer.

4. In a small skillet, heat oil over medium-high heat. Add green pepper; cook and stir 5-7 minutes or until crisp-tender. Serve on top of pork mixture.

**1½ cups pork mixture with ¼ cup pepper strips:** 423 cal., 12g fat (4g sat. fat), 82mg chol., 573mg sod., 40g carb. (6g sugars, 4g fiber), 38g pro.
**Diabetic exchanges:** 5 lean meat, 2½ starch, 1 vegetable.

---

# SAUSAGE & SPINACH CRESCENT BAKE

A classic Florentine casserole has spinach and cheese. I make a yummy version with mozzarella, mushrooms and sausage. It's gone in the blink of an eye at our house.
—Noelle Carle, Bristow, OK

**PREP:** 20 MIN. • **BAKE:** 25 MIN. • **MAKES:** 8 SERVINGS

1 lb. bulk pork sausage
2 cups sliced fresh mushrooms
1 medium onion, chopped
2 garlic cloves, minced
1 pkg. (10 oz.) frozen chopped spinach, thawed and squeezed dry
1 cup shredded part-skim mozzarella cheese
4 oz. cream cheese, softened
1 cup half-and-half cream
1 tube (8 oz.) refrigerated crescent rolls

1. Preheat the oven to 350°. In a large skillet, cook sausage, mushrooms, onion and garlic over medium heat 6-8 minutes or until sausage is crumbly and no longer pink. Drain.

2. Add spinach, mozzarella cheese, cream cheese and cream to sausage mixture; cook and stir until blended. Transfer to a greased 13x9-in. baking dish.

3. Unroll dough into 1 long rectangle; press perforations to seal. Place over the sausage mixture. Bake, covered, 10 minutes. Bake, uncovered, until golden brown and filling is bubbly, 12-15 minutes longer. Let stand 5-10 minutes before cutting.

**1 piece:** 401 cal., 29g fat (12g sat. fat), 70mg chol., 758mg sod., 18g carb. (5g sugars, 1g fiber), 15g pro.

CAJUN PORK
& RICE

66
One of the best
meals I've made
in a while. It
reminded me of
jambalaya but
it's much easier
to make! Loved
it and husband
did too!
—SANDYC1940
TASTEOFHOME.COM

WINNING CRANBERRY GLAZED HAM

# WINNING CRANBERRY GLAZED HAM

A friend shared the recipe for this tender ham with me. I've served it at reunions, weddings, graduations, baptisms and holiday gatherings. It's a delicious way to please a crowd.
—*Sue Seymour, Valatie, NY*

PREP: 15 MIN. + MARINATING • BAKE: 2½ HOURS • MAKES: 16 SERVINGS

2 cans (16 oz. each) whole-berry cranberry sauce
1 cup orange juice
⅓ cup steak sauce
2 Tbsp. canola oil
2 Tbsp. prepared mustard
2 Tbsp. brown sugar
1 fully cooked bone-in ham (7 to 9 lbs.)

1. In a large bowl, combine the cranberry sauce, orange juice, steak sauce, oil, mustard and brown sugar. Score surface of ham with shallow diagonal cuts, making diamond shapes.

2. Place ham in a 2-gallon resealable bag. Add half of cranberry mixture; seal bag and turn to coat. Cover and refrigerate 8 hours or overnight, turning several times. Cover and refrigerate the remaining cranberry mixture.

3. Preheat oven to 325°. Drain ham, discarding marinade. Place ham on a rack in a foil-lined roasting pan; cover with foil. Bake for 1¾ hours.

4. Place reserved cranberry mixture in a small saucepan; heat through. Uncover ham; brush with cranberry mixture.

5. Bake 45-60 minutes longer or until a thermometer reads 140°, brushing with cranberry mixture every 15 minutes. Warm the remaining cranberry mixture; serve with ham.

**4 oz. cooked ham:** 264 cal., 7g fat (2g sat. fat), 87mg chol., 1164mg sod., 22g carb. (15g sugars, 1g fiber), 29g pro.

# BAKED PORK CHOPS WITH STUFFING

For a lip-smacking change, I combine plain pork chops with green beans and a mild cheese sauce for a swift supper. Round out the menu with a salad and brownies for dessert.
—*Linda Martin, Bartlett, TN*

PREP: 15 MIN. • BAKE: 30 MIN. • MAKES: 4 SERVINGS

2 Tbsp. canola oil
4 boneless pork loin chops (6 oz. each)
3 cups day-old French bread cubes
¼ cup butter, melted
¼ cup chicken broth
2 Tbsp. chopped celery
2 Tbsp. chopped onion
¼ tsp. poultry seasoning
1 can (10¾ oz.) condensed cream of mushroom soup, undiluted
⅓ cup water

1. Preheat oven to 350°. In a large skillet, heat oil over medium heat and brown pork chops on both sides. Place in an ungreased 13x9-in. baking pan. In a large bowl, toss bread cubes, butter, broth, celery, onion and poultry seasoning. Spoon about ½ cup stuffing onto each pork chop.

2. Combine soup and water; pour over the chops. Cover and bake 20 minutes. Uncover; bake 10-15 minutes longer or until a thermometer inserted in the pork reads 145°. Let stand 5 minutes before serving.

**1 stuffed pork chop:** 356 cal., 25g fat (10g sat. fat), 54mg chol., 841mg sod., 19g carb. (2g sugars, 2g fiber), 11g pro.

# COUNTRY-STYLE BARBECUE RIBS

These ribs get a good sear under the broiler, then go into the slow cooker to become fall-apart tender.
—Shannon Copley, Upper Arlington, OH

PREP: 15 MIN. • COOK: 3 HOURS • MAKES: 10 SERVINGS

2 Tbsp. paprika
2 Tbsp. brown sugar
2 tsp. salt
2 tsp. garlic powder
2 tsp. chili powder
1 tsp. onion powder
1 tsp. ground chipotle pepper
1 tsp. pepper
¾ tsp. dried thyme
4 lbs. boneless country-style pork ribs
1 bottle (18 oz.) barbecue sauce
¾ cup amber beer or reduced-sodium chicken broth

1. Preheat broiler. Mix first 9 ingredients. Place pork in a foil-lined 15x10x1-in. pan; rub with seasonings. Broil 4-5 in. from heat until browned, 2-3 minutes per side.

2. Transfer to a 5-qt. slow cooker. Whisk together barbecue sauce and beer; pour over ribs. Cook, covered, on low until tender, 3-4 hours.

3. Remove ribs. Reserve 2 cups cooking juices and skim fat. Serve juices with ribs.

1 serving: 393 cal., 17g fat (6g sat. fat), 105mg chol., 1098mg sod., 26g carb. (20g sugars, 1g fiber), 33g pro.

## TEST KITCHEN TIP

*Country-style are the meatiest of all pork ribs. Look for highly marbled ribs; they might be labeled pork shoulder country-style ribs. Country-style ribs from the loin are leaner and won't be as tender and moist.*

# LAMB KABOBS WITH BULGUR PILAF

This is a great old family recipe that shows my Armenian heritage. The tender, slightly sweet lamb is complemented perfectly by the savory bulgur pilaf.
—Ruth Hartunian Alumbaugh, Willimantic, CT

PREP: 15 MIN. + MARINATING • COOK: 35 MIN. • MAKES: 6 SERVINGS

30 garlic cloves, crushed (1½ to 2 bulbs)
½ cup balsamic vinegar
¾ cup chopped fresh mint
¼ cup olive oil
2 lbs. lean boneless lamb, cut into 1½-in. cubes

**PILAF**
½ cup butter, cubed
1 large onion, chopped
1 cup uncooked mini spiral pasta
2 cups bulgur
3 cups beef broth

1. In a bowl or a shallow dish, combine garlic, vinegar, mint and oil. Add lamb and turn to coat; refrigerate for several hours or overnight.

2. For pilaf, in a large skillet, melt butter. Add onion and pasta; saute until pasta is browned. Add bulgur and stir to coat. Stir in broth. Bring to a boil. Reduce heat; cover and simmer 25-30 minutes. Remove from heat; let stand 5 minutes.

3. Drain lamb; discard marinade. Thread onto 6 metal or soaked wooden skewers.

4. Grill kabobs, covered, over medium heat 8-10 minutes or until meat reaches desired doneness, turning frequently. Serve with pilaf.

1 serving: 626 cal., 31g fat (14g sat. fat), 132mg chol., 644mg sod., 52g carb. (4g sugars, 10g fiber), 38g pro.

COUNTRY-STYLE
BARBECUE RIBS

66
This was a hit
with the family.
My spouse
took leftovers
for lunch and
said that it was
even better
the next day.
—HELENGOFF
TASTEOFHOME.COM

SPINACH &
CHEESE
LASAGNA
ROLLS,
PAGE 231

"
Five stars!
Everyone asks
for this recipe!
Even bona fide
carnivores
are won over
by this dish.
—BUNCHOFFLUFF
TASTEOFHOME.COM

# CHAPTER 8

# SEAFOOD & MEATLESS MAINS

From meatless Mondays to fish-fry Fridays, mixing up dinner routines is a great way to make the most of your family's time around the table. Here, you'll find more than a dozen comforting dishes everyone will love—whether following a particular diet or not.

# AIR-FRYER FISH TACOS

These crispy tacos are good enough to challenge the best food truck. I love that
the fish is deliciously guilt-free because it's air-fried instead of deep-fried.
—*Lena Lim, Seattle, WA*

**PREP:** 30 MIN. • **COOK:** 10 MIN./BATCH • **MAKES:** 8 SERVINGS

¾ cup reduced-fat sour cream
1 can (4 oz.) chopped green chiles
1 Tbsp. fresh cilantro leaves
1 Tbsp. lime juice
4 tilapia fillets (4 oz. each)
½ cup all-purpose flour
1 large egg white, beaten
½ cup panko bread crumbs
 Cooking spray
½ tsp. salt
½ tsp. each white pepper,
 cayenne pepper and paprika
8 corn tortillas (6 in.), warmed
1 large tomato, finely chopped

**1.** Place sour cream, chiles, cilantro and lime juice in a food processor; cover and process until blended. Set aside.

**2.** Cut each tilapia fillet lengthwise into 2 portions. Place flour, egg white and bread crumbs in separate shallow bowls. Dip tilapia in flour, then egg white, then crumbs.

**3.** Preheat air fryer to 400°. In batches, arrange fillets in a single layer on greased tray in air-fryer basket; spritz with cooking spray. Cook until the fish flakes easily with a fork, 10-12 minutes, turning once.

**4.** Combine the seasonings; sprinkle over fish. Place a portion of fish on each tortilla; top with about 2 Tbsp. sour cream mixture. Sprinkle with tomato. If desired, top with additional cilantro.

**Note:** In our testing, we find that cook times vary dramatically among different brands of air fryers. As a result, we give wider than normal ranges on suggested cook times. Begin checking at the first time listed and adjust as needed.

**1 taco:** 178 cal., 3g fat (1g sat. fat), 30mg chol., 269mg sod., 22g carb. (2g sugars, 2g fiber), 16g pro. **Diabetic exchanges:** 2 lean meat, 1½ starch, ½ fat.

## TEST KITCHEN TIP

*You can use other kinds of fish to make these yummy tacos. A mild whitefish like tilapia works well. Other options include snapper, mahi mahi, grouper, flounder, halibut or cod. Of course, if you have a local fresh fish you want to use, that's good too.*
—MAGGIE KNOEBEL, *TASTE OF HOME* RECIPE EDITOR/TESTER

# CAULIFLOWER ALFREDO

My family loves this quick and healthy cauliflower Alfredo sauce on any kind of pasta.
—*Shelly Bevington, Hermiston, OR*

PREP: 20 MIN. • COOK: 20 MIN. • MAKES: 6 SERVINGS

2 Tbsp. extra virgin olive oil
3 garlic cloves, minced
1 shallot, minced
1 medium head cauliflower, chopped
2 vegetable bouillon cubes
⅔ cup shredded Parmesan cheese, plus additional for garnish
¼ tsp. crushed red pepper flakes
1 pkg. (16 oz.) fettuccine
Chopped fresh parsley

1. In a Dutch oven, heat oil over medium-high heat. Add garlic and shallot; cook and stir until fragrant, 1-2 minutes. Add cauliflower, 4 cups water and bouillon; bring to a boil. Cook, covered, until tender, 5-6 minutes. Drain; cool slightly. Transfer to a food processor; add ⅔ cup Parmesan cheese and pepper flakes. Process until pureed smooth.

2. Meanwhile, cook fettuccine according to package directions for al dente. Drain fettuccine; place in a large bowl. Add cauliflower mixture; toss to coat. Sprinkle with parsley and additional Parmesan cheese.

**1⅓ cups:** 371 cal., 9g fat (3g sat. fat), 6mg chol., 533mg sod., 60g carb. (5g sugars, 5g fiber), 16g pro.

---

# PINEAPPLE SHRIMP STIR-FRY

I came up with this recipe for a luau-themed party and served it with sliced papaya, mango and avocado. My family loved it! If you don't care for coconut, sprinkle it with chopped macadamia nuts instead.
—*Trisha Kruse, Eagle, ID*

TAKES: 30 MIN. • MAKES: 4 SERVINGS

1 can (20 oz.) unsweetened pineapple tidbits
2 Tbsp. cornstarch
1 cup chicken broth
1 Tbsp. brown sugar
1 Tbsp. orange juice
1 Tbsp. reduced-sodium soy sauce
1 Tbsp. sesame or canola oil
1 medium sweet red pepper, thinly sliced
1 medium green pepper, thinly sliced
1 medium sweet onion, thinly sliced
1 lb. uncooked shrimp (31-40 per lb.), peeled and deveined
¼ cup sweetened shredded coconut, toasted
Hot cooked rice

1. Drain pineapple, reserving juice. In a bowl, mix cornstarch, broth, brown sugar, orange juice, soy sauce and reserved pineapple juice until smooth.

2. In a large skillet, heat oil over medium-high heat. Add peppers and onion; stir-fry 1-2 minutes or just until crisp-tender. Add shrimp; stir-fry 2-3 minutes longer or until shrimp turn pink. Remove from pan.

3. Place pineapple in skillet. Stir cornstarch mixture into the pan. Bring to a boil; cook and stir 4-5 minutes or until sauce is thickened. Return shrimp mixture to pan; heat through, stirring to combine. Sprinkle with coconut; serve with rice.

**1 cup:** 301 cal., 7g fat (3g sat. fat), 139mg chol., 568mg sod., 38g carb. (27g sugars, 3g fiber), 20g pro.

# PESTO VEGETABLE PIZZA

My family loves pizza night, but we have rarely ordered takeout since I created this fresh and flavorful version. It is a fast and scrumptious meal that is always a winner in my house.
—Kate Selner, Lino Lakes, MN

**TAKES:** 30 MIN. • **MAKES:** 6 SERVINGS

1  prebaked 12-in. thin pizza crust
2  garlic cloves, halved
½  cup pesto sauce
¾  cup packed fresh spinach, chopped
2  large portobello mushrooms, sliced
1  medium sweet yellow pepper, julienned
2  plum tomatoes, seeded and sliced
⅓  cup packed fresh basil, chopped
1  cup shredded part-skim mozzarella cheese
¼  cup grated Parmesan cheese
½  tsp. fresh or dried oregano

**1.** Preheat oven to 450°. Place crust on an ungreased 12-in. pizza pan. Rub the cut side of garlic cloves over crust; discard garlic. Spread pesto sauce over crust. Top with spinach, mushrooms, yellow pepper, tomatoes and basil. Sprinkle with cheeses and oregano.

**2.** Bake until pizza is heated through and cheese is melted, 10-15 minutes.

**1 piece:** 310 cal., 15g fat (4g sat. fat), 15mg chol., 707mg sod., 31g carb. (4g sugars, 2g fiber), 13g pro. **Diabetic exchanges:** 2 starch, 2 fat, 1 lean meat, 1 medium-fat meat.

## TEST KITCHEN TIP

*If you enjoy a gluten-free, cauliflower or homemade pizza crust, feel free to use it in this recipe.*

---

# FOIL-BAKED SALMON

Baking salmon in foil is an easy technique that can also be used on the grill. This quick recipe uses lemon zest and slices plus garlic for flavor, but you could also try other citrus fruits, herbs and spices.
—Taste of Home *Test Kitchen*

**PREP:** 10 MIN. • **BAKE:** 25 MIN. • **MAKES:** 6 SERVINGS

1  salmon fillet (about 2 lbs.)
2  Tbsp. butter, melted
2  garlic cloves, minced
2  tsp. grated lemon zest
1  Tbsp. minced fresh parsley
¾  tsp. salt
¼  tsp. pepper
6  lemon slices

**1.** Preheat the oven to 350°. Line a 15x10x1-in. baking pan with heavy-duty foil; grease lightly. Place salmon skin side down on foil. Combine butter, garlic and lemon zest; drizzle over salmon. Sprinkle with parsley, salt and pepper. Top with lemon. Fold foil around salmon; seal tightly.

**2.** Bake for 20 minutes. Open foil carefully, allowing steam to escape. Broil 4-6 in. from the heat until fish flakes easily with a fork, 3-5 minutes.

**4 oz. cooked salmon:** 273 cal., 18g fat (5g sat. fat), 86mg chol., 402mg sod., 1g carb. (0 sugars, 0 fiber), 26g pro. **Diabetic exchanges:** 4 lean meat, 1 fat.

QUICK BEAN &
RICE BURRITOS

# QUICK BEAN & RICE BURRITOS

These hearty and zippy burritos can be whipped up in a jiffy.
—*Kimberly Hardison, Maitland, FL*

TAKES: 25 MIN. • MAKES: 8 SERVINGS

1½ cups water
1½ cups uncooked instant brown rice
1 Tbsp. olive oil
1 medium green pepper, diced
½ cup chopped onion
1 tsp. minced garlic
1 Tbsp. chili powder
1 tsp. ground cumin
⅛ tsp. crushed red pepper flakes
1 can (15 oz.) black beans,
    rinsed and drained
1 cup salsa
10 flour tortillas (8 in.), warmed
    Optional: Avocado slices, lime
    wedges, vegan sour cream and salsa

**1.** In a small saucepan, bring water to a boil. Add rice. Return to a boil. Reduce heat; cover and simmer 5 minutes. Remove from heat. Let stand until water is absorbed, about 5 minutes.

**2.** Meanwhile, in a large skillet, heat oil over medium-high heat. Add green pepper and onion; cook and stir 3-4 minutes or until tender. Add garlic; cook 1 minute longer. Stir in chili powder, cumin and pepper flakes until combined. Add beans and rice; cook and stir 4-6 minutes or until heated through. Stir in the salsa and remove from heat.

**3.** Spoon about ½ cup of filling off-center on each tortilla. Fold sides and ends over filling and roll up. Serve with optional toppings as desired.

**1 burrito:** 345 cal., 7g fat (1g sat. fat), 0 chol., 544mg sod., 61g carb. (2g sugars, 6g fiber), 10g pro.

# SHRIMP EGG FOO YOUNG

If you love Chinese food as much as I do, you'll appreciate this shrimp egg foo young that features all the flavor without all the fat and calories. The secret lies in using just the egg white instead of the whole egg.
—*Quimberley Rice, Decatur, GA*

PREP: 25 MIN. • COOK: 5 MIN./BATCH • MAKES: 8 PATTIES (1 CUP SAUCE)

1 cup chicken broth
1 Tbsp. oyster sauce
1 Tbsp. reduced-sodium soy sauce
1 Tbsp. cornstarch
¼ cup cold water

**EGG FOO YOUNG**
8 oz. uncooked shrimp (31-40 per lb.),
    peeled, deveined and chopped
⅔ cup coarsely chopped
    fresh mushrooms
½ cup bean sprouts
1 green onion, sliced
3 Tbsp. canola oil, divided
8 large egg whites
1 Tbsp. reduced-sodium soy sauce
    Black and white sesame seeds

**1.** In a small saucepan, combine broth, oyster sauce and soy sauce. Bring to a boil. Combine cornstarch and water until smooth; gradually stir into the pan. Bring to a boil; cook and stir until thickened, about 2 minutes. Set aside and keep warm.

**2.** In a large skillet, saute shrimp, mushrooms, bean sprouts and green onion in 1 Tbsp. oil until shrimp turn pink and vegetables are crisp-tender, about 2 minutes. Remove from heat; cool slightly. In a large bowl, whisk egg whites and soy sauce. Stir in the cooked shrimp mixture.

**3.** In another large skillet, heat the remaining oil. Drop shrimp mixture in batches by ⅓ cupfuls into oil. Cook until golden brown, 2-3 minutes on each side. Serve with sauce. If desired, sprinkle with black and white sesame seeds and additional green onion.

**2 patties with ¼ cup sauce:** 115 cal., 7g fat (1g sat. fat), 40mg chol., 477mg sod., 3g carb. (1g sugars, 0 fiber), 10g pro.

# BURRATA RAVIOLI

Using burrata cheese as ravioli filling is very easy and really delivers on flavor.
Instead of mixing ingredients for the filling, this quicker version uses pieces of burrata
and fresh basil to create a luscious interior. Serve the ravioli with your favorite sauce.
—Taste of Home *Test Kitchen*

**PREP: 35 MIN. • COOK: 10 MIN. • MAKES: 4 SERVINGS**

2½ to 3 cups all-purpose flour
3 large eggs
¼ cup water
1½ tsp. olive oil

**SAUCE**
1½ tsp. olive oil
¼ cup finely chopped onion
1 garlic clove, minced
1 can (28 oz.) Italian crushed tomatoes
1½ tsp. Italian seasoning
2 to 3 tsp. sugar
¼ tsp. salt
¼ tsp. pepper

**FILLING**
8 oz. burrata cheese, cut into 30 quarter-sized pieces
¼ cup minced fresh basil

**1.** Place 2½ cups flour in a large bowl. Make a well in the center. Beat eggs, water and oil; pour into well. Stir together, forming a ball. Turn onto a floured surface; knead until smooth and elastic, 4-6 minutes, adding remaining flour if necessary to keep dough from sticking. Cover and let rest 30 minutes.

**2.** Meanwhile, in a small saucepan, heat oil over medium heat. Add onion; cook and stir until tender, 2-3 minutes. Add garlic; cook and stir 1 minute longer. Stir in remaining sauce ingredients. Bring to a boil. Reduce heat; cover and simmer until flavors are blended, about 30 minutes, stirring occasionally. Keep warm.

**3.** Divide pasta dough in half; on a lightly floured surface (or using a pasta roller), roll 1 portion to ¹⁄₁₆-in. thickness. (Keep pasta covered until ready to use.) Working quickly, arrange burrata pieces 1 in. apart over half of pasta sheet. Top each piece of burrata with a scant ½ tsp. basil. Fold sheet over; press down to seal. Cut into squares with a pastry wheel. Repeat with remaining dough and filling.

**4.** In a Dutch oven, bring salted water to a boil; add ravioli. Reduce heat to a gentle simmer; cook until ravioli float to the top and are tender, 1-2 minutes. Drain. Serve with sauce.

**8 ravioli with about ¾ cup sauce:** 607 cal., 20g fat (10g sat. fat), 180mg chol., 781mg sod., 75g carb. (11g sugars, 6g fiber), 26g pro.

## TEST KITCHEN TIP

*Don't have time for the homemade sauce? Any simple marinara sauce would work with Burrata Ravioli. You can also serve the pasta with a pesto, Alfredo or red clam sauce.*
—SAMMI DIVITO, *TASTE OF HOME* ASSOCIATE EDITOR

# THAI LIME SHRIMP & NOODLES

The flavors keep popping in this quick dinner! Use as much lime peel and chili paste as you like.
—*Teri Rasey, Cadillac, MI*

**TAKES: 25 MIN. • MAKES: 6 SERVINGS**

1 cup minced fresh basil
3 Tbsp. lime juice
4 tsp. Thai red chili paste
1 garlic clove, minced
1 tsp. minced fresh gingerroot
1½ lbs. uncooked shrimp (26-30 per lb.), peeled and deveined
12 oz. uncooked angel hair pasta
4 tsp. olive oil, divided
1 can (14½ oz.) chicken broth
1 can (13.66 oz.) coconut milk
1 tsp. salt
1 Tbsp. cornstarch
2 Tbsp. cold water
2 Tbsp. grated lime zest

1. Place the first 5 ingredients in a blender; cover and process until blended. Remove 1 Tbsp. mixture; toss with shrimp.

2. Cook pasta according to package directions. Meanwhile, in a large nonstick skillet, heat 2 tsp. oil over medium-high heat. Add half of the shrimp mixture; stir-fry 2-4 minutes or until shrimp turn pink. Remove from pan; keep warm. Repeat with remaining oil and shrimp mixture.

3. Add broth, coconut milk, salt and remaining basil mixture to the same pan. In a small bowl, mix cornstarch and water until smooth. Stir into broth mixture. Bring to a boil; cook and stir 1-2 minutes or until slightly thickened. Stir in lime zest.

4. Drain pasta; add pasta and shrimp to sauce, tossing to coat.

**1 serving:** 462 cal., 17g fat (11g sat. fat), 141mg chol., 874mg sod., 48g carb. (4g sugars, 2g fiber), 28g pro.

# VEG JAMBALAYA

This flavorful entree won't leave you hungry since it uses convenient canned beans in place of meat.
—*Crystal Jo Bruns, Iliff, CO*

**PREP: 10 MIN. • COOK: 30 MIN. • MAKES: 6 SERVINGS**

1 Tbsp. canola oil
1 medium green pepper, chopped
1 medium onion, chopped
1 celery rib, chopped
3 garlic cloves, minced
2 cups water
1 can (14½ oz.) diced tomatoes, undrained
1 can (8 oz.) tomato sauce
½ tsp. Italian seasoning
¼ tsp. salt
¼ tsp. crushed red pepper flakes
⅛ tsp. fennel seed, crushed
1 cup uncooked long grain rice
1 can (16 oz.) butter beans, drained
1 can (16 oz.) red beans, drained

1. In a Dutch oven, heat oil over medium heat. Add green pepper, onion and celery; cook and stir until tender. Add garlic; cook for 1 minute longer.

2. Add water, diced tomatoes, tomato sauce, Italian seasoning, salt, red pepper flakes and fennel. Bring to a boil; stir in rice. Reduce heat; cover and simmer 15-18 minutes or until liquid is absorbed and rice is tender. Stir in butter beans and red beans; heat through.

**1⅓ cups:** 281 cal., 3g fat (0 sat. fat), 0 chol., 796mg sod., 56g carb. (6g sugars, 9g fiber), 11g pro.

# OVER-THE-TOP BAKED ZITI

I adapted a ziti recipe to remove ingredients my kids did not like, such as ground beef. The revised recipe was a success not only with my family but at potlucks too. It's so versatile: You can use jarred sauce, double or triple the recipe, and even freeze it.
—*Kimberley Pitman, Smyrna, DE*

**PREP:** 20 MIN. • **COOK:** 4 HOURS 20 MIN. • **MAKES:** 8 SERVINGS

2 cans (29 oz. each) tomato puree
1 can (12 oz.) tomato paste
1 medium onion, chopped
¼ cup minced fresh parsley
2 Tbsp. dried oregano
4 tsp. sugar
3 garlic cloves, minced
1 Tbsp. dried basil
1 tsp. salt
½ tsp. pepper

**ZITI**
1 pkg. (16 oz.) ziti
1 large egg, beaten
1 carton (15 oz.) reduced-fat ricotta cheese
2 cups shredded part-skim mozzarella cheese, divided
¾ cup grated Parmesan cheese
¼ cup minced fresh parsley
½ tsp. salt
¼ tsp. pepper
Additional minced fresh parsley, optional

**1.** In a 3-qt. or 4-qt. slow cooker, combine the first 10 ingredients. Cover and cook on low for 4 hours.

**2.** Cook ziti according to the package directions. In a large bowl, combine egg, ricotta cheese, 1 cup mozzarella, Parmesan cheese, parsley, salt, pepper and 5 cups slow-cooked sauce. Drain ziti; stir into sauce mixture.

**3.** Transfer to a 13x9-in. baking dish coated with cooking spray. Pour remaining sauce over top; sprinkle with remaining mozzarella cheese. Bake at 350° until bubbly, 20-25 minutes. If desired, garnish with additional parsley.

**1 serving:** 499 cal., 10g fat (6g sat. fat), 62mg chol., 826mg sod., 72g carb. (16g sugars, 6g fiber), 29g pro.

## TEST KITCHEN TIP

*Keep this recipe's slow-cooked tomato sauce in mind the next time you want to include a little homemade flair in any pasta meal without much work on your part.*

# VEGETABLE TOFU POTPIE

I wanted to give my vegetarian daughters more options than just pizza and pasta. This recipe is still a hit.
—Mark Sirota, New York, NY

**PREP: 25 MIN. • COOK: 45 MIN. + STANDING • MAKES: 6 SERVINGS**

1½ cups frozen mixed vegetables
   (about 8 oz.)
1  large potato, peeled , chopped
2  cups chopped cauliflower
2  Tbsp. water
8  oz. extra-firm tofu
3  Tbsp. cornstarch
½  tsp. onion salt
2  Tbsp. canola oil
2  large eggs, lightly beaten
1  can (10½ oz.) condensed cream
   of potato soup, undiluted
½  cup 2% milk
½  tsp. dried thyme
¼  tsp. pepper
¼  tsp. salt
   Dough for double-crust pie (9 in.)

1. Preheat oven to 375°. In a large microwave-safe bowl, combine frozen mixed vegetables, potato, cauliflower and water. Cover and microwave on high 8-10 minutes or until potato is almost tender; drain.

2. Cut tofu into ½-in. cubes; pat dry with paper towels. In a large bowl, combine cornstarch and onion salt. Add tofu and toss to coat. In a large skillet, heat oil over medium-high heat. Add tofu; cook until crisp and golden brown, 5-7 minutes, stirring occasionally. Remove from pan; drain on paper towels.

3. In another large bowl, whisk eggs, soup, milk, thyme, pepper and salt until combined. Stir in the vegetable mixture and tofu. On a lightly floured surface, roll half the dough to a ⅛-in.-thick circle; transfer to a 9-in. pie plate. Trim even with rim. Add filling. Roll remaining dough to a ⅛-in.-thick circle. Place over filling. Trim, seal and flute edge. Cut slits in top.

4. Bake on a lower oven rack until crust is golden brown and filling is bubbly, 45-50 minutes. Let stand 15 minutes before cutting.

**Dough for double-crust pie:** Combine 2½ cups flour and ½ tsp. salt; cut in 1 cup cold butter until crumbly. Gradually add ⅓-⅔ cup ice water, tossing with a fork until dough holds together. Divide dough in half. Shape each into a disk; wrap and refrigerate 1 hour.

**1 piece:** 679 cal., 40g fat (21g sat. fat), 146mg chol., 973mg sod., 65g carb. (5g sugars, 6g fiber), 15g pro.

# MODERN TUNA CASSEROLE

Tuna casserole was my favorite as a kid, and I found myself craving it as an adult.
I reconfigured the recipe to include more vegetables, and the result is perfection.
—*Rebecca Blanton, St. Helena, CA*

PREP: 20 MIN. • COOK: 20 MIN. • MAKES: 6 SERVINGS

3 Tbsp. butter, divided
4 medium carrots, chopped
1 medium onion, chopped
1 medium sweet red pepper, chopped
1 cup sliced portobello mushrooms
2 cans (5 oz. each) albacore white tuna in water, drained and flaked
2 cups fresh baby spinach
1 cup frozen peas
3 cups uncooked spiral pasta
1 Tbsp. all-purpose flour
⅔ cup reduced-sodium chicken broth
⅓ cup half-and-half cream
½ cup shredded Parmesan cheese
¾ tsp. salt
¼ tsp. pepper

**1.** In a large skillet, heat 1 Tbsp. butter over medium-high heat. Add carrots, onion, red pepper and mushrooms. Cook and stir until tender, 8-10 minutes. Add tuna, spinach and peas; cook until spinach is just wilted, 2-3 minutes.

**2.** Meanwhile, cook pasta according to package directions for al dente. Drain pasta, reserving 1 cup pasta water. Place pasta and tuna mixture in a large bowl; toss to combine. Wipe skillet clean.

**3.** In the same skillet, melt remaining butter over medium heat. Stir in flour until smooth; gradually whisk in broth and cream. Bring to a boil, stirring constantly; cook and stir until thickened, 1-2 minutes, adding reserved pasta water if needed. Stir in Parmesan cheese, salt and pepper. Pour over pasta; toss to coat.

**1¾ cups:** 372 cal., 11g fat (6g sat. fat), 47mg chol., 767mg sod., 44g carb. (7g sugars, 5g fiber), 23g pro. **Diabetic exchanges:** 3 lean meat, 2½ starch, 1½ fat, 1 vegetable.

---

# BAKED HALIBUT

I got this easy, protein-rich recipe from the Puffin Bed & Breakfast located in Gustavus, Alaska.
—*Edward Mahnke, Houston, TX*

PREP: 5 MIN. • BAKE: 30 MIN. • MAKES: 6 SERVINGS

3 lbs. halibut steaks (1 in. thick)
1 cup sour cream
½ cup grated Parmesan cheese
¼ cup butter, softened
½ tsp. dill weed
½ tsp. salt
¼ tsp. pepper
  Paprika

**1.** Preheat the oven to 375°. Place halibut steaks in a greased 13x9-in. baking dish. Combine sour cream, Parmesan cheese, butter, dill, salt and pepper; spoon over halibut.

**2.** Cover and bake for 20 minutes. Uncover; sprinkle with paprika. Bake until fish just begins to flake easily with a fork, 10-15 minutes.

**6 oz. cooked fish:** 378 cal., 20g fat (11g sat. fat), 146mg chol., 545mg sod., 2g carb. (1g sugars, 0 fiber), 45g pro.

# SEARED SCALLOPS WITH POLENTA & AVOCADO CREAM

This is a really impressive dish. It's beautiful but simple and a wonderful dinner party entree. If you can find them, Peppadew peppers add a bit of zing, but if you can't, roasted red peppers work just fine.
—*Katie Pelczar, West Hartford, CT*

PREP: 30 MIN. • COOK: 35 MIN. • MAKES: 4 SERVINGS

1   small onion, chopped
3   Tbsp. butter, divided
½   cup fresh corn or
    frozen corn, thawed
¼   cup roasted sweet red peppers,
    drained and chopped
4   cups reduced-sodium chicken broth
¾   tsp. salt, divided
1   cup yellow cornmeal
½   cup grated Parmesan cheese
1   medium ripe avocado,
    peeled and chopped
¼   to ½ cup water
2   Tbsp. heavy whipping cream
8   sea scallops (about 1 lb.)
½   tsp. pepper

1. In a large skillet, saute onion in half the butter until tender, 5-7 minutes. Add corn and peppers; cook 4-5 minutes longer. Stir in broth and ¼ tsp. salt; bring to a boil. Reduce heat to a gentle boil; slowly whisk in cornmeal. Cook and stir with a wooden spoon until polenta is thickened and pulls away from the sides of the pan, 15-20 minutes. Stir in cheese. Remove from heat; set aside and keep warm.

2. Meanwhile, in a blender, combine avocado, ¼ cup water, cream and ¼ tsp. salt. Blend until smooth, about 30 seconds. Add additional water as needed to reach the desired consistency. Cover and refrigerate until serving.

3. Sprinkle scallops with remaining salt and pepper. In a large skillet, saute the scallops in remaining butter until firm and opaque, 1-2 minutes per side. Serve with polenta and avocado cream.

**2 scallops with 1 cup polenta and 2 Tbsp. avocado cream:** 467 cal., 21g fat (10g sat. fat), 67mg chol., 1773mg sod., 46g carb. (4g sugars, 5g fiber), 24g pro.

# SPINACH & CHEESE LASAGNA ROLLS

These Italian-inspired roll-ups are fast and fun to make. They may look elegant but are also very kid-friendly.
—*Cindy Romberg, Mississauga, ON*

PREP: 25 MIN. + CHILLING • BAKE: 35 MIN. • MAKES: 6 SERVINGS

1   pkg. (10 oz.) frozen chopped spinach,
    thawed and squeezed dry
1   cup shredded part-skim
    mozzarella cheese
1   cup 2% cottage cheese
¾   cup grated Parmesan cheese,
    divided
1   large egg, lightly beaten
6   lasagna noodles,
    cooked and drained
1   jar (24 oz.) marinara sauce

1. In a bowl, combine thawed spinach, mozzarella, cottage cheese, ½ cup Parmesan cheese and egg. Spread ⅓ cupful over each noodle. Roll up; place seam side down in a 9-in. square baking dish coated with cooking spray. Cover and refrigerate overnight.

2. Remove from the refrigerator 30 minutes before baking. Pour marinara sauce over the top.

3. Cover and bake at 350° for 33-38 minutes. Sprinkle with remaining cheese.

**1 lasagna roll:** 301 cal., 11g fat (5g sat. fat), 56mg chol., 963mg sod., 33g carb. (9g sugars, 4g fiber), 18g pro.

# GREEK SHRIMP ORZO

This is one of our go-to meals. It's finger-licking good and so satisfying, and it reheats well. My husband would rather have the shrimp orzo than go out to eat. Serve it with crusty bread and a green salad.
—Molly Seidel, Edgewood, NM

**PREP: 45 MIN. • COOK: 2 HOURS • MAKES: 6 SERVINGS**

- 2 cups uncooked orzo pasta
- 2 Tbsp. minced fresh basil
- 3 Tbsp. olive oil, divided
- 1½ Tbsp. chopped shallot
- 2 Tbsp. butter
- 1 can (14½ oz.) diced tomatoes, drained
- 2 Tbsp. minced fresh oregano
- 3 garlic cloves, minced
- 1 lb. uncooked shrimp (26-30 per lb.), peeled and deveined
- 1 cup oil-packed sun-dried tomatoes, chopped
- 2½ cups (10 oz.) crumbled feta cheese
- 1½ cups pitted Greek olives

**1.** Cook orzo according to package directions; rinse in cold water and drain. Transfer to a large bowl. Add basil and 1 Tbsp. oil; toss to coat and set aside.

**2.** In a large skillet, saute shallot in butter and remaining oil until tender. Add diced tomatoes, oregano and garlic; cook and stir 1-2 minutes. Add shrimp and sun-dried tomatoes; cook and stir until shrimp turn pink, 2-3 minutes.

**3.** Transfer to a greased 5-qt. slow cooker. Stir in the orzo mixture, feta cheese and olives. Cover and cook on low 2-3 hours or until heated through.

**Note:** Also known as kalamata olives, Greek olives are almond-shaped and range in size from ½ to 1 in. long. Dark eggplant in color, the kalamata olive is rich and fruity in flavor and can be found packed in either a vinegar brine or olive oil.

**1½ cups:** 673 cal., 32g fat (10g sat. fat), 127mg chol., 1262mg sod., 63g carb. (5g sugars, 6g fiber), 31g pro.

---

# SICILIAN PIZZA (SFINCIONE)

My favorite pizza from childhood is still my favorite today. The crunchy bread-crumb topping sets it apart from its American counterpart. I like to top this pie with fresh basil.
—Susan Falk, Sterling Heights, MI

**PREP: 20 MIN. • BAKE: 20 MIN. • MAKES: 12 SERVINGS**

- 2 loaves (1 lb. each) fresh or frozen pizza dough, thawed
- 3 Tbsp. olive oil, divided
- 1 can (28 oz.) whole tomatoes, drained and crushed
- 1 medium onion, finely chopped
- 1 can (2 oz.) anchovy fillets, drained and broken into ¼-in. pieces
- 1 cup shredded mozzarella cheese
- ½ cup soft bread crumbs
- Fresh torn basil leaves

**1.** Preheat oven to 425°. Grease a 15x10x1-in. baking pan. Press dough to fit the bottom and ½ in. up the sides of pan. Brush with 2 Tbsp. oil; top with tomatoes, onion and anchovies. Sprinkle with mozzarella. Combine the bread crumbs and remaining 1 Tbsp. oil; sprinkle over pizza.

**2.** Bake on a lower oven rack until edges are golden brown and cheese is melted, 20-25 minutes. Sprinkle with basil before serving.

**1 piece:** 277 cal., 9g fat (2g sat. fat), 11mg chol., 527mg sod., 38g carb. (4g sugars, 3g fiber), 11g pro.

> **Super easy, quick and yummy. This one is a keeper.**
> —KATIE156
> TASTEOFHOME.COM

# VEGETARIAN SKILLET ENCHILADAS

Whether served for meatless Monday or your family's everyday vegetarian meal, these unconventional enchiladas will leave everyone asking for more.
—*Susan Court, Pewaukee, WI*

TAKES: 25 MIN. • MAKES: 4 SERVINGS

1 Tbsp. canola oil
1 medium onion, chopped
1 medium sweet red pepper, chopped
2 garlic cloves, minced
1 can (15 oz.) black beans,
   rinsed and drained
1 can (10 oz.) enchilada sauce
1 cup frozen corn
2 tsp. chili powder
½ tsp. ground cumin
⅛ tsp. pepper
8 corn tortillas, cut into ½-in. strips
1 cup shredded Mexican cheese blend
   Optional: Chopped fresh cilantro,
   sliced avocado, sliced radishes,
   sour cream and lime wedges

1. Preheat oven to 400°. Heat oil in a 10-in. cast-iron or other ovenproof skillet over medium-high heat. Add onion and pepper; cook and stir until tender, 2-3 minutes. Add garlic; cook 1 minute longer. Stir in beans, enchilada sauce, corn, chili powder, cumin and pepper. Stir in tortilla strips.

2. Bring to a boil. Reduce the heat; simmer, uncovered, until tortilla strips are softened, 3-5 minutes. Sprinkle with cheese. Bake, uncovered, until sauce is bubbly and cheese is melted, 3-5 minutes. Garnish with optional ingredients.

**1½ cups:** 307 cal., 14g fat (5g sat. fat), 25mg chol., 839mg sod., 33g carb. (5g sugars, 7g fiber), 14g pro.

## TEST KITCHEN TIP

*Leftovers of this vegetarian entree last about 2-3 days in the fridge or you can freeze them in an airtight container for up to 3 months.*

# GARLIC TILAPIA WITH MUSHROOM RISOTTO

Boxed risotto makes it quick; mushrooms, shallots and cheese make it tasty.
—*Lynn Moretti, Oconomowoc, WI*

TAKES: 30 MIN. • MAKES: 4 SERVINGS

1 pkg. (5½ oz.) Parmesan risotto mix
1 cup sliced fresh mushrooms
¼ cup chopped shallots
1½ lbs. tilapia fillets
1½ tsp. seafood seasoning
4 Tbsp. butter, divided
3 garlic cloves, sliced
¼ cup grated Parmesan cheese

1. Cook risotto according to package directions, adding mushrooms and shallots with water.

2. Sprinkle tilapia fillets with seafood seasoning. In a skillet, heat 2 Tbsp. butter over medium heat. Cook tilapia with garlic until fish begins to flake easily, about 5 minutes, turning fillets halfway through cooking.

3. Stir Parmesan cheese and remaining butter into risotto; remove from the heat. Serve with tilapia.

**1 serving:** 432 cal., 18g fat (10g sat. fat), 118mg chol., 964mg sod., 32g carb. (3g sugars, 1g fiber), 39g pro.

# SAMOSA POTPIE

The go-to appetizer at any Indian restaurant, samosas are reimagined as a delicious main-dish potpie. The heavily spiced potato and pea filling is surrounded by a flaky homemade crust. Serve with green or tamarind chutney.

—*Shri Repp, Seattle, WA*

**PREP:** 40 MIN. + CHILLING • **BAKE:** 40 MIN. + COOLING • **MAKES:** 8 SERVINGS

2½ cups all-purpose flour
1 tsp. salt
1 tsp. dried ajwain seeds or dried thyme
1 cup cold unsalted butter
6 to 8 Tbsp. ice water

**FILLING**
4 cups cubed peeled potatoes
½ cup frozen peas, thawed
1 Tbsp. lemon juice
1 Tbsp. chat masala seasoning
1 tsp. ground cumin
1 tsp. ground coriander
½ tsp. chili powder
¼ tsp. ground turmeric
½ tsp. salt
1 to 2 red chili peppers, minced, optional
Green or tamarind chutney, optional

**1.** In a large bowl, mix flour, salt and ajwain seeds; cut in butter until crumbly. Gradually add ice water, tossing with a fork until dough holds together when pressed. Divide dough in half. Shape each into a disk; wrap and refrigerate 1 hour or overnight.

**2.** Preheat oven to 375°. For filling, place potatoes in a large saucepan; add water to cover. Bring to a boil. Reduce heat; cook, uncovered, until tender, 15-20 minutes. Drain; return to pan. Mash potatoes gently, leaving some chunks. Stir in peas, lemon juice, seasonings and, if desired, chili peppers.

**3.** On a lightly floured surface, roll half of dough to a ⅛-in.-thick circle; transfer to a 9-in. pie plate greased well with butter. Trim even with rim. Add filling. Roll remaining dough to a ⅛-in.-thick circle. Place over filling. Trim, seal and flute edge. Cut slits in top.

**4.** Bake until crust is golden brown, 40-45 minutes. Cool for 10 minutes before cutting. If desired, serve with chutney.

**1 piece:** 430 cal., 24g fat (14g sat. fat), 61mg chol., 715mg sod., 48g carb. (1g sugars, 3g fiber), 6g pro.

# BISTRO MAC & CHEESE

I like mac and cheese with a salad and crusty bread. It's a satisfying meal that feels upscale but will fit just about any budget. And because the Gorgonzola is so mild in this dish, even the kiddos will go for it.

—*Charlotte Giltner, Mesa, AZ*

**TAKES: 25 MIN. • MAKES: 8 SERVINGS**

- 1 pkg. (16 oz.) uncooked elbow macaroni
- 5 Tbsp. butter, divided
- 3 Tbsp. all-purpose flour
- 2½ cups 2% milk
- 1 tsp. salt
- ½ tsp. onion powder
- ½ tsp. pepper
- ¼ tsp. garlic powder
- 1 cup shredded part-skim mozzarella cheese
- 1 cup shredded cheddar cheese
- ½ cup crumbled Gorgonzola cheese
- 3 oz. cream cheese, softened
- ½ cup sour cream
- ½ cup seasoned panko bread crumbs
  Minced fresh parsley, optional

1. Cook macaroni according to package directions; drain. Meanwhile, in a Dutch oven, melt 3 Tbsp. butter over low heat. Stir in the flour until smooth; gradually whisk in milk and seasonings. Bring to a boil, stirring constantly; cook and stir 2 minutes or until thickened.

2. Reduce heat; stir in cheeses until melted. Stir in sour cream. Add the macaroni; toss to coat. In a small skillet, heat remaining butter over medium heat. Add bread crumbs; cook and stir until golden brown. Sprinkle over top. If desired, sprinkle with parsley.

**1 cup:** 468 cal., 22g fat (14g sat. fat), 68mg chol., 649mg sod., 49g carb. (7g sugars, 2g fiber), 20g pro.

**Baked Bistro Mac:** Place prepared macaroni in a greased 3-qt. baking dish. Combine ⅓ cup seasoned bread crumbs and 2 Tbsp. melted butter; sprinkle over macaroni. Bake, uncovered, at 350° for 20-25 minutes or until bubbly.

## TEST KITCHEN TIP

*The combination of cheeses takes this recipe over the top, but feel free to substitute any cheeses you like. Just keep the total cup amount the same.*

CHOCOLATE OAT
SQUARES, PAGE 258

" 

My kids have loved this recipe since I first made it. They request that I make these bars every year at Christmas.

—ICROOMS
TASTEOFHOME.COM

# CHAPTER 9

# COOKIES, BROWNIES & BARS

When it comes to best-shared recipes, sweet treats are a staple. Here, home cooks share the finger-licking bites their families request most. From after-school snacks to late-night nibbles, these delights are sure to become new favorites in your kitchen too.

# BITE-SIZED CINNAMON ROLL COOKIES

If you love cinnamon rolls and spiced cookies as much as I do, make this bite-sized version that combines the best of both worlds.
—*Jasmine Sheth, New York, NY*

**PREP:** 1 HOUR + CHILLING • **BAKE:** 10 MIN./BATCH + COOLING • **MAKES:** 6 DOZEN

½ cup packed brown sugar
4 tsp. ground cinnamon
1¼ cups butter, softened
4 oz. cream cheese, softened
1½ cups sugar
2 large eggs, room temperature
2 tsp. vanilla extract
2 tsp. grated orange zest
4¼ cups all-purpose flour
1 tsp. baking powder
1 tsp. active dry yeast
½ tsp. salt

**GLAZE**
1 cup confectioners' sugar
2 Tbsp. 2% milk
1 tsp. vanilla extract

**1.** In a small bowl, mix brown sugar and cinnamon until blended. In a large bowl, cream butter, cream cheese and sugar until light and fluffy, 5-7 minutes. Beat in eggs, vanilla and orange zest. In another bowl, whisk flour, baking powder, yeast and salt; gradually beat into creamed mixture.

**2.** Divide dough into 4 portions; chill 30 minutes or until no longer sticky. On a lightly floured surface, roll each into an 8x6-in. rectangle; sprinkle with about 2 Tbsp. brown sugar mixture. Roll up tightly jelly-roll style, starting with a long side. Wrap in waxed paper; refrigerate 1 hour or until firm.

**3.** Preheat oven to 350°. Unwrap dough and cut crosswise into ⅜-in. slices. Place 1 in. apart on greased baking sheets. Bake 8-10 minutes or until bottoms are light brown. Remove from pans to wire racks to cool completely.

**4.** In a small bowl, whisk glaze ingredients. Dip tops of cookies in glaze. Let stand until set. Store in an airtight container.

**1 cookie:** 92 cal., 4g fat (2g sat. fat), 16mg chol., 52mg sod., 13g carb. (7g sugars, 0 fiber), 1g pro.

## TEST KITCHEN TIP

*You can make these adorable cookies ahead of time. In fact, they make wonderful freezer or icebox cookies. Keep wrapped (unsliced) cookie dough logs in your freezer until you're ready to bake. It's a good idea to wrap an extra layer of foil around the dough to prevent freezer burn and freezer odors.*

—MARK NEUFANG, *TASTE OF HOME* CULINARY ASSISTANT

> **These were a fun cookie to make, and they turned out so well. Good flavor. Grandkids loved them.**
> —GRAMRENE
> TASTEOFHOME.COM

# CHOCOLATE HAZELNUT BROWNIES

Toasted nuts, Nutella and liqueur transform fudgy homemade brownies into a hazelnut-lover's dream. They're perfect for a casual dessert or as a yummy gift.
—*Genesis Navasca, Shoreline, WA*

PREP: 25 MIN. • BAKE: 30 MIN. + COOLING • MAKES: 16 BROWNIES

¾ cup butter, cubed
4 oz. unsweetened chocolate, coarsely chopped
3 large eggs, room temperature
2 cups sugar
⅓ cup Nutella
¼ cup hazelnut liqueur
1 cup all-purpose flour
¾ tsp. salt
1¼ cups coarsely chopped hazelnuts, toasted, divided

1. Preheat oven to 325°. In a microwave, melt butter and chocolate; stir until smooth. Cool slightly. In a large bowl, beat eggs and sugar. Stir in chocolate mixture, Nutella and liqueur. Combine flour and salt; gradually add to mixture. Fold in 1 cup nuts.

2. Transfer to a greased 9-in. square baking pan. Sprinkle with the remaining nuts. Bake until a toothpick inserted in the center comes out with moist crumbs (do not overbake), 30-40 minutes. Cool on a wire rack. Cut into bars.

**1 brownie:** 371 cal., 23g fat (9g sat. fat), 62mg chol., 189mg sod., 40g carb. (30g sugars, 3g fiber), 5g pro.

---

# WHITE CHOCOLATE PUMPKIN DREAMS

If you like pumpkin pie, you'll love these delicious pumpkin cookies dotted with white chocolate chips and chopped pecans. Drizzled with a brown sugar icing, they're irresistible.
—*Jean Kleckner, Seattle, WA*

PREP: 25 MIN. • BAKE: 15 MIN./BATCH + COOLING • MAKES: 6½ DOZEN

1 cup butter, softened
½ cup sugar
½ cup packed brown sugar
1 large egg, room temperature
2 tsp. vanilla extract
1 cup canned pumpkin
2 cups all-purpose flour
3½ tsp. pumpkin pie spice
1 tsp. baking powder
1 tsp. baking soda
¼ tsp. salt
1 pkg. (10 to 12 oz.) white baking chips
1 cup chopped pecans

**PENUCHE FROSTING**
½ cup packed brown sugar
3 Tbsp. butter
¼ cup 2% milk
1½ to 2 cups confectioners' sugar

1. Preheat oven to 350°. In a large bowl, cream butter and sugars until light and fluffy, 5-7 minutes. Beat in egg, vanilla and pumpkin. Combine the dry ingredients; gradually add to the creamed mixture and mix well. Stir in chips and pecans.

2. Drop by tablespoonfuls 2 in. apart onto ungreased baking sheets. Bake until firm, 12-14 minutes. Remove to wire racks to cool.

3. For frosting, combine brown sugar and butter in a small saucepan. Bring to a boil; cook over medium heat until slightly thickened, about 1 minute. Cool for 10 minutes. Add milk; beat until smooth. Beat in enough confectioners' sugar to reach desired consistency. Spread over cooled cookies.

**1 cookie:** 93 cal., 5g fat (3g sat. fat), 11mg chol., 58mg sod., 12g carb. (9g sugars, 0 fiber), 1g pro.

# GRANDMA'S SCOTTISH SHORTBREAD

My Scottish grandmother was renowned for baked goods, and these chunky shortbread bars are an example of why.
—*Jane Kelly, Wayland, MA*

**PREP: 15 MIN. • BAKE: 45 MIN. + COOLING • MAKES: 4 DOZEN**

1 lb. butter, softened
8 oz. superfine sugar (about 1¼ cups)
1 lb. all-purpose flour (3⅔ cups)
8 oz. white rice flour (1⅓ cups)

1. Preheat the oven to 300°. Cream butter and sugar until light and fluffy, 5-7 minutes. Combine flours; gradually beat into creamed mixture. Press dough into an ungreased 13x9-in. baking pan. Prick with a fork.

2. Bake until light brown, 45-50 minutes. Cut into 48 bars or triangles while warm. Cool completely on a wire rack.

**1 bar:** 139 cal., 8g fat (5g sat. fat), 20mg chol., 61mg sod., 16g carb. (5g sugars, 0 fiber), 1g pro.

---

# CHOCOLATE-MINT CREME COOKIES

A minty filling sandwiched between rich chocolate cookies—what's not to love?
—*Gaylene Anderson, Sandy, UT*

**PREP: 20 MIN. • BAKE: 10 MIN. + COOLING • MAKES: 4 DOZEN**

1½ cups packed brown sugar
¾ cup butter, cubed
2 Tbsp. water
2 cups semisweet chocolate chips
2 large eggs, room temperature
3 cups all-purpose flour
1¼ tsp. baking soda
1 tsp. salt

**FILLING**
⅓ cup butter, softened
3 cups confectioners' sugar
3 to 4 Tbsp. 2% milk
⅛ tsp. peppermint extract
Dash salt

1. In a small saucepan, combine brown sugar, butter and water. Cook and stir over medium heat until sugar is dissolved. Remove from heat; stir in chocolate chips until melted and smooth. Transfer to a large bowl; cool slightly.

2. Add eggs, 1 at a time, beating well after each addition. Combine flour, baking soda and salt; gradually add to chocolate mixture and mix well.

3. Drop by rounded teaspoonfuls onto greased baking sheets. Bake at 350° until set, 8-10 minutes. Remove to wire racks; flatten slightly. Cool completely.

4. Combine the filling ingredients; spread on the bottoms of half of the cookies. Top with remaining cookies. Store in the refrigerator.

**1 serving:** 157 cal., 7g fat (4g sat. fat), 20mg chol., 134mg sod., 25g carb. (18g sugars, 1g fiber), 1g pro.

> Delicious! The
> first biscotti
> recipe I made.
> Worked great,
> tasted great
> and looked
> great. What
> more could you
> ask for?
> —LAUREN BEDFORD
> TASTEOFHOME.COM

# CRANBERRY WALNUT BISCOTTI

A chocolate drizzle lends extra sweetness to biscotti loaded with walnuts and dried cranberries.
—*Joan Duckworth, Lee's Summit, MO*

PREP: 25 MIN. • BAKE: 30 MIN. + COOLING • MAKES: ABOUT 1½ DOZEN

2 cups all-purpose flour
¾ cup sugar
1 tsp. baking powder
⅛ tsp. salt
3 large eggs, room temperature
1½ tsp. vanilla extract
1 cup chopped walnuts, toasted
1 cup dried cranberries, chopped
½ cup milk chocolate chips
1 tsp. shortening

1. Preheat oven to 350°. In a large bowl, combine flour, sugar, baking powder and salt. In a small bowl, whisk eggs and vanilla; add to the dry ingredients just until moistened. Fold in walnuts and cranberries (dough will be sticky).

2. Divide dough in half. On a greased baking sheet, with floured hands, shape each half into a 10x2½-in. rectangle. Bake 20-25 minutes or until golden brown.

3. Carefully remove to wire racks; cool 10 minutes. Transfer to a cutting board; cut diagonally with a serrated knife into 1-in. slices. Place cut side down on ungreased baking sheets. Bake 8-10 minutes on each side or until lightly browned. Remove to wire racks to cool completely.

4. In a microwave, melt chocolate chips and shortening; stir until smooth. Drizzle over biscotti. Let stand until set. Store in an airtight container.

**1 cookie:** 166 cal., 6g fat (1g sat. fat), 33mg chol., 49mg sod., 25g carb. (14g sugars, 1g fiber), 4g pro.

# CHOCOLATE MACADAMIA MACAROONS

This perfect macaroon has dark chocolate, chewy coconut and macadamia nuts, and is dipped in chocolate—sinful and delicious!
—*Darlene Brenden, Salem, OR*

PREP: 20 MIN. • BAKE: 15 MIN. + COOLING • MAKES: 1½ DOZEN

2 cups sweetened shredded coconut
½ cup finely chopped macadamia nuts
⅓ cup sugar
3 Tbsp. baking cocoa
2 Tbsp. all-purpose flour
Pinch salt
2 large egg whites, room temperature, lightly beaten
1 Tbsp. light corn syrup
1 tsp. vanilla extract
4 oz. semisweet chocolate, melted

1. Preheat the oven to 325°. In a large bowl, mix the first 6 ingredients. Stir in egg whites, corn syrup and vanilla until blended.

2. Drop by tablespoonfuls 2 in. apart onto greased baking sheets. Bake until set and dry to the touch, 15-20 minutes. Cool on pans 5 minutes. Remove to wire racks to cool completely.

3. Dip half of each cookie into melted chocolate, allowing excess to drip off. Place on waxed paper; let stand until set.

**1 cookie:** 136 cal., 9g fat (5g sat. fat), 0 chol., 52mg sod., 15g carb. (11g sugars, 1g fiber), 2g pro.

# CHRISTMAS COOKIES IN A JAR

With layers of vanilla chips, oats and dried cranberries, this delectable cookie mix looks as good as it tastes! For a special gift, tuck a jar in a pretty basket with wooden spoon, cookie sheet and instructions.
—*Lori Daniels, Beverly, WV*

PREP: 15 MIN. + CHILLING • BAKE: 10 MIN. • MAKES: 3 DOZEN

⅓ cup sugar
⅓ cup packed brown sugar
¾ cup all-purpose flour
½ tsp. baking powder
⅛ tsp. baking soda
⅛ tsp. salt
1 cup quick-cooking oats
1 cup dried cranberries
1 cup vanilla or white chips

**ADDITIONAL INGREDIENTS**
½ cup butter, melted
1 large egg, room temperature
1 tsp. vanilla extract

1. In a 1-qt. glass jar, layer sugar and brown sugar, packing well between each layer. Combine flour, baking powder, baking soda and salt; spoon into jar. Top with oats, cranberries and chips. Cover and store in a cool, dry place.

2. To prepare cookies, preheat oven to 375°. Pour cookie mix into a large bowl; stir to combine. Beat in butter, egg and vanilla. Cover and refrigerate 30 minutes.

3. Drop by tablespoonfuls 2 in. apart onto ungreased baking sheets. Bake until browned, 8-10 minutes. Remove to wire racks to cool.

**1 cookie:** 97 cal., 4g fat (3g sat. fat), 13mg chol., 47mg sod., 14g carb. (10g sugars, 1g fiber), 1g pro.

## TEST KITCHEN TIP

*The dry ingredients for these cookies will last up to 6 months when tightly sealed and stored properly in a cool, dry place.*

# PEANUT BUTTER CAKE BARS

These cakelike bars are packed with peanut butter and chocolate chips, and they're perfect for any occasion.
—*Charlotte Ennis, Lake Arthur, NM*

PREP: 15 MIN. • BAKE: 45 MIN. + COOLING • MAKES: 2 DOZEN

⅔ cup butter, softened
⅔ cup peanut butter
1 cup sugar
1 cup packed brown sugar
4 large eggs, room temperature
2 tsp. vanilla extract
2 cups all-purpose flour
2 tsp. baking powder
½ tsp. salt
1 pkg. (11½ oz.) milk chocolate chips

1. Preheat oven to 350°. In a large bowl, cream first 4 ingredients until light and fluffy, 5-7 minutes. Add eggs, 1 at a time, beating well after each addition. Beat in vanilla. Combine flour, baking powder and salt; gradually add to the creamed mixture. Stir in chocolate chips.

2. Spread onto a greased 13x9-in. baking pan. Bake until a toothpick inserted in the center comes out clean, 45-50 minutes. Cool on a wire rack. Cut into bars.

**1 bar:** 277 cal., 14g fat (6g sat. fat), 52mg chol., 178mg sod., 35g carb. (25g sugars, 1g fiber), 5g pro.

# CHERRY ALMOND SNOWDROPS

As soon as I was old enough, I helped make these distinctive almond cookies.
You can freeze the dough, so they're perfect for the busy holidays.
—*Trisha Kruse, Eagle, ID*

PREP: 25 MIN. • BAKE: 10 MIN./BATCH • MAKES: ABOUT 3 DOZEN

2 cups plus 2 Tbsp. cake flour
¾ cup plus ½ cup confectioners' sugar, divided
¼ tsp. salt
1 cup cold butter, cubed
2 tsp. vanilla extract
½ tsp. almond extract
½ cup dried cherries, chopped
¼ cup finely chopped almonds, toasted

1. Preheat the oven to 350°. Place cake flour, ¾ cup confectioner's sugar and salt in a food processor; pulse until blended. Add the butter and extracts; pulse until butter is the size of peas. Add cherries and almonds; pulse until combined (dough will be crumbly).

2. Shape dough into 1-in. balls, pressing firmly to adhere; place 1 in. apart on ungreased baking sheets. Bake 10-12 minutes or until lightly browned.

3. Cool on pans 10 minutes. Roll warm cookies in remaining confectioners' sugar. Cool on wire racks.

**Note:** To toast nuts, place in a dry skillet and heat over low heat until lightly browned, stirring occasionally.

**1 cookie:** 113 cal., 6g fat (4g sat. fat), 15mg chol., 59mg sod., 13g carb. (5g sugars, 0 fiber), 1g pro.

# PEPPERMINT PUFF PASTRY STICKS

I wanted to impress my husband's family with something you'd expect to find in a European bakery, and these chocolaty treats are what I came up with.
—*Darlene Brenden, Salem, OR*

PREP: 15 MIN. • BAKE: 15 MIN./BATCH + COOLING • MAKES: 3 DOZEN

1 sheet frozen puff pastry, thawed
1½ cups crushed peppermint candies
10 oz. milk chocolate candy coating, coarsely chopped

1. Preheat oven to 400°. Unfold pastry sheet. Cut in half to form 2 rectangles. Cut each rectangle crosswise into 18 strips, about ½ in. wide. Place on ungreased baking sheets. Bake until golden brown, 12-15 minutes. Remove pastry sticks from pans to wire racks to cool completely.

2. Place crushed candies in a shallow bowl. In a microwave, melt candy coating; stir until smooth. Dip each cookie halfway in coating; allow excess to drip off. Sprinkle with peppermint candies. Place on waxed paper; let stand until set. Store in an airtight container.

**1 cookie:** 89 cal., 4g fat (2g sat. fat), 0 chol., 24mg sod., 13g carb. (7g sugars, 1g fiber), 1g pro.

# COFFEE SHORTBREAD

When you need a treat for brunch, bake some of these coffee-flavored
shortbreads. The chocolate drizzle is surprisingly easy to do.

—*Dixie Terry, Goreville, IL*

PREP: 15 MIN. • BAKE: 20 MIN./BATCH + COOLING • MAKES: ABOUT 2½ DOZEN

1  cup butter, softened
½  cup packed brown sugar
¼  cup sugar
2  Tbsp. instant coffee granules
¼  tsp. salt
2  cups all-purpose flour
½  cup semisweet chocolate chips
2  tsp. shortening, divided
½  cup white baking chips

**1.** Preheat oven to 300°. In a large bowl, cream butter, sugars, coffee granules and salt until light and fluffy, 5-7 minutes; gradually beat flour into creamed mixture.

**2.** On a lightly floured surface, roll dough to ¼-in. thickness. Cut with floured 2-in. cookie cutters. Place 2 in. apart on ungreased baking sheets.

**3.** Bake 20-22 minutes or until set. Remove to wire racks to cool completely. In a microwave, melt chocolate chips and 1 tsp. shortening; stir until smooth. Repeat with baking chips and remaining shortening. Drizzle over cookies; refrigerate until set. Store between pieces of waxed paper in an airtight container.

**1 cookie:** 137 cal., 8g fat (5g sat. fat), 17mg chol., 73mg sod., 15g carb. (8g sugars, 0 fiber), 1g pro.

---

# CHERRY CHOCOLATE CHUNK COOKIES

These rich, fudgy cookies are chewy and studded with
tangy dried cherries. It's a good thing the recipe makes
only a small batch, because we eat them all in one night!

—*Trisha Kruse, Eagle, ID*

PREP: 15 MIN. • BAKE: 15 MIN./BATCH • MAKES: ABOUT 1½ DOZEN

½  cup butter, softened
¾  cup sugar
1  large egg, room temperature
2  Tbsp. 2% milk
½  tsp. vanilla extract
1  cup all-purpose flour
6  Tbsp. baking cocoa
¼  tsp. baking soda
¼  tsp. salt
1  cup semisweet chocolate chunks
½  cup dried cherries

**1.** Preheat the oven to 350°. Cream butter and sugar until light and fluffy, 5-7 minutes. Beat in egg, milk and vanilla. In a separate bowl, whisk flour, cocoa, baking soda and salt; gradually beat into creamed mixture. Stir in chocolate chunks and dried cherries.

**2.** Drop by rounded tablespoonfuls 2 in. apart onto baking sheets lightly coated with cooking spray. Bake until firm, 12-14 minutes. Cool for 1 minute before removing to a wire rack.

**1 cookie:** 159 cal., 8g fat (5g sat. fat), 22mg chol., 88mg sod., 22g carb. (15g sugars, 1g fiber), 2g pro.

# BLUE-RIBBON CARROT CAKE COOKIES

I created this recipe because I just love carrot cake. I entered my recipe in the Los Angeles County Fair, and the cookies not only won first place but were also named best of the division.
—Marina Castle-Kelley, Canyon Country, CA

**PREP: 50 MIN. • BAKE: 10 MIN./BATCH + COOLING • MAKES: 4 DOZEN**

1 cup butter, softened
1 cup packed brown sugar
¾ cup sugar
2 large eggs, room temperature
1½ tsp. vanilla extract
½ tsp. rum extract
3 cups all-purpose flour
½ cup old-fashioned oats
1½ tsp. ground cinnamon
¾ tsp. salt
¾ tsp. baking soda
½ tsp. ground ginger
½ tsp. ground nutmeg
1 cup chopped walnuts, toasted
¾ cup shredded carrots
¾ cup raisins

**FILLING**
1 pkg. (8 oz.) cream cheese, softened
½ cup butter, softened
1¼ cups confectioners' sugar
1 tsp. vanilla extract
½ cup chopped walnuts, toasted
2 Tbsp. crushed pineapple
Additional confectioners' sugar

1. Preheat the oven to 350°. In a large bowl, cream butter and sugars until light and fluffy, 5-7 minutes. Beat in eggs and extracts. Combine flour, oats, cinnamon, salt, baking soda, ginger and nutmeg; gradually add to creamed mixture and mix well. Stir in walnuts, carrots and raisins.

2. Drop by rounded teaspoonfuls 2 in. apart onto greased baking sheets. Flatten with a glass dipped in sugar. Bake at 350° until lightly browned, 9-11 minutes. Remove to wire racks to cool completely.

3. In a small bowl, beat cream cheese, butter, confectioners' sugar and vanilla until light and fluffy. Stir in walnuts and pineapple. Spread over the bottoms of half the cookies; top with remaining cookies. Sprinkle both sides with additional confectioners' sugar. Store in the refrigerator.

**1 sandwich cookie:** 176 cal., 10g fat (5g sat. fat), 29mg chol., 117mg sod., 20g carb. (12g sugars, 1g fiber), 2g pro.

## TEST KITCHEN TIP

*To make these cookies ahead of time, store the baked cookies in an airtight container, separating layers with waxed paper, and freeze for up to 1 month. Thaw in a single layer before filling.*

# BUTTER PECAN COOKIES

When my daughter was a teen, these cookies earned her blue ribbons from two county fairs. Then a few years ago, her own daughter took home a blue ribbon for the same cookie. Needless to say, these mouthwatering morsels are winners!
—Martha Thefield, Cedartown, GA

**PREP:** 25 MIN. + CHILLING • **BAKE:** 10 MIN./BATCH • **MAKES:** 4 DOZEN

1¾ cups chopped pecans
1 Tbsp. plus 1 cup butter, softened, divided
1 cup packed brown sugar
1 large egg, separated, room temperature
1 tsp. vanilla extract
2 cups self-rising flour
1 cup pecan halves

1. Preheat oven to 325°. Place chopped pecans and 1 Tbsp. butter in a baking pan. Bake 5-7 minutes or until pecans are toasted and browned, stirring frequently. Set aside to cool.

2. In a large bowl, cream brown sugar and remaining butter until light and fluffy, 5-7 minutes. Beat in egg yolk and vanilla. Gradually add flour and mix well. Cover and refrigerate 1 hour or until easy to handle.

3. Preheat the oven to 375°. Roll dough into 1-in. balls, then roll balls in toasted pecans, pressing nuts into dough. Place 2 in. apart on ungreased baking sheets. Beat egg white until foamy. Dip pecan halves into egg white, then gently press 1 into each ball.

4. Bake at 375° until golden brown, 10-12 minutes. Cool for 2 minutes before removing to wire racks.

**Note:** As a substitute for each cup of self-rising flour, place 1½ tsp. baking powder and ½ tsp. salt in a measuring cup. Add all-purpose flour to measure 1 cup.

**1 cookie:** 115 cal., 9g fat (3g sat. fat), 15mg chol., 97mg sod., 9g carb. (5g sugars, 1g fiber), 1g pro.

## TEST KITCHEN TIP

*These butter pecan cookies freeze well. Store baked cookies in an airtight container in the freezer for up to 6 months. To freeze the dough raw, form the dough into balls as directed and freeze in a single layer on parchment. Once they are solid enough, transfer the frozen dough balls into airtight containers and freeze for up to 3 months. When you are ready to use the dough, remove it from the freezer and thaw in the refrigerator overnight. Continue with the recipe as directed.*

# SNICKERDOODLE CRISPS

This classic cookie from New England can be made two ways: soft or crunchy.
My happy version with cinnamon, ginger and nutmeg is crispy to perfection.
—*Jenni Sharp, Milwaukee, WI*

PREP: 20 MIN. + CHILLING • BAKE: 10 MIN./BATCH • MAKES: ABOUT 5 DOZEN

1 cup butter, softened
2 cups sugar
2 large eggs, room temperature
2 tsp. vanilla extract
3 cups all-purpose flour
4 tsp. ground cinnamon
2 tsp. ground ginger
¾ tsp. ground nutmeg
½ tsp. ground allspice
2 tsp. cream of tartar
1 tsp. baking soda
½ tsp. salt

**SPICED SUGAR**
⅓ cup sugar
1 tsp. ground cinnamon
¾ tsp. ground ginger
¼ tsp. ground nutmeg
¼ tsp. ground allspice

**1.** In a large bowl, cream butter and sugar until light and fluffy, 5-7 minutes. Beat in eggs and vanilla. In another bowl, whisk flour, spices, cream of tartar, baking soda and salt; gradually beat into creamed mixture.

**2.** Divide dough in half; shape each into an 8-in.-long roll. Wrap in waxed paper and refrigerate 2 hours or until firm.

**3.** Preheat oven to 350°. In a small bowl, mix spiced sugar ingredients. Unwrap and cut dough crosswise into ¼-in. slices; press cookies into sugar mixture to coat both sides or sprinkle sugar mixture over cookies. Place 2 in. apart on greased baking sheets. Bake 7-9 minutes or until edges are light brown. Cool on pans for 2 minutes. Remove to wire racks to cool.

**Freeze option:** Freeze wrapped logs in an airtight freezer container. To use, unwrap frozen logs and cut into slices. If necessary, let dough stand a few minutes at room temperature before cutting. Bake as directed.

**1 cookie:** 84 cal., 3g fat (2g sat. fat), 14mg chol., 68mg sod., 13g carb. (8g sugars, 0 fiber), 1g pro.

# WHITE CHOCOLATE CHIP HAZELNUT COOKIES

You will want to make these cookies again and again. I like to take them to church get-togethers and family reunions. They are rich and scrumptious—crispy on the outside and chewy on the inside.
—*Denise DeJong, Pittsburgh, PA*

**PREP:** 15 MIN. • **BAKE:** 10 MIN./BATCH • **MAKES:** 3 DOZEN

1¼ cups whole hazelnuts, toasted, divided
9 Tbsp. butter, softened, divided
½ cup sugar
½ cup packed brown sugar
1 large egg, room temperature
1 tsp. vanilla extract
1½ cups all-purpose flour
½ tsp. baking soda
½ tsp. salt
1 cup white baking chips

1. Preheat oven to 350°. Coarsely chop ½ cup hazelnuts; set aside. Melt 2 Tbsp. butter. In a food processor, combine melted butter and the remaining hazelnuts. Cover and process until the mixture forms a crumbly paste.

2. In a bowl, cream the remaining 7 Tbsp. butter. Beat in the sugars. Add egg and vanilla; beat until light and fluffy, 5-7 minutes. Beat in ground hazelnut mixture until blended. Combine flour, baking soda and salt; add to batter and mix just until combined. Stir in chips and remaining chopped hazelnuts.

3. Drop by rounded tablespoonfuls 2 in. apart onto greased baking sheets. Bake until lightly browned, 10-12 minutes. Remove to wire racks to cool.

**1 cookie:** 132 cal., 8g fat (3g sat. fat), 14mg chol., 80mg sod., 14g carb. (9g sugars, 1g fiber), 2g pro.

---

# CHOCOLATE OAT SQUARES

SHOWN ON PAGE 238

When you bring these chewy treats to a group meal, guests will be tempted to start at the dessert table. Chock-full of chocolate and walnuts, they'll satisfy any sweet tooth.
—*Jennifer Eilts, Lincoln, NE*

**PREP:** 20 MIN. • **BAKE:** 20 MIN. • **MAKES:** 4 DOZEN

1 cup plus 2 Tbsp. butter, softened, divided
2 cups packed brown sugar
2 large eggs, room temperature
4 tsp. vanilla extract, divided
3 cups quick-cooking oats
2½ cups all-purpose flour
1½ tsp. salt, divided
1 tsp. baking soda
1 can (14 oz.) sweetened condensed milk
2 cups semisweet chocolate chips
1 cup chopped walnuts

1. Preheat the oven to 350°. In a large bowl, beat 1 cup butter and brown sugar until light and fluffy, 5-7 minutes. Beat in eggs and 2 tsp. vanilla. Combine oats, flour, 1 tsp. salt and baking soda; gradually add to the creamed mixture and mix well. Press two-thirds of oat mixture into a greased 15x10x1-in. baking pan.

2. In a large saucepan, combine condensed milk, chocolate chips, and remaining 2 Tbsp. butter and ½ tsp. salt. Cook and stir over low heat until chocolate is melted. Remove from heat; stir in chopped walnuts and remaining 2 tsp. vanilla. Spread over crust. Sprinkle with remaining oat mixture.

3. Bake 20-25 minutes or until golden brown. Cool on a wire rack. Cut into squares.

**1 square:** 205 cal., 10g fat (5g sat. fat), 23mg chol., 155mg sod., 28g carb. (19g sugars, 1g fiber), 3g pro.

WHITE CHOCOLATE CHIP
HAZELNUT COOKIES

# TRIPLE GINGER COOKIES

My dad loved ginger cookies. I tinkered with the recipe my grandma handed down by using fresh, ground and crystallized ginger for more pizazz.
—*Trisha Kruse, Eagle, ID*

PREP: 20 MIN. + CHILLING • BAKE: 15 MIN./BATCH + COOLING • MAKES: 2½ DOZEN

½ cup butter, softened
½ cup packed brown sugar
1 large egg, room temperature
3 Tbsp. molasses
½ tsp. grated fresh gingerroot
2¼ cups all-purpose flour
½ tsp. baking powder
½ tsp. ground ginger
¼ tsp. salt
¼ tsp. baking soda

**ICING**
½ cup confectioners' sugar
2 to 3 tsp. water
¼ cup finely chopped
    crystallized ginger

1. Preheat oven to 350°. In a large bowl, cream butter and brown sugar until light and fluffy, 5-7 minutes. Beat in egg, molasses and fresh ginger. In another bowl, whisk flour, baking powder, ground ginger, salt and baking soda; gradually beat into the creamed mixture. Refrigerate, covered, until firm enough to handle, about 2 hours.

2. Shape dough by tablespoonfuls into balls; place 1 in. apart on ungreased baking sheets. Flatten slightly with the bottom of a glass. Bake until cookies are set and edges begin to brown, 12-14 minutes. Remove from pans to wire racks to cool completely.

3. For icing, in a small bowl, mix confectioners' sugar and enough water to reach the desired consistency. Drizzle over cookies; sprinkle with crystallized ginger.

**1 cookie:** 97 cal., 3g fat (2g sat. fat), 15mg chol., 64mg sod., 16g carb. (7g sugars, 0 fiber), 1g pro.

---

# SWEDISH RASPBERRY ALMOND BARS

My neighbor brought me and my daughter these treats one Christmas. My daughter is 36 now, and I still make these wonderful bars.
—*Marina Castle-Kelley, Canyon Country, CA*

PREP: 35 MIN. • BAKE: 20 MIN. + COOLING • MAKES: 2 DOZEN

¾ cup butter, softened
¾ cup confectioners' sugar
1½ cups all-purpose flour
¾ cup seedless raspberry jam
3 large egg whites
6 Tbsp. sugar
½ cup sweetened shredded coconut
1 cup sliced almonds, divided
    Additional confectioners' sugar,
    optional

1. Preheat the oven to 350°. In a large bowl, cream butter and confectioners' sugar until light and fluffy, 3-4 minutes. Gradually add flour and mix well. Press onto the bottom of a greased 13x9-in. baking pan. Bake 18-20 minutes or until lightly browned.

2. Spread jam over crust. In a large bowl, beat egg whites until soft peaks form. Gradually beat in sugar, 1 Tbsp. at a time, on high until stiff peaks form. Fold in coconut and ½ cup almonds. Spread over jam. Sprinkle with remaining almonds. Bake 18-22 minutes or until golden brown. Cool completely on a wire rack. Dust with additional confectioners' sugar as desired.

**1 bar:** 165 cal., 8g fat (4g sat. fat), 15mg chol., 53mg sod., 21g carb. (14g sugars, 1g fiber), 2g pro.

# MONSTER COOKIES

This recipe combines several favorites flavors—peanut butter, butterscotch and chocolate—in one monster cookie. Before baking, press a few extra M&M's on top for added color.
—*Patricia Schroedl, Jefferson, WI*

PREP: 15 MIN. + STANDING • BAKE: 15 MIN./BATCH • MAKES: ABOUT 2½ DOZEN

1 cup peanut butter
½ cup butter, softened
1¼ cups packed brown sugar
1 cup sugar
3 large eggs, room temperature
2 tsp. baking soda
1 tsp. vanilla extract
4 cups quick-cooking oats
1 cup M&M's
1 cup butterscotch chips
1 cup salted peanuts
2 cups all-purpose flour

1. In a large bowl, cream peanut butter, butter and sugars. Add eggs, 1 at a time, beating well after each addition. Add baking soda and vanilla. Add oats, M&M's, butterscotch chips and peanuts; let stand for 10 minutes. Stir in flour (the dough will be crumbly).

2. Shape by ¼ cupfuls into balls. Place on greased baking sheets, about 9 cookies on each sheet. Gently flatten cookies. Bake at 325° for 15-18 minutes or until edges are lightly browned. Remove to wire racks.

**1 cookie:** 318 cal., 15g fat (6g sat. fat), 28mg chol., 180mg sod., 41g carb. (25g sugars, 2g fiber), 7g pro.

# CHOCOLATE-PEANUT BUTTER TOPPERS

My mother-in-law was known for her Sunday dinners, which sometimes included these cookies. She always enjoyed baking and even worked in a bakery to help put her sons through college.
—*Cathy Pawlowski, Naperville, IL*

PREP: 30 MIN. • BAKE: 15 MIN./BATCH + COOLING • MAKES: 5 DOZEN

1 cup butter, softened
½ cup sugar
2 tsp. vanilla extract
2 cups all-purpose flour
Additional sugar

**PEANUT BUTTER TOPPING**
⅓ cup packed brown sugar
⅓ cup creamy peanut butter
¼ cup butter, softened

**CHOCOLATE GLAZE**
½ cup semisweet chocolate chips, melted
⅓ cup confectioners' sugar
2 Tbsp. 2% milk

1. Preheat oven to 325°. In a large bowl, cream butter and sugar until light and fluffy, 5-7 minutes. Beat in vanilla. Gradually add flour to creamed mixture and mix well.

2. Shape into ¾-in. balls. Coat bottom of a glass with cooking spray, then dip it in sugar. Flatten cookies with prepared glass, re-dipping glass in sugar as needed. Place on baking sheets. Bake until set, 12-15 minutes. Remove to wire racks to cool completely.

3. In a small bowl, beat the brown sugar, peanut butter and butter until smooth. Spread 1 tsp. over each cookie. Combine glaze ingredients; gently spread ¾ tsp. over each peanut butter layer. Store in a single layer in airtight containers.

**1 cookie:** 157 cal., 10g fat (6g sat. fat), 20mg chol., 75mg sod., 16g carb. (9g sugars, 1g fiber), 2g pro.

> ❝
> My friend made
> these for my
> family, and we
> loved them so
> much that we
> couldn't believe
> they were
> homemade.
> —PUNKYBOOLADY
> TASTEOFHOME.COM

# ULTIMATE FUDGY BROWNIES

Coffee granules enhance the chocolate flavor in these amazingly fudgy brownies.
Add chocolate chips to the batter and you've got some seriously irresistible treats.
—*Sarah Farmer, Waukesha, WI*

**PREP: 20 MIN. • BAKE: 40 MIN. + COOLING • MAKES: 16 SERVINGS**

1 cup sugar
½ cup packed brown sugar
⅔ cup butter, cubed
¼ cup water
2 tsp. instant coffee granules, optional
2¾ cups bittersweet chocolate chips, divided
4 large eggs, room temperature
2 tsp. vanilla extract
1½ cups all-purpose flour
½ tsp. baking soda
½ tsp. salt

1. Preheat oven to 325°. Line a 9-in. square baking pan with parchment, letting ends extend up the sides. In a large heavy saucepan, combine sugars, butter, water and, if desired, coffee granules; bring to a boil, stirring constantly. Remove from heat; add 1¾ cups chocolate chips and stir until melted. Cool slightly.

2. In a large bowl, whisk eggs until foamy, about 3 minutes. Add vanilla; gradually whisk in chocolate mixture. In another bowl, whisk flour, baking soda and salt; stir into chocolate mixture. Fold in remaining chocolate chips.

3. Pour into pan. Bake on a lower oven rack 40-50 minutes or until a toothpick inserted in center comes out with moist crumbs. Cool in pan on a wire rack.

4. Lifting with parchment, remove brownies from pan. Cut into squares.

**1 brownie:** 344 cal., 18g fat (10g sat. fat), 67mg chol., 197mg sod., 47g carb. (35g sugars, 2g fiber), 4g pro.

# STAR ANISE-HONEY COOKIES

When I was growing up, my mother made many desserts and pastries
with anise. Today, I continue the tradition with these cookies.
—*Darlene Brenden, Salem, OR*

**PREP: 25 MIN. • BAKE: 5 MIN./BATCH • MAKES: 6 DOZEN**

1 cup sugar
1 cup honey
3 large eggs
5 cups all-purpose flour
2½ tsp. baking soda
1 tsp. ground star anise

1. Preheat oven to 350°. In a large bowl, beat sugar and honey until blended. Beat in eggs. In another bowl, whisk flour, baking soda and star anise; gradually beat into sugar mixture.

2. On a floured surface, roll dough to ¼-in. thickness. Cut with a floured 1½-in. star-shaped cookie cutter. Place 1 in. apart on greased baking sheets.

3. Bake 4-6 minutes or until edges are light brown. Remove from pans to wire racks to cool.

**1 cookie:** 60 cal., 0 fat (0 sat. fat), 8mg chol., 47mg sod., 13g carb. (7g sugars, 0 fiber), 1g pro.

BLUEBERRY
UPSIDE-DOWN CAKE,
PAGE 280

"

I made this
for my father's
birthday. It
tasted really
good and was
a refreshing
change from
frosted cake.
—JENNOELLE13
TASTEOFHOME.COM

CHAPTER 10

# TASTY CAKES
# & PIES

There's always room for dessert, particularly when that dinner finale
is a tender cake or luscious pie! Turn here for the secrets behind the
decadent treats that today's home cooks are asked to share most.

# OREO MOUSSE CAKE

Oreo mousse cake is so simple to put together, but it tastes as decadent as fancy restaurant desserts. Have fun garnishing it as you like, using crushed or whole Oreos, whipped cream rosettes or chocolate shavings.
—Taste of Home *Test Kitchen*

PREP: 15 MIN. • COOK: 10 MIN. + CHILLING • MAKES: 16 SERVINGS

1 pkg. (14.3 oz.) Oreo cookies, crushed
⅓ cup butter, melted
8 oz. semisweet chocolate, chopped
3 cups heavy whipping cream, divided
½ cup confectioners' sugar
Additional whole or crushed Oreos, optional

1. In a small bowl, mix 2 cups crushed cookies and butter. Press onto the bottom of a greased 9-in. springform pan. Refrigerate until ready to use.

2. In a large microwave-safe bowl, microwave chocolate on high just until melted; stir until smooth. Cool to room temperature.

3. In another bowl, beat cream and confectioners' sugar until stiff peaks form; fold 4 cups into chocolate mixture. Spread over crust. Spread remaining whipped cream over top. Cover and refrigerate until set, about 3 hours. If desired, garnish with additional Oreos.

**1 piece:** 402 cal., 30g fat (17g sat. fat), 61mg chol., 143mg sod., 32g carb. (21g sugars, 2g fiber), 3g pro.

# APPLE PIE A LA MODE

I was planning a dinner party and wanted a dessert that wowed. My caramel apple ice cream pie certainly does the trick. Now it's a family favorite.
—Trisha Kruse, Eagle, ID

PREP: 15 MIN. + FREEZING • MAKES: 8 SERVINGS

1 can (21 oz.) apple pie filling
1 graham cracker crust (9 in.)
2 cups butter pecan ice cream, softened if necessary
1 jar (12 oz.) hot caramel ice cream topping
¼ cup chopped pecans, toasted

1. Spread half of the pie filling over crust. Top with half of the ice cream; freeze 30 minutes. Drizzle with half of the caramel topping; layer with the remaining pie filling. Freeze for 30 minutes. Scoop remaining ice cream over top. Freeze, covered, until firm.

2. Remove from the freezer 30 minutes before serving. In a microwave, warm the remaining caramel topping. Serve pie with warm caramel topping; sprinkle with pecans.

**Note:** To toast nuts, bake in a shallow pan in a 350° oven for 5-10 minutes or cook in a skillet over low heat until lightly browned, stirring occasionally.

**1 piece:** 398 cal., 14g fat (4g sat. fat), 13mg chol., 357mg sod., 69g carb. (59g sugars, 2g fiber), 3g pro.

> ❝
> This is my
> favorite lemon
> pie recipe. I've
> made it several
> times, and it
> always turns
> out perfect!
> My husband
> loves it.
> —CHUCKSGIRL87
> TASTEOFHOME.COM

# WORLD'S BEST LEMON PIE

Mother's pies were always so memorable, with tender, flaky crusts. In summer the order of the day was lemon meringue!
—*Phyllis Kirsling, Junction City, WI*

PREP: 45 MIN. + CHILLING • BAKE: 15 MIN. + COOLING • MAKES: 8 SERVINGS

Dough for single-crust pie
1 cup sugar
¼ cup cornstarch
3 Tbsp. all-purpose flour
¼ tsp. salt
2 cups water
3 large egg yolks, beaten
1 Tbsp. butter
¼ cup lemon juice
1 tsp. grated lemon zest

## MERINGUE
3 large egg whites,
 room temperature
¼ tsp. salt
½ cup sugar

1. On a lightly floured surface, roll dough to a ⅛-in.-thick circle; transfer to a 9-in. pie plate. Trim to ½ in. beyond rim of plate; flute the edge. Refrigerate 30 minutes. Preheat oven to 425°.

2. Line crust with a double thickness of foil. Fill with pie weights, dried beans or uncooked rice. Bake on a lower oven rack 20-25 minutes or until edge is golden brown. Remove foil and weights; bake until bottom is golden brown, 3-6 minutes longer. Cool on a wire rack. Reduce oven setting to 350°.

3. In a medium saucepan, combine sugar, cornstarch, flour and salt. Gradually stir in water. Cook and stir over medium heat until thickened and bubbly. Reduce heat; cook and stir 2 minutes more. Remove from the heat.

4. Gradually stir 1 cup hot mixture into egg yolks; return all to saucepan. Bring to a boil. Cook and stir 2 minutes. Remove from the heat. Stir in butter, lemon juice and zest until smooth. Pour into pie crust.

5. In a bowl, beat egg whites and salt until stiff (but not dry) peaks form. Gradually beat in sugar until soft peaks form. Spread over pie, sealing the edge to crust. Bake at 350° until meringue is golden, 12-15 minutes. Cool. Store any leftovers in the refrigerator.

**Dough for single-crust pie:** Combine 1¼ cups all-purpose flour and ¼ tsp. salt; cut in ½ cup cold butter until crumbly. Gradually add 3-5 Tbsp. ice water, tossing with a fork until dough holds together when pressed. Shape into a disk; wrap and refrigerate 1 hour.

**1 piece:** 321 cal., 9g fat (4g sat. fat), 74mg chol., 272mg sod., 58g carb. (39g sugars, 0 fiber), 4g pro.

## TEST KITCHEN TIP

*Lemon meringue pie is definitely best served fresh, but you can keep your pie in the refrigerator for up to 3 days, loosely covered with aluminum foil.*

# GRANDMA'S STRAWBERRY SHORTCAKE

I can still taste the juicy berries piled over warm biscuits and topped with a dollop of fresh whipped cream.
My father added even more indulgence to the dessert by first buttering his biscuits.
—*Shirley Joan Helfenbein, Lapeer, MI*

PREP: 30 MIN. • BAKE: 20 MIN. + COOLING • MAKES: 8 SERVINGS

2 cups all-purpose flour
2 Tbsp. sugar
3 tsp. baking powder
½ tsp. salt
½ cup cold butter, cubed
1 large egg, room temperature
⅔ cup half-and-half cream
1 cup heavy whipping cream
2 Tbsp. confectioners' sugar
⅛ tsp. vanilla extract
 Additional butter
1½ cups fresh strawberries, sliced

**1.** Preheat oven to 450°. In a large bowl, combine flour, sugar, baking powder and salt. Cut in butter until mixture resembles coarse crumbs. In another bowl, whisk egg and half-and-half. Add all at once to crumb mixture; stir just until moistened.

**2.** Spread batter into a greased 8-in. round baking pan, building up the edge. Bake until golden brown, 16-18 minutes. Remove from pan; cool on a wire rack.

**3.** Beat heavy cream until it begins to thicken. Add confectioners' sugar and vanilla; beat until stiff peaks form. Split cake in half crosswise; butter bottom layer. Spoon half the strawberries over bottom layer. Spread with whipped cream. Cover with top cake layer. Top with remaining berries and whipped cream. Cut into wedges.

**1 piece:** 381 cal., 25g fat (16g sat. fat), 98mg chol., 447mg sod., 32g carb. (8g sugars, 1g fiber), 6g pro.

# MOCHA FROSTING

Our Test Kitchen culinary experts dress up purchased cupcakes and angel food cake with this easy-to-make coffee-flavored frosting.
—Taste of Home *Test Kitchen*

TAKES: 20 MIN. • MAKES: 2½ CUPS

2 Tbsp. instant coffee granules
3 Tbsp. boiling water
1 cup butter, softened
2 Tbsp. baking cocoa
4 cups confectioners' sugar

In a small bowl, dissolve the coffee granules in water and set aside. In a bowl, cream butter until light and fluffy. Beat in cocoa. Gradually beat in confectioners' sugar and coffee mixture until smooth. Use immediately or refrigerate.

**2 Tbsp.:** 177 cal., 9g fat (6g sat. fat), 24mg chol., 74mg sod., 24g carb. (23g sugars, 0 fiber), 0 pro.

## TEST KITCHEN TIP

*When making this frosting, use espresso or instant coffee granules instead of brewed coffee. Using regular brewed coffee will not give you a particularly strong flavor.*

"My daughter asked for pie for her birthday party. Out of all the pies we made, this was the only one that was completely devoured.

—JOINME4COFFEE
TASTEOFHOME.COM

# DARK CHOCOLATE CREAM PIE

This is one of my favorite desserts to make for my chocolate-loving friends.
—*Kezia Sullivan, Sackets Harbor, NY*

PREP: 30 MIN. + CHILLING • MAKES: 8 SERVINGS

Dough for single-crust pie
1¼ cups sugar
¼ cup cornstarch
¼ tsp. salt
3 cups whole milk
3 oz. unsweetened chocolate, chopped
4 large egg yolks, lightly beaten
3 Tbsp. butter
1½ tsp. vanilla extract
Optional: Whipped cream and grated chocolate

1. On a lightly floured surface, roll dough to a ⅛-in.-thick circle; transfer to a 9-in. pie plate. Trim crust to ½ in. beyond rim of plate; flute the edge. Refrigerate 30 minutes. Preheat the oven to 425°. Line crust with a double thickness of foil. Fill with pie weights, dried beans or uncooked rice. Bake on a lower oven rack until edge is golden brown, 20-25 minutes. Remove foil and weights; bake until bottom is golden brown, 3-6 minutes longer. Cool on a wire rack.

2. In a large saucepan, combine sugar, cornstarch and salt. Stir in milk and chocolate. Cook and stir over medium-high heat until thickened and bubbly. Reduce heat; cook and stir 2 minutes longer. Remove from the heat.

3. Stir a small amount of hot filling into egg yolks; return all to the pan, stirring constantly. Bring to a gentle boil; cook and stir 2 minutes. Remove from heat.

4. Gently stir in butter and vanilla until butter is melted. Spoon into crust. Cool on a wire rack. Cover and chill at least 3 hours. If desired, serve with whipped cream and grated chocolate.

**Dough for single-crust pie:** Combine 1¼ cups all-purpose flour and ¼ tsp. salt; cut in ½ cup cold butter until crumbly. Gradually add 3-5 Tbsp. ice water, tossing with a fork until dough holds together when pressed. Shape into a disk; wrap and refrigerate 1 hour.

**1 piece:** 390 cal., 19g fat (10g sat. fat), 128mg chol., 218mg sod., 52g carb. (37g sugars, 2g fiber), 7g pro.

# PECAN SHORTBREAD TEA CAKES

My Grandma Ellis made her shortbread cookies only at Christmas because the ingredients were so indulgent. The results are too!
—*Trisha Kruse, Eagle, ID*

PREP: 45 MIN. • BAKE: 10 MIN./BATCH + COOLING • MAKES: ABOUT 6 DOZEN

2   cups butter, softened
½   cup sugar
½   cup packed brown sugar
2   tsp. vanilla extract
4   cups all-purpose flour
½   tsp. salt
72  pecan halves, toasted

**CARAMEL GLAZE**
½   cup packed brown sugar
3   Tbsp. 2% milk
2   Tbsp. butter
1½  cups confectioners' sugar
1   Tbsp. brandy

**1.** Preheat the oven to 350°. Cream the butter and sugars until light and fluffy, 5-7 minutes. Beat in vanilla. In a bowl, whisk together flour and salt; gradually add to the creamed mixture and mix well. Roll into 1-in. balls; place in greased mini-muffin cups. Lightly press a pecan half into the center of each. Bake until edges are lightly browned, 10-12 minutes. Cool 10 minutes before removing from pans to wire racks.

**2.** For caramel glaze, combine brown sugar, milk and butter in a small saucepan over medium heat. Bring to a boil; cook and stir 1 minute. Remove from heat; cool 5 minutes. Gradually beat in confectioners' sugar and brandy. Drizzle over cookies.

**1 cookie:** 112 cal., 7g fat (4g sat. fat), 14mg chol., 61mg sod., 12g carb. (7g sugars, 0 fiber), 1g pro.

---

# ROOT BEER FLOAT PIE

This is the kind of recipe your kids will look back on and always remember. And you don't even need to use an oven!
—*Cindy Reams, Philipsburg, PA*

PREP: 15 MIN. + FREEZING • MAKES: 8 SERVINGS

1   carton (8 oz.) frozen reduced-fat whipped topping, thawed, divided
¾   cup cold diet root beer
½   cup fat-free milk
1   pkg. (1 oz.) sugar-free instant vanilla pudding mix
1   graham cracker crust (9 in.)
    Maraschino cherries, optional

**1.** Reserve and refrigerate ½ cup whipped topping for garnish. In a large bowl, whisk together root beer, milk and pudding mix for 2 minutes. Fold in half of the whipped topping. Spread into graham cracker crust.

**2.** Spread the remaining whipped topping over pie. Freeze at least 8 hours or overnight.

**3.** Dollop the reserved whipped topping over each serving. If desired, top each serving with a maraschino cherry.

**1 piece:** 184 cal., 8g fat (4g sat. fat), 0 chol., 268mg sod., 27g carb. (14g sugars, 0 fiber), 1g pro. **Diabetic exchanges:** 2 starch, 1½ fat.

> Such a yummy and easy little snack. It's not too sweet but it's just right for those little cravings!
> —LUCASCARR
> TASTEOFHOME.COM

PEACH BLUEBERRY PIE

# PEACH BLUEBERRY PIE

What a flavor! That's what I hear most often when guests taste this pie.
—Sue Thumma, Shepherd, MI

**PREP: 15 MIN. • BAKE: 40 MIN. + COOLING • MAKES: 8 SERVINGS**

1 cup sugar
⅓ cup all-purpose flour
½ tsp. ground cinnamon
⅛ tsp. ground allspice
3 cups sliced peeled fresh peaches
1 cup fresh or frozen unsweetened blueberries
Dough for double-crust pie
1 Tbsp. butter
1 Tbsp. 2% milk
Cinnamon sugar

1. In a large bowl, combine sugar, flour, cinnamon and allspice. Add peaches and blueberries; toss to coat.

2. Preheat oven to 400°. On a floured surface, roll half of the dough to a ⅛-in.-thick circle; transfer to a 9-in. pie plate. Trim even with rim. Add filling; dot with butter.

3. Roll remaining dough to a ⅛-in.-thick circle; cut into ½-in.-wide strips. Arrange over filling in a lattice pattern. Trim and seal strips to edge of bottom crust; flute edge. Brush lattice strips with milk; sprinkle with cinnamon sugar.

4. Bake until crust is golden brown, 40-45 minutes. Cool on a wire rack.

**Dough for double-crust pie:** Combine 2½ cups flour and ½ tsp. salt; cut in 1 cup cold butter until crumbly. Gradually add ⅓-⅔ cup ice water, tossing with a fork until dough holds together. Divide dough in half. Shape each into a disk; wrap and refrigerate 1 hour.

**1 piece:** 406 cal., 16g fat (7g sat. fat), 14mg chol., 215mg sod., 65g carb. (34g sugars, 2g fiber), 3g pro.

---

# MAKEOVER GOOEY CHOCOLATE PEANUT BUTTER CAKE

My dad made sure this dessert was on the menu for Father's Day—or else! This makeover version is great. I can't believe so much fat was cut and it still tastes like the original.
—Trisha Kruse, Eagle, ID

**PREP: 25 MIN. • BAKE: 40 MIN. + COOLING • MAKES: 24 SERVINGS**

1 pkg. chocolate cake mix
1 large egg, room temperature
¼ cup canola oil
¼ cup unsweetened applesauce

**TOPPING**
1 pkg. reduced-fat cream cheese
½ cup creamy peanut butter
½ cup reduced-fat butter, melted
2 large eggs, room temperature
2 large egg whites, room temperature
1 tsp. vanilla extract
2 cups confectioners' sugar

1. In a large bowl, beat chocolate cake mix, egg, oil and applesauce on low until combined. Press into a 13x9-in. baking pan coated with cooking spray.

2. In another large bowl, beat cream cheese and peanut butter until smooth. Add the butter, eggs, egg whites and vanilla; beat on low until combined. Add confectioners' sugar; mix well. Pour over crust.

3. Bake at 350° until edges are golden brown, 40-45 minutes. Cool on a wire rack for 20 minutes before cutting. Refrigerate leftovers.

**1 piece:** 228 cal., 11g fat (4g sat. fat), 38mg chol., 255mg sod., 29g carb. (21g sugars, 1g fiber), 4g pro.

# BLUEBERRY UPSIDE-DOWN CAKE

SHOWN ON PAGE 266

This cake is a family favorite when blueberries are in season.
—*Charlotte Harrison, North Providence, RI*

PREP: 10 MIN. • BAKE: 40 MIN. • MAKES: 9 SERVINGS

6 Tbsp. butter, softened, divided
¼ cup packed brown sugar
2 cups fresh blueberries
¾ cup sugar
1 large egg, room temperature
1 tsp. vanilla extract
1¼ cups cake flour
1½ tsp. baking powder
½ cup whole milk
  Whipped topping

1. Preheat oven to 350°. In a small saucepan, melt 2 Tbsp. butter; stir in brown sugar. Spread into an ungreased 8-in. square baking dish. Arrange blueberries in a single layer over brown sugar mixture; set aside.

2. In a bowl, cream remaining 4 Tbsp. butter and the sugar until light and fluffy, 5-7 minutes. Beat in egg and vanilla. Combine flour and baking powder; add to butter mixture alternately with milk, beating well. Carefully pour over blueberries.

3. Bake until a toothpick inserted in the center comes out clean, 40-45 minutes. Immediately invert onto a serving platter. Cool. Serve with whipped topping.

**1 piece:** 261 cal., 9g fat (5g sat. fat), 42mg chol., 157mg sod., 43g carb. (27g sugars, 1g fiber), 3g pro.

---

# GERMAN CHOCOLATE TRES LECHES CAKE

I first tried tres leches cake while I was in Ecuador several years ago. Since then, I've changed it up by adding chocolate and coconut.
—*Lisa Varner, El Paso, TX*

PREP: 20 MIN. • BAKE: 25 MIN. + CHILLING • MAKES: 15 SERVINGS

1 pkg. chocolate cake mix (regular size)
1 can (14 oz.) sweetened condensed milk
1 can (12 oz.) evaporated milk
1½ cups heavy whipping cream, divided
¼ cup rum
3 Tbsp. confectioners' sugar
½ cup sweetened shredded coconut, toasted
½ cup chopped pecans, toasted
  Chocolate syrup, optional

1. Preheat oven to 350°. Prepare and bake cake mix according to package directions. Cool on a wire rack.

2. In a bowl, whisk milks, ½ cup cream and rum. With a skewer, poke holes in cake about ½ in. apart. Pour milk mixture over cake, allowing the cake to absorb the mixture. Let stand for 30 minutes. Refrigerate, covered, for 8 hours.

3. In a bowl, beat remaining 1 cup cream until it thickens. Add sugar; beat until stiff peaks form. Spread over the top. Sprinkle with coconut and pecans, and, if desired, drizzle with syrup.

**1 piece:** 416 cal., 23g fat (11g sat. fat), 81mg chol., 299mg sod., 44g carb. (33g sugars, 0 fiber), 7g pro.

# RAINBOW BIRTHDAY CAKE

How fun is this rainbow birthday cake? It will add a festive touch to any celebration. Be sure to use gel food coloring for the most vibrant look.
—Taste of Home *Test Kitchen*

**PREP: 1 HOUR • BAKE: 30 MIN. + COOLING • MAKES: 16 SERVINGS**

1 cup butter, softened
2½ cups sugar
4 large eggs, room temperature
4 cups all-purpose flour
3 tsp. baking powder
1 tsp. salt
½ tsp. baking soda
1½ cups sour cream
6 different colors gel food coloring

## FROSTING

2 cups butter, softened
6 cups confectioners' sugar, sifted
2 tsp. vanilla extract
¼ to ⅓ cup heavy whipping cream
Sprinkles

1. Preheat oven to 350°. Line bottoms of 3 greased and floured 8-in. round baking pans with parchment; grease paper. In a large bowl, cream butter and sugar until fluffy, 5-7 minutes. Add eggs, 1 at a time, beating well after each addition. Combine flour, baking powder, salt and baking soda; add to the creamed mixture alternately with sour cream, beating well after each addition. Divide batter into equal portions, with 1¼ cup in 6 separate bowls. Tint each portion a different color with food coloring. Cover and refrigerate 3 portions.

2. Transfer 3 remaining portions to prepared pans. Bake until edges begin to just brown, 13-15 minutes. Cool for 10 minutes before removing from pans to wire racks to cool completely. Cool, wash and dry pans. Repeat with the remaining batter.

3. For frosting, in a large bowl, beat butter until fluffy. Gradually beat in the confectioners' sugar. Beat in vanilla and enough cream to reach the desired consistency. Spread the frosting between layers and over the top and side of cake. Decorate with sprinkles.

**1 piece:** 793 cal., 42g fat (26g sat. fat), 158mg chol., 579mg sod., 101g carb. (77g sugars, 1g fiber), 6g pro.

## TEST KITCHEN TIP

*To make sure your cake layers are uniformly thick, give your cake tins a good tap on the counter before putting them in the oven. Doing so will help release extra air bubbles trapped beneath the surface and level everything out, so the batter is evenly dispersed.*
—SAMMI DIVITO, *TASTE OF HOME* ASSISTANT EDITOR

# WHIPPED CREAM POUND CAKE

This cake never lasts long at family gatherings. Slices taste
terrific whether served alone or topped with fresh fruit.
—*Shirley Tincher, Zanesville, OH*

PREP: 15 MIN. • BAKE: 1 HOUR 20 MIN. + COOLING • MAKES: 2 CAKES (12 PIECES EACH)

1   cup butter, softened
3   cups sugar
6   large eggs, room temperature
1   tsp. lemon extract
1   tsp. vanilla extract
3   cups all-purpose flour
1   cup heavy whipping cream
    Sliced fresh fruit, optional

**1.** Preheat oven to 325°. Grease and flour two 9x5-in. loaf pans. In a large bowl, cream butter and sugar until light and fluffy, 5-7 minutes. Add eggs, 1 at a time, beating well after each addition. Beat in extracts. Add flour alternately with cream, beating just until blended. Pour into prepared pans.

**2.** Bake until a toothpick inserted in the center comes out clean, 80-85 minutes. Cool 10 minutes before removing from pans to wire racks to cool completely. Serve with fresh fruit if desired.

**1 piece:** 275 cal., 13g fat (8g sat. fat), 78mg chol., 82mg sod., 38g carb. (26g sugars, 0 fiber), 4g pro.

---

# S'MORES CUPCAKES

Marshmallow frosting puts these cupcakes over the top. Chocolate bar
pieces and graham cracker crumbs make them extra indulgent.
—*Erin Rachwal, Hartland, WI*

PREP: 30 MIN. • BAKE: 20 MIN. + COOLING • MAKES: 2 DOZEN

¾   cup water
¾   cup buttermilk
2   large eggs, room temperature
3   Tbsp. canola oil
1   tsp. vanilla extract
1½  cups all-purpose flour
1½  cups sugar
¾   cup baking cocoa
1½  tsp. baking soda
¾   tsp. salt
¾   tsp. baking powder

**FROSTING**
1½  cups butter, softened
2   cups confectioners' sugar
½   tsp. vanilla extract
2   jars (7 oz. each) marshmallow creme
2   Tbsp. graham cracker crumbs
2   milk chocolate candy bars
    Optional: Toasted marshmallows
    and graham cracker pieces

**1.** Preheat oven to 350°. In a large bowl, beat water, buttermilk, eggs, oil and vanilla until well blended. Combine flour, sugar, cocoa, baking soda, salt and baking powder; gradually beat into buttermilk mixture until blended.

**2.** Fill paper-lined muffin cups half full with batter. Bake 16-20 minutes or until a toothpick inserted in the center comes out clean. Cool in pans for 10 minutes before removing from pans to wire racks to cool completely.

**3.** For frosting, in a bowl, beat butter until fluffy; beat in confectioners' sugar and vanilla until smooth. Add marshmallow creme; beat until fluffy. Spread frosting over cupcakes. Sprinkle with cracker crumbs. Break candy bars into 24 pieces; garnish cupcakes. If desired, top with toasted marshmallows and cracker pieces.

**1 cupcake:** 330 cal., 15g fat (8g sat. fat), 47mg chol., 298mg sod., 43g carb. (35g sugars, 1g fiber), 3g pro.

> "This gets rave reviews from everyone. People often ask me to bring it to parties. Enjoy!
>
> —OUTDOORGAL
> TASTEOFHOME.COM

BANANA
CREAM PIE

# BANANA CREAM PIE

Mom's pie recipe is a real treasure, and I've never found one that tastes better!
—Bernice Morris, Marshfield, MO

PREP: 35 MIN. + COOLING • COOK: 10 MIN. + CHILLING • MAKES: 8 SERVINGS

Dough for single-crust pie
¾ cup sugar
⅓ cup all-purpose flour
¼ tsp. salt
2 cups whole milk
3 large egg yolks, lightly beaten
2 Tbsp. butter
1 tsp. vanilla extract
3 firm medium bananas
Whipped cream, optional

1. On a lightly floured surface, roll dough to a ⅛-in.-thick circle; transfer to a 9-in. pie plate. Trim to ½ in. beyond rim of plate; flute edge. Refrigerate for 30 minutes. Preheat oven to 425°.

2. Line crust with a double thickness of foil. Fill with pie weights, dried beans or uncooked rice. Bake on a lower oven rack 20-25 minutes or until edge is golden brown. Remove foil and weights; bake until bottom is golden brown, 3-6 minutes longer. Cool on a wire rack.

3. Meanwhile, in a saucepan, combine sugar, flour and salt; stir in milk and mix well. Cook over medium-high heat until mixture is thickened and bubbly. Cook and stir 2 minutes longer. Remove from heat. Stir a small amount of hot mixture into egg yolks; return all to saucepan. Bring to a gentle boil. Cook and stir 2 minutes; remove from heat. Add butter and vanilla; cool slightly.

4. Slice bananas into crust; pour filling over top. Cover and refrigerate until set, about 2 hours. If desired, garnish with whipped cream and sliced bananas.

Dough for single-crust pie: Combine 1¼ cups all-purpose flour and ¼ tsp. salt; cut in ½ cup cold butter until crumbly. Gradually add 3-5 Tbsp. ice water, tossing with a fork until dough holds together when pressed. Shape into a disk; wrap and refrigerate 1 hour.

1 piece: 338 cal., 14g fat (7g sat. fat), 101mg chol., 236mg sod., 49g carb. (30g sugars, 1g fiber), 5g pro.

# BLACKBERRY BUTTERCREAM

Juicy blackberry buttercream frosting has a stunning color and sophisticated flavor.
This frosting works especially well on rich, decadent chocolate cake.
—Jocelyn Adams, Grandbaby-cakes.com

TAKES: 10 MIN. • MAKES: 5 CUPS

1 cup fresh blackberries
2 cups unsalted butter, softened
1 tsp. vanilla extract
Dash salt
7 cups confectioners' sugar

1. Place blackberries in a blender; cover and process until pureed. Press through a fine mesh strainer into a bowl; discard seeds.

2. In a large bowl, beat butter until creamy. Beat in vanilla and salt. Gradually beat in confectioners' sugar until smooth. Add blackberry puree; beat until blended.

2 Tbsp.: 165 cal., 9g fat (6g sat. fat), 24mg chol., 5mg sod., 21g carb. (21g sugars, 0 fiber), 0 pro.

# CARROT CUPCAKES

To try to get my family to eat more vegetables, I often hide nutritional foods inside sweet treats. Now we can have our cake and eat our vegetables too!
—*Doreen Kelly, Roslyn, PA*

**PREP:** 15 MIN. • **BAKE:** 20 MIN. • **MAKES:** 2 DOZEN

4  large eggs, room temperature
2  cups sugar
1  cup canola oil
2  cups all-purpose flour
2  tsp. ground cinnamon
1  tsp. baking soda
1  tsp. baking powder
1  tsp. ground allspice
½  tsp. salt
3  cups grated carrots

**CHUNKY FROSTING**
1  pkg. (8 oz.) cream cheese, softened
¼  cup butter, softened
2  cups confectioners' sugar
½  cup sweetened shredded coconut
½  cup chopped pecans
½  cup chopped raisins

**1.** Preheat oven to 325°. In a large bowl, beat eggs, sugar and oil. Combine flour, cinnamon, baking soda, baking powder, allspice and salt; gradually add to the egg mixture. Stir in carrots.

**2.** Fill 24 greased or paper-lined muffin cups two-thirds full with batter. Bake until a toothpick inserted in the center comes out clean, 20-25 minutes. Cool 5 minutes before removing from pans to wire racks.

**3.** For the frosting, in a large bowl, beat cream cheese and butter until fluffy. Gradually beat in confectioners' sugar until smooth. Stir in coconut, pecans and raisins. Frost cupcakes. Store in the refrigerator.

**Note:** Thicken the frosting by adding more confectioners' sugar until you reach the desired consistency. Alternatively, thin it out by adding a few more teaspoons of water, 1 tsp. at a time.

**1 cupcake:** 326 cal., 18g fat (5g sat. fat), 51mg chol., 187mg sod., 40g carb. (30g sugars, 1g fiber), 3g pro.

---

# FLUFFY WHITE FROSTING

For a heavenly light and fluffy frosting, you can't top this variation of the classic seven-minute frosting.
—*Georgia Bohmann, West Allis, WI*

**TAKES:** 20 MIN. • **MAKES:** 4 CUPS

4  large egg whites
1⅓  cups sugar
1  Tbsp. water
½  tsp. cream of tartar
1  tsp. vanilla extract

**1.** In a stand mixer, whisk egg whites, sugar, water and cream of tartar until blended. Place mixture over simmering water in a large saucepan over medium heat. Whisking constantly, heat mixture 3-5 minutes or until a thermometer reads 160°.

**2.** Remove from heat; add vanilla. With the whisk attachment, beat on high until stiff glossy peaks form, about 7 minutes. Use immediately.

**2 Tbsp.:** 35 cal., 0 fat (0 sat. fat), 0 chol., 7mg sod., 8g carb. (8g sugars, 0 fiber), 0 pro.

66
Everyone's favorite for sure! I make them time and time again. I even get requests to bring these to birthdays!
—DANIELLEYLEE
TASTEOFHOME.COM

# SPECIAL-OCCASION CHOCOLATE CAKE

This recipe won Grand Champion at the Alaska State Fair, and with just one bite, you'll see why! The decadent chocolate cake boasts a luscious ganache filling and fudge buttercream frosting.
—*Cindi DeClue, Anchorage, AK*

**PREP:** 40 MIN. • **BAKE:** 25 MIN. + COOLING • **MAKES:** 16 SERVINGS

1 cup baking cocoa
2 cups boiling water
1 cup butter, softened
2¼ cups sugar
4 large eggs, room temperature
1½ tsp. vanilla extract
2¾ cups all-purpose flour
2 tsp. baking soda
½ tsp. baking powder
½ tsp. salt

**GANACHE**
10 oz. semisweet chocolate, chopped
1 cup heavy whipping cream
2 Tbsp. sugar

**FROSTING**
1 cup butter, softened
4 cups confectioners' sugar
½ cup baking cocoa
¼ cup 2% milk
2 tsp. vanilla extract

**GARNISH**
¾ cup sliced almonds, toasted

**1.** Preheat the oven to 350°. In a small bowl, combine baking cocoa and water; set aside to cool completely. In a large bowl, cream butter and sugar until light and fluffy, 5-7 minutes. Add eggs, 1 at a time, beating well after each addition. Beat in vanilla. Whisk together flour, baking soda, baking powder and salt; add to creamed mixture alternately with cocoa mixture, beating well after each addition.

**2.** Pour into 3 greased and floured 9-in. round baking pans. Bake until a toothpick inserted in the center comes out clean, 25-30 minutes. Cool for 10 minutes before removing from pans to wire racks to cool completely.

**3.** For ganache, place semisweet chocolate in a bowl. In a small heavy saucepan over low heat, bring whipping cream and sugar to a boil. Pour over chocolate; whisk gently until smooth. Allow to cool until it reaches a spreadable consistency, stirring occasionally.

**4.** For frosting, in a large bowl, beat butter until fluffy. Add confectioners' sugar, cocoa, milk and vanilla; beat until smooth.

**5.** Place the first cake layer on a serving plate; spread with 1 cup frosting. Top with the second layer and 1 cup ganache; sprinkle with ½ cup almonds. Top with the third layer; frost the top and side of cake. Warm ganache until pourable; pour over cake, allowing some to flow down the side. Sprinkle with remaining almonds. Refrigerate until serving.

**1 piece:** 736 cal., 39g fat (22g sat. fat), 125mg chol., 454mg sod., 86g carb. (63g sugars, 3g fiber), 8g pro.

# WINNING RHUBARB-STRAWBERRY PIE

While growing up on a farm, I often ate rhubarb, so it's natural for me to use it in a pie.
I prefer to use lard for the flaky pie crust, and thin red rhubarb stalks for the filling.
These two little secrets helped this recipe win top honors at the Iowa State Fair.
—*Marianne Carlson, Jefferson, IA*

**PREP:** 50 MIN. + CHILLING • **BAKE:** 65 MIN. + COOLING • **MAKES:** 8 SERVINGS

1 large egg
4 to 5 Tbsp. ice water, divided
¾ tsp. white vinegar
2¼ cups all-purpose flour
¾ tsp. salt
¾ cup cold lard

**FILLING**
1¼ cups sugar
6 Tbsp. quick-cooking tapioca
3 cups sliced fresh or frozen rhubarb, thawed
3 cups halved fresh strawberries
3 Tbsp. butter
1 Tbsp. 2% milk
Coarse sugar

**1.** In a small bowl, whisk egg, 4 Tbsp. ice water and vinegar until blended. In a large bowl, mix flour and salt; cut in lard until crumbly. Gradually add egg mixture, tossing with a fork, until dough holds together when pressed. If mixture is too dry, slowly add additional ice water, 1 tsp. at a time, just until dough comes together.

**2.** Divide dough in half. Shape each into a disk; wrap and refrigerate 1 hour or overnight.

**3.** Preheat oven to 400°. In a large bowl, mix sugar and tapioca. Add rhubarb and strawberries; toss to coat evenly. Let stand 15 minutes.

**4.** On a lightly floured surface, roll half the dough to a ⅛-in.-thick circle; transfer to a 9-in. pie plate. Trim crust even with rim.

**5.** Add filling; dot with butter. Roll remaining dough to a ⅛-in.-thick circle. Place over filling. Trim, seal and flute edge. Cut slits in top. Brush milk over top crust; sprinkle with coarse sugar. Place pie on a baking sheet; bake 20 minutes.

**6.** Reduce oven setting to 350°. Bake 45-55 minutes longer or until crust is golden brown and filling is bubbly. Cool pie on a wire rack.

**Note** If using frozen rhubarb, measure rhubarb while still frozen, then thaw completely. Drain in a colander, but do not press liquid out.

**1 piece:** 531 cal., 25g fat (11g sat. fat), 53mg chol., 269mg sod., 73g carb. (35g sugars, 3g fiber), 5g pro.

LAYERED STRAWBERRY
POUND CAKE DESSERT,
PAGE 302

" This is a wonderful recipe. The three layers make it a showstopper.
—KM1995
TASTEOFHOME.COM

# CHAPTER 11

# MUST-TRY DESSERTS

When you need a special surprise to cap off a meal, turn to this mouthwatering collection of ideas. For everything from tarts and ice cream to cheesecake and mousse, you'll always find the perfect family-favorite finale here.

# PEANUT BUTTER MOUSSE

This is a nice light mousse that packs plenty of peanut butter flavor. It can be prepared and frozen ahead of time.
—*Cindi DeClue, Anchorage, AK*

**PREP TIME: 15 MIN. + CHILLING • MAKES: 12 SERVINGS**

2 cups heavy whipping cream
3 Tbsp. vanilla extract
1 pkg. (8 oz.) cream cheese, softened
¾ cup confectioners' sugar
1 jar (16 oz.) creamy peanut butter
Optional: Chocolate shavings and chopped salted peanuts

**1.** In a large bowl, beat cream and vanilla until stiff peaks form. In another bowl, beat cream cheese and sugar until smooth. Gradually beat in peanut butter to cream cheese mixture until smooth; fold in whipped cream.

**2.** Spoon into dessert dishes; top with chocolate and peanuts, if desired. Refrigerate at least 1 hour before serving.

**½ cup mousse:** 514 cal., 43g fat (17g sat. fat), 64mg chol., 252mg sod., 25g carb. (19g sugars, 2g fiber), 12g pro.

# SOUTHERN BRULEED PEACH TARTS

This is my creative homage to our southern fresh peach cobbler. It is an upscale presentation with delicious peaches and is very easy to prepare.
—*Mary Louise Lever, Rome, GA*

**PREP: 15 MIN. + STANDING • BROIL: 5 MIN. • MAKES: 12 SERVINGS**

3 medium ripe peaches, peeled and thinly sliced
3 Tbsp. peach preserves
1 tsp. lemon juice
¼ tsp. minced fresh gingerroot
¼ tsp. ground cinnamon
6 English muffins, split and toasted
1 carton (8 oz.) mascarpone cheese
⅓ cup packed light brown sugar
Fresh mint leaves

**1.** In a large bowl, combine the first 5 ingredients. Let stand for 15 minutes, stirring occasionally. Spread cut sides of English muffins with mascarpone cheese. Drain peaches, reserving liquid. Arrange peaches over muffins; brush with some of the reserved liquid. Place on a foil-lined baking sheet; sprinkle with brown sugar.

**2.** Broil 3-4 in. from heat until caramelized and bubbly, 3-4 minutes. Garnish with mint.

**1 tart:** 202 cal., 9g fat (5g sat. fat), 24mg chol., 136mg sod., 27g carb. (13g sugars, 1g fiber), 4g pro.

## TEST KITCHEN TIP

*For an adult version, use 1 tablespoon peach schnapps or Grand Marnier instead of peach preserves.*

> **Amazing! I plan on making these gems again and again. Delicious.**
> —JELLYBUG
> TASTEOFHOME.COM

# NONNI'S FRITOLE

My Italian grandmother was famous for her fritole and made these treats for her family and friends. Years later we found her recipe card and tried making them without success for several years. We finally figured out the missing part —the self-rising flour! Now we can have these as often as we like.
—Ann Marie Eberhart, Gig Harbor, WA

**PREP:** 15 MIN. • **COOK:** 5 MIN./BATCH • **MAKES:** 4 DOZEN

4 cups self-rising flour
½ cup sugar
3 large eggs, room temperature
1 cup whole milk
3 oz. whiskey, rum or orange juice
2 medium apples, peeled and grated
8 tsp. grated orange zest
   Oil for deep-fat frying
   Confectioners' sugar

1. In a large bowl, whisk flour and sugar. In another bowl, whisk eggs, milk and whiskey until blended. Add to dry ingredients, stirring just until moistened. Fold in apples and zest.

2. In an electric skillet or deep fryer, heat oil to 375°. Drop batter by tablespoonfuls, a few at a time, into hot oil. Fry until golden brown, about 2 minutes on each side. Drain on paper towels. Dust with confectioners' sugar.

**Note:** As a substitute for each cup of self-rising flour, place 1½ tsp. baking powder and ½ tsp. salt in a measuring cup. Add all-purpose flour to measure 1 cup.

**1 fritter:** 69 cal., 2g fat (0 sat. fat), 12mg chol., 131mg sod., 11g carb. (3g sugars, 0 fiber), 2g pro.

# REFRESHING RHUBARB ICE CREAM

No matter where my military family is stationed, this ice cream always makes me think of my parents' backyard rhubarb patch in Rochester, New York.
—Rachel Garcia, Honolulu, HI

**PREP:** 25 MIN. + FREEZING • **BAKE:** 30 MIN. • **MAKES:** ABOUT 2¾ CUPS

3 cups sliced fresh rhubarb
2 cups sugar
1 tsp. lemon juice
1 cup heavy whipping cream

1. Preheat oven to 375°. In an ungreased baking dish, combine rhubarb and sugar; toss to combine. Bake, covered, 30-40 minutes, stirring occasionally. Cool slightly.

2. Place rhubarb mixture in a blender; cover and process until pureed. Transfer to a bowl; refrigerate, covered.

3. Stir lemon juice into rhubarb. In a small bowl, beat cream until stiff peaks form; fold into rhubarb mixture. Transfer to a shallow 1-qt. freezer container. Freeze 1 hour, stirring every 15 minutes. Freeze, covered, overnight or until firm.

**½ cup:** 489 cal., 18g fat (11g sat. fat), 65mg chol., 22mg sod., 85g carb. (81g sugars, 1g fiber), 2g pro.

# SPICY MOLE BARK

Traditional Mexican mole sauces are made with chocolate, chiles, fruit, nuts and seeds,
so it makes sense all of these ingredients would work well in bark. One bite and you'll be hooked.
—*James Schend, Pleasant Prairie, WI*

**PREP:** 15 MIN. + CHILLING • **MAKES:** ABOUT 1 LB.

1 pkg. (12 oz.) milk chocolate chips
½ cup golden raisins, divided
⅓ cup crushed tortilla chips
¼ cup salted pumpkin seeds or pepitas, divided
2 Tbsp. sesame seeds, divided
1 tsp. ground cinnamon
1 tsp. ground ancho chile pepper
¼ tsp. crushed red pepper flakes, divided

1. Line a 15x10x1-in. pan with parchment; set aside.

2. In a double boiler or metal bowl over hot water, melt chocolate until ⅔ chips are melted. Remove from heat; stir until smooth. Stir in ¼ cup raisins, tortilla chips, 2 Tbsp. salted pumpkin seeds, 1 Tbsp. sesame seeds, cinnamon, ancho chile, and ⅛ tsp. pepper flakes. Spread into prepared pan; top with remaining ingredients (pan will not be full). Refrigerate until firm, 15-20 minutes. Break or cut into pieces. Store in an airtight container.

**1 oz.:** 142 cal., 8g fat (4g sat. fat), 5mg chol., 26mg sod., 17g carb. (13g sugars, 1g fiber), 2g pro.

# AIR-FRYER PEAR POTPIES

I love to make potpies when pears are in season. I love them
so much more than apples because they have a better flavor.
—*Bee Engelhart, Bloomfield Township, MI*

**PREP:** 20 MIN. • **COOK:** 20 MIN. • **MAKES:** 4 SERVINGS

2 Tbsp. butter, divided
2 Tbsp. sugar
1 Tbsp. cornflake crumbs
1 Tbsp. brown sugar
¼ tsp. ground ginger
2 cups finely chopped peeled Anjou pears
2 cups finely chopped peeled Bartlett pears
1 Tbsp. orange juice
½ sheet frozen puff pastry, thawed
    Vanilla ice cream

1. Grease bottoms and sides of four 8-oz. ramekins with 1 Tbsp. butter (do not butter rims).

2. In a small bowl, mix sugar, cornflake crumbs, brown sugar and ginger. In a large bowl, toss pears with orange juice. Add crumb mixture and toss to combine. Divide mixture among ramekins; dot with remaining butter.

3. Preheat air fryer to 325°. Unfold pastry; cut into ½-in. strips. Arrange over the ramekins in a lattice pattern, trimming to fit. Gently press ends onto ramekin rims.

4. Place ramekins in air fryer. Cook until filling is bubbly and pastry is golden brown, 20-25 minutes. Serve warm, with ice cream.

**1 potpie:** 343 cal., 15g fat (6g sat. fat), 62mg chol., 177mg sod., 50g carb. (24g sugars, 7g fiber), 5g pro.

# COPYCAT CELEBRATION CHEESECAKE

*My children were born on the same day five years apart, so I go all out for their celebration.
A takeoff on a Cheesecake Factory classic, this seven-layer beauty is impressive. The baking
and prep is easy, but assembly does take some time, so set aside an afternoon.*
—*Kristyne McDougle Walter, Lorain, OH*

PREP: 1 HOUR + FREEZING • BAKE: 30 MIN. + COOLING • MAKES: 16 SERVINGS

4  cups cold 2% milk
3  pkg. (3.4 oz. each) instant white chocolate pudding mix
1  pkg. white cake mix (regular size)
1⅓ cups rainbow sprinkles, divided
1  pkg. (1 oz.) freeze-dried strawberries
3  to 12 drops blue food coloring
¼  cup baking cocoa
2  cartons (24.3 oz. each) Philadelphia ready-to-serve cheesecake filling
2  cans (16 oz. each) cream cheese frosting
2  Tbsp. rainbow sequin sprinkles

**1.** Preheat oven to 350°. In each of 3 small bowls, whisk 1⅓ cups milk and 1 pudding mix for 2 minutes. Refrigerate, covered, while baking cake layers.

**2.** Line bottoms of 2 greased 9-in. round baking pans with parchment; grease paper. Prepare cake mix batter according to package directions, folding ⅔ cup sprinkles into batter. Transfer to prepared pans. Bake and cool as package directs.

**3.** Using a long serrated knife, trim tops of cake layers to level. Crumble trimmings; transfer to a parchment-lined baking sheet. Bake at 350° until crisp but not browned, about 5 minutes. Cool completely on pan on wire rack.

**4.** Line two 9-in. springform pans with plastic wrap, letting ends extend over sides. Place strawberries in a food processor; process until ground. Stir ground strawberries into 1 bowl of pudding. To another bowl of pudding, whisk in blue food coloring. To the third bowl, whisk in cocoa; refrigerate chocolate pudding.

**5.** Place 1 cake layer in 1 prepared springform pan; spread with strawberry pudding. Place remaining cake layer in remaining prepared springform pan; spread with blue pudding. Freeze both pans at least 1 hour. Top each with 1 carton cheesecake filling. Freeze at least 1 hour longer.

**6.** Remove strawberry-layered pan from freezer; spread chocolate pudding over top. Return to freezer for 3 hours. Meanwhile, stir remaining ⅔ cup sprinkles into cooled cake crumbs.

**7.** Remove rims from springform pans; discard plastic. Place strawberry-layered cake on a serving plate; top with blue-layered cake. Frost top and side with frosting. Gently press crumb mixture into frosting on side of cake; sprinkle with sequins. Freeze until ready to serve. Remove 10 minutes before cutting.

**Note:** This recipe was tested with Hershey's White Chocolate Instant Pudding Mix.

**1 piece:** 871 cal., 43g fat (19g sat. fat), 120mg chol., 929mg sod., 114g carb. (90g sugars, 1g fiber), 9g pro.

# DARK CHOCOLATE BOURBON BALLS

Here's a chocolate classic made easy. The blended flavor of bourbon and pecans is irresistible!

—Taste of Home *Test Kitchen*

PREP: 30 MIN. + CHILLING • MAKES: 4 DOZEN

1¼ cups finely chopped
    pecans, divided
¼  cup bourbon
½  cup butter, softened
3¾ cups confectioners' sugar
1  lb. dark chocolate candy
    coating, melted

1. Combine 1 cup pecans and bourbon; let stand, covered, for 8 hours or overnight.

2. Cream butter and confectioners' sugar, ¼ cup at a time, until crumbly; stir in pecan mixture. Refrigerate, covered, until firm, 45 minutes. Shape into 1-in. balls; place on waxed paper-lined baking sheets. Refrigerate until firm, about 1 hour.

3. Dip in chocolate coating; allow excess to drip off. Sprinkle with remaining ¼ cup pecans. Let stand until set.

**1 bourbon ball:** 124 cal., 7g fat (4g sat. fat), 5mg chol., 15mg sod., 16g carb. (15g sugars, 0 fiber), 0 pro.

## TEST KITCHEN TIP

*If you want these treats to be alcohol-free, simply replace the bourbon with apple juice.*

# LAYERED STRAWBERRY POUND CAKE DESSERT

SHOWN ON PAGE 292

My mother's cousin shared this recipe more than 50 years ago. Our family has enjoyed it ever since, especially on a hot New Mexico day! It can be made the day before.

—*Vickie Britton, Hobbs, NM*

PREP: 20 MIN. + CHILLING • MAKES: 24 SERVINGS

1  loaf (10¾ oz.) frozen pound cake,
    thawed
1  pkg. (8 oz.) cream cheese, softened
1  can (14 oz.) sweetened
    condensed milk
⅓  cup lemon juice
1  carton (12 oz.) frozen whipped
    topping, thawed, divided
1  container (16 oz.) frozen sweetened
    sliced strawberries, thawed, divided

1. Cut pound cake into ½-in. slices; place in bottom of a 13x9-in. baking dish. In a large bowl, beat cream cheese until smooth. Beat in milk and lemon juice until blended. Fold in 2⅔ cups whipped topping and 1½ cups strawberries with juice.

2. Spread mixture over pound cake. Top with remaining whipped topping. Refrigerate, covered, at least 4 hours or overnight. Top with the remaining ½ cup strawberries in juice before serving.

**1 piece:** 195 cal., 10g fat (7g sat. fat), 34mg chol., 88mg sod., 24g carb. (20g sugars, 0 fiber), 3g pro.

DARK CHOCOLATE
BOURBON BALLS

# FRESH PLUM KUCHEN

In summer when plums are in season, this tender fruit-topped cake is delectable! For variety, you can use fresh pears or apples instead.
—Anna Daley, Montague, PE

PREP: 20 MIN. • BAKE: 40 MIN. + COOLING • MAKES: 12 SERVINGS

¼ cup butter, softened
¾ cup sugar
2 large eggs, room temperature
1 cup all-purpose flour
1 tsp. baking powder
¼ cup 2% milk
1 tsp. grated lemon zest
2 cups sliced fresh plums (about 4 medium)
½ cup packed brown sugar
1 tsp. ground cinnamon
Confectioners' sugar, optional

1. Preheat oven to 350°. In a small bowl, cream butter and sugar until light and fluffy, 5-7 minutes. Beat in eggs. Combine flour and baking powder; add to the creamed mixture alternately with milk, beating well after each addition. Add lemon zest. Pour into a greased 10-in. springform pan. Arrange plums on top; gently press into batter. Sprinkle the top with brown sugar and cinnamon.

2. Place pan on a baking sheet. Bake until top is golden and a toothpick inserted in the center comes out clean, 40-50 minutes. Cool 10 minutes. Run a knife around edge of pan; remove rim. Cool on a wire rack. If desired, dust with confectioners' sugar just before serving.

**1 piece:** 185 cal., 5g fat (3g sat. fat), 46mg chol., 89mg sod., 33g carb. (24g sugars, 1g fiber), 3g pro.

# STRAWBERRY PRETZEL DESSERT MINIS

Need to bring a dish to pass this weekend? This make-ahead layered dessert, adorable in individual Mason jars, will disappear quickly at any potluck.
—Aldene Belch, Flint, MI

PREP: 30 MIN. • BAKE: 15 MIN. + CHILLING • MAKES: 32 SERVINGS

2 cups crushed pretzels (about 8 oz.)
¾ cup butter, melted
3 Tbsp. sugar

**FILLING**
2 cups whipped topping
1 pkg. (8 oz.) cream cheese, softened
1 cup sugar

**TOPPING**
2 pkg. (3 oz. each) strawberry gelatin
2 cups boiling water
2 pkg. (16 oz. each) frozen sweetened sliced strawberries, thawed

1. Preheat oven to 350°. In a small bowl, combine pretzels, butter and sugar; spread onto a baking sheet. Bake until crisp and lightly browned, 12-15 minutes. Cool completely on a wire rack; break into small pieces.

2. For filling, in a bowl, beat whipped topping, cream cheese and sugar until smooth. Refrigerate until chilled.

3. For topping, in a bowl, dissolve gelatin in boiling water. Stir in strawberries; chill until partially set, about 1 hour. Layer pretzel mixture, filling and topping into glass jars. Chill at least 2 hours. If desired, serve with whipped topping and pretzels.

**1 jar:** 172 cal., 8g fat (5g sat. fat), 19mg chol., 151mg sod., 25g carb. (20g sugars, 1g fiber), 2g pro.

# PRESSURE-COOKER BUTTERNUT RICE PUDDING

This tasty rice pudding blends all our favorite flavors of
fall into one comforting dessert. The ease of the pressure
cooker allows you to limit your dishes and cuts cooking time.
—*Gretchen Monahan, Palmyra, PA*

**PREP: 35 MIN. • COOK: 15 MIN. + RELEASING • MAKES: 10 SERVINGS**

3 Tbsp. butter, divided
½ cup chopped walnuts
2 Tbsp. plus ¾ cup packed
   brown sugar, divided
1 medium butternut squash,
   halved and seeds removed
2¼ cups water, divided
⅓ cup dried cranberries
1¼ cups uncooked jasmine rice, rinsed
4 cups whole milk
¼ cup cornstarch
1 medium apple, finely chopped
1 tsp. vanilla extract
½ tsp. ground cinnamon
   Whipped cream, optional

**1.** Select saute setting on a 6-qt. electric pressure cooker. Adjust for low heat; add 2 Tbsp. butter. When butter is melted, add the walnuts and 2 Tbsp. brown sugar. Cook and stir until nuts are coated, 5-7 minutes. Press cancel. Transfer nuts to a bowl; set aside. Wipe inner pot clean.

**2.** In the same inner pot, add squash, in batches, cut side down. Select saute setting; adjust for medium heat. Cook for 2 minutes. Press cancel. Return all squash to cooker. Add 1 cup water and cranberries. Lock lid; close pressure-release valve. Adjust to pressure-cook on high for 7 minutes. Allow pressure to release naturally for 10 minutes; quick-release any remaining pressure. Remove squash. Drain cranberries. Place cranberries in a large bowl.

**3.** When cool enough to handle, remove flesh from squash; discard skins. Place squash in a blender; cover and process until smooth. Wipe inner pot clean. Add rice and remaining 1¼ cups water. Lock lid; close pressure-release valve. Adjust to pressure-cook on high for 4 minutes. Allow pressure to release naturally for 10 minutes; quick-release any of the remaining pressure. Stir rice into cranberries.

**4.** In the same inner pot, whisk milk, cornstarch and remaining 1 Tbsp. butter. Select saute setting; adjust for low heat. Simmer until thickened, about 5 minutes. Stir in 1 cup pureed squash (save remaining for another use), apple and remaining ¾ cup brown sugar. Stir in rice mixture, vanilla and cinnamon. Cook and stir for 5-7 minutes or until thickened. Press cancel. Pudding will continue to thicken upon standing. Serve warm with candied walnuts and, if desired, whipped cream and additional ground cinnamon. Refrigerate leftovers.

**¾ cup:** 342 cal., 11g fat (4g sat. fat), 19mg chol., 77mg sod., 56g carb. (29g sugars, 2g fiber), 6g pro.

> 66
> This is so easy
> and incredibly
> delicious. It was
> even good cold
> for breakfast
> the next day.
> —BUTCHER2BOY
> TASTEOFHOME.COM

# ROASTED GRAPE & SWEET CHEESE PHYLLO GALETTE

Faced with an abundant crop of grapes, I had to come up with a creative way to use them.
In this recipe, a layer of orange-kissed cream cheese is topped with roasted grapes.
Then a bit of honey is drizzled on, and a sprinkle of coarse sugar is added to finish it off.
—*Kallee Krong-McCreery, Escondido, CA*

PREP: 25 MIN. • BAKE: 35 MIN. + COOLING • MAKES: 10 SERVINGS

1 pkg. (8 oz.) cream cheese, softened
2 Tbsp. orange marmalade
1 tsp. sugar
8 sheets phyllo dough (14x9-in. size)
4 Tbsp. butter, melted
1 cup seedless grapes
1 Tbsp. honey
2 tsp. coarse sugar

1. Preheat oven to 350°. In a large bowl, beat cream cheese, marmalade and sugar until smooth; set aside.

2. Place 1 sheet of phyllo on a parchment-lined baking sheet; brush with butter. Layer with remaining phyllo sheets, brushing each layer. (Keep remaining phyllo covered with a damp towel to prevent it from drying out.) Spread cream cheese mixture over phyllo to within 2 in. of edges. Arrange grapes over cream cheese.

3. Fold edges of phyllo over filling, leaving center uncovered. Brush folded phyllo with any remaining butter; drizzle with honey and sprinkle with coarse sugar. Bake until phyllo is golden brown, 35-40 minutes. Transfer to a wire rack to cool completely. Refrigerate leftovers.

**1 piece:** 177 cal., 13g fat (8g sat. fat), 35mg chol., 148mg sod., 15g carb. (9g sugars, 0 fiber), 2g pro.

# CHOCOLATE SQUASH MOUSSE

I love that this recipe is rich and decadent yet is made with healthy ingredients!
—*Andy Huffman, Reno, NV*

PREP: 15 MIN. + CHILLING • MAKES: 8 SERVINGS

1½ cups raw cashews
1 can (13.66 oz.) unsweetened coconut cream
1 cup sweet potato puree or canned pumpkin
⅓ cup baking cocoa
¼ cup maple syrup
½ tsp. salt
Optional: Cashews, chocolate shavings and flake sea salt

1. Rinse cashews in cold water; drain. Place in a large bowl; add enough water to cover by 3 in. Cover and let stand overnight.

2. Drain and rinse cashews. Place cashews in a food processor. Add coconut cream, puree, cocoa, syrup and salt; cover and process until pureed. Transfer to 8 dessert dishes. Refrigerate, covered, at least 4 hours. Top with cashews, chocolate shavings and flake sea salt.

**½ cup:** 286 cal., 19g fat (11g sat. fat), 0 chol., 177mg sod., 23g carb. (11g sugars, 2g fiber), 6g pro.

# GANACHE-TOPPED PUMPKIN TART

I love the combination of spiced pumpkin and chocolate, which inspired me to create this tart. Sometimes I like to sprinkle chopped crystallized ginger over the chocolate ganache for extra flavor and texture.
—*Bernice Janowski, Stevens Point, WI*

**PREP:** 20 MIN. + CHILLING • **BAKE:** 55 MIN. • **MAKES:** 8 SERVINGS

1 cup all-purpose flour
¾ cup sugar
½ cup baking cocoa
1 tsp. pumpkin pie spice
½ tsp. salt
½ cup butter, melted

**FILLING**
1 can (15 oz.) pumpkin
3 large eggs
¾ cup packed dark brown sugar
2 tsp. grated orange zest
2 tsp. pumpkin pie spice
¼ tsp. salt
½ cup heavy whipping cream

**GANACHE**
¾ cup semisweet chocolate chips
½ cup heavy whipping cream
 Crystallized ginger, chopped, optional

**1.** Preheat oven to 425°. In a large bowl, combine flour, sugar, baking cocoa, pie spice and salt. Stir in butter until crumbly. Press onto bottom and up side of a 9-in. tart pan with removable bottom; place on a baking sheet. Bake 10 minutes; cool on a wire rack.

**2.** Meanwhile, in another bowl, whisk pumpkin, eggs, brown sugar, orange zest, pie spice and salt. Slowly whisk in cream. Pour into crust. Bake 15 minutes. Reduce temperature to 350°. Bake until filling is set, 40-45 minutes. Cool on a wire rack.

**3.** For ganache, place chocolate chips in a small bowl. In a saucepan, bring cream just to a boil. Pour over chocolate; let stand 10 minutes. Stir with a whisk until smooth. Spread over tart; chill until set. If desired, garnish with crystallized ginger.

**1 piece:** 551 cal., 30g fat (18g sat. fat), 134mg chol., 358mg sod., 70g carb. (50g sugars, 4g fiber), 7g pro.

## TEST KITCHEN TIP

*This recipe was tested with canned pumpkin. You can use fresh pumpkin puree instead, but the texture and flavor will differ. Make sure you know the differences between canned and fresh pumpkin before you decide!*

# STRAWBERRY, BASIL & HONEY PALETAS

This recipe for strawberry paletas is one of my favorites. It's fruity, fragrant, sweet and refreshing—perfect for a warm summer day outdoors.
—*Ericka Sanchez, La Habra, CA*

**PREP:** 15 MIN. + FREEZING • **MAKES:** 10 SERVINGS

1 lb. chopped fresh strawberries
⅓ cup fresh basil leaves
1½ tsp. fresh lime juice
¼ cup raw honey
3 fresh strawberries

In a blender, puree chopped strawberries, basil and lime juice until smooth. Add honey and blend to combine. Hull and slice remaining strawberries. Divide among pop molds or cups. Pour pureed mixture into molds, filling almost full. Top molds with holders. If using cups, top with foil and insert sticks through foil. Freeze until firm, at least 4 hours.

**1 pop:** 42 cal., 0 fat (0 sat. fat), 0 chol., 1mg sod., 11g carb. (9g sugars, 1g fiber), 0 pro.
**Diabetic exchanges:** ½ starch.

GANACHE-TOPPED PUMPKIN TART

# AIR-FRYER CREME BRULEE

There is something so elegant and regal about creme brulee but when you really think about it, it's just a baked custard. I love to make these, and no one has any idea how easy it is.
—*Joylyn Trickel, Helendale, CA*

PREP: 15 MIN. • COOK: 20 MIN. + CHILLING • MAKES: 4 SERVINGS

2   cups heavy whipping cream
5   large egg yolks
6   Tbsp. sugar
½   tsp. vanilla extract
2   Tbsp. brown sugar

1. In a large saucepan, combine cream, egg yolks and sugar. Cook and stir over medium heat until mixture reaches 160° or is thick enough to coat the back of a metal spoon. Stir in vanilla.

2. Preheat air fryer to 275°. Transfer mixture to four 8-oz. ramekins. In batches if necessary, place ramekins in air fryer. Cook until centers are just set (mixture will jiggle), 20-25 minutes. Cool for 10 minutes; cover and refrigerate for 4 hours.

3. One hour before serving, sprinkle each with 1½ tsp. brown sugar. Using a kitchen torch or blow torch, caramelize sugar until dark golden brown. Or broil 8 in. from the heat until sugar is caramelized, 4-7 minutes. Refrigerate leftovers.

**1 creme brulee:** 577 cal., 49g fat (30g sat. fat), 366mg chol., 45mg sod., 30g carb. (29g sugars, 0 fiber), 7g pro.

# SOUTHERN PEACH COBBLER

When fresh peaches are in season, cobblers are the first thing I think about. This is perfect for any cookout or family gathering.
—*Betty Clark, Mt. Vernon, MO*

PREP: 10 MIN. • BAKE: 35 MIN. • MAKES: 12 SERVINGS

1   cup packed brown sugar
¼   cup cornstarch
1   cup water
9   cups sliced fresh or frozen peaches
¼   cup butter
1   Tbsp. fresh lemon juice

**TOPPING**
2   cups all-purpose flour
¾   cup sugar
1   Tbsp. baking powder
¼   tsp. salt
¾   cup 2% milk
½   cup butter, melted
1½  tsp. grated orange zest, optional
    Vanilla ice cream, optional

1. Preheat oven to 400°. In a Dutch oven, combine brown sugar, cornstarch and water until smooth. Add the peaches; bring to a boil. Cook and stir for 2 minutes. Reduce heat to low; stir in butter and lemon juice.

2. For topping, combine flour, sugar, baking powder and salt in a bowl. Stir in milk, butter and orange zest if desired. Transfer hot peach mixture to an ungreased 13x9-in. baking dish. Spoon topping over peaches. Bake, uncovered, until golden brown, 30 to 35 minutes. If desired, serve with vanilla ice cream.

**1 serving:** 360 cal., 12g fat (8g sat. fat), 32mg chol., 274mg sod., 61g carb. (41g sugars, 2g fiber), 4g pro.

# PEACH SUGAR COOKIE CRUMBLE

This is like peach crisp with a sugar cookie topping. It's delicious with ice cream.
—*Teri Rasey, Cadillac, MI*

**PREP:** 30 MIN. • **BAKE:** 35 MIN. • **MAKES:** 12 SERVINGS

2 Tbsp. butter
4 cans (15¼ oz. each) sliced peaches, drained
1¾ cups sugar, divided
3 tsp. vanilla extract, divided
1 tsp. crystallized ginger, chopped
½ tsp. ground cinnamon
1 cup shortening
¼ cup packed brown sugar
1 large egg, room temperature
1 tsp. almond extract
2½ cups all-purpose flour
1 Tbsp. cornstarch
1 tsp. baking soda
½ tsp. baking powder
Optional: Chopped pecans, coarse sugar and vanilla ice cream

**1.** Preheat oven to 350°. Melt butter in a 12-in. cast-iron or other ovenproof skillet over medium heat. Add canned sliced peaches, ¾ cup sugar, 2 tsp. vanilla, crystallized chopped ginger and cinnamon. Cook and stir until peaches soften and begin to break down, about 10 minutes. Remove from the heat.

**2.** In a large bowl, cream shortening, brown sugar and remaining 1 cup sugar until light and fluffy, 5-7 minutes. Beat in egg, almond extract and remaining 1 tsp. vanilla. In another bowl, whisk flour, cornstarch, baking soda and baking powder; gradually beat into creamed mixture. Crumble dough over peach mixture. If desired, sprinkle with pecans and coarse sugar.

**3.** Bake until a toothpick inserted in center comes out clean, 35-40 minutes. Cool on a wire rack. If desired, serve with vanilla ice cream.

**1 serving:** 480 cal., 19g fat (5g sat. fat), 21mg chol., 156mg sod., 73g carb. (52g sugars, 2g fiber), 3g pro.

---

# PEANUT BUTTER & JELLY ICE CREAM

What could be better than peanut butter and jelly ice cream? You'll love the sweet-salty combination.
—*Taste of Home Test Kitchen*

**PREP:** 20 MIN. + CHILLING • **PROCESS:** 20 MIN. + FREEZING • **MAKES:** 10 SERVINGS (1¼ QT.)

1½ cups whole milk
⅔ cup packed brown sugar
½ tsp. salt
1 large egg, lightly beaten
⅔ cup creamy peanut butter
2 cups heavy whipping cream
2 tsp. vanilla extract
½ cup grape jelly or strawberry jelly

**1.** In a large heavy saucepan, heat the milk, brown sugar and salt until bubbles form around side of pan. Whisk a small amount of hot mixture into the egg. Return all to the pan, whisking constantly.

**2.** Cook and stir over low heat until mixture is thickened and coats the back of a spoon. Remove from the heat; whisk in peanut butter. Quickly transfer to a bowl; place in ice water and stir for 2 minutes. Stir in cream and vanilla. Press waxed paper onto surface of custard. Refrigerate for several hours or overnight.

**3.** Fill cylinder of ice cream maker two-thirds full; freeze according to the manufacturer's directions. When ice cream is frozen, spoon into a freezer container, layering with jelly; freeze for 2-4 hours before serving.

**½ cup:** 393 cal., 28g fat (14g sat. fat), 77mg chol., 231mg sod., 32g carb. (29g sugars, 1g fiber), 7g pro.

> **Makes a lovely presentation. Easy to make, and very nice crumble on top.**
> —MISSCOFFEEPOT
> TASTEOFHOME.COM

PEACH
SUGAR COOKIE
CRUMBLE

# CHOCOLATE-PECAN CRACKER CUPCAKES

A local restaurant made a pie that was so unique and delicious, I decided to tweak the recipe to make it my own. I made rich and yummy cupcakes and added a marshmallow frosting.
—*Bonnie De Jong, Holland, MI*

PREP: 25 MIN. • BAKE: 15 MIN. + COOLING • MAKES: 1 DOZEN

3 large egg whites, room temperature
1 tsp. baking powder
1 tsp. vanilla extract
¾ cup sugar
4 oz. German sweet chocolate, grated
1 cup crushed Ritz crackers
 (about 25 crackers)
½ cup chopped pecans

**FILLING**
¼ cup butter, softened
½ cup confectioners' sugar
½ tsp. vanilla extract
1 cup marshmallow creme

**1.** Preheat oven to 350°. Line 12 muffin cups with foil liners. Place egg whites, baking powder and vanilla in a bowl; beat on medium until soft peaks form. Add sugar, 1 Tbsp. at a time, beating on high until sugar is dissolved. Continue beating just until stiff but not dry. Gradually fold in grated chocolate, crackers and pecans.

**2.** Fill prepared cups. Bake on lowest oven rack until puffed and tops appear dry, 13-15 minutes. Cool in pans 10 minutes before removing to wire racks.

**3.** For filling, in a large bowl, beat butter, confectioners' sugar and vanilla until smooth. Gently fold in marshmallow creme. If centers of cupcakes have not already collapsed, gently press center with a small spoon to open cavity inside. Fill cupcakes; top with additional chocolate. Refrigerate leftovers.

**1 cupcake:** 263 cal., 12g fat (5g sat. fat), 10mg chol., 153mg sod., 31g carb. (26g sugars, 1g fiber), 3g pro.

# PRESSURE-COOKER CRANBERRY STUFFED APPLES

Cinnamon and walnuts add a homey autumn flavor to these stuffed apples.
—*Grace Sandvigen, Rochester, NY*

PREP: 10 MIN. • COOK: 5 MIN. • MAKES: 5 SERVINGS

5 medium apples
⅓ cup fresh or frozen cranberries, thawed and chopped
¼ cup packed brown sugar
2 Tbsp. chopped walnuts
¼ tsp. ground cinnamon
⅛ tsp. ground nutmeg
 Vanilla ice cream or whipped cream

**1.** Core apples, leaving bottoms intact. Peel top third of each apple. Place trivet insert and 1 cup water in cooker. Combine cranberries, brown sugar, walnuts, cinnamon and nutmeg; spoon into apples. Place apples on trivet.

**2.** Lock lid; close pressure-release valve. Adjust to pressure-cook on high for 3 minutes. Quick-release pressure. Serve with ice cream or whipped cream.

**1 stuffed apple:** 142 cal., 2g fat (0 sat. fat), 0 chol., 5mg sod., 33g carb. (27g sugars, 4g fiber), 1g pro. **Diabetic exchanges:** 1 starch, 1 fruit.

# NO-BAKE MANGO STRAWBERRY CHEESECAKE

Cheesecake is my mom's favorite dessert. I made this especially for her on
Mother's Day to thank her for being such an awesome mom. Decorate to your own taste!

—*Elizabeth Ding, El Cerrito, CA*

**PREP:** 45 MIN. + CHILLING • **MAKES:** 12 SERVINGS

1¼ cups graham cracker crumbs
⅓ cup butter, melted
¼ cup sugar

**FILLING**
1 envelope unflavored gelatin
3 Tbsp. cold water
2 pkg. (8 oz. each) cream cheese, softened
1⅓ cups sugar
1 cup heavy whipping cream
2 tsp. vanilla extract
½ large mango, peeled and cubed (about ¾ cup)
4 fresh strawberries, chopped

**GLAZE**
1 envelope unflavored gelatin
3 Tbsp. plus ½ cup cold water, divided
½ large mango, peeled and cubed (about ¾ cup)
Optional: Whipped cream, mango pieces and sliced strawberries

1. In a small bowl, mix crumbs, butter and sugar. Press into bottom of a greased 8-in. springform pan.

2. For filling, in a microwave-safe bowl, sprinkle gelatin over cold water; let stand 1 minute. Microwave on high for 10-20 seconds or just until water is warm but not hot. Stir and let stand until gelatin is completely dissolved, about 1 minute. Cool until partially set.

3. In a large bowl, beat cream cheese and sugar until smooth. Gradually beat in cream, vanilla and gelatin mixture until blended. Fold in mango and strawberries. Pour over crust. Refrigerate while preparing glaze.

4. For glaze, in another microwave-safe bowl, sprinkle gelatin over 3 Tbsp. cold water; let stand 1 minute. Microwave on high 10-20 seconds or just until water is warm but not hot. Stir and let stand until gelatin is completely dissolved, about 1 minute. Cool until partially set. Meanwhile, place mango and remaining ½ cup water in a food processor; process until pureed. Stir in gelatin mixture; pour over filling. Refrigerate, loosely covered, overnight.

5. Loosen side from pan with a knife. Remove rim from pan. If desired, garnish cheesecake with whipped cream, additional mango pieces and strawberry slices.

**1 piece:** 417 cal., 27g fat (16g sat. fat), 74mg chol., 215mg sod., 42g carb. (35g sugars, 1g fiber), 5g pro.

# RECIPE INDEX